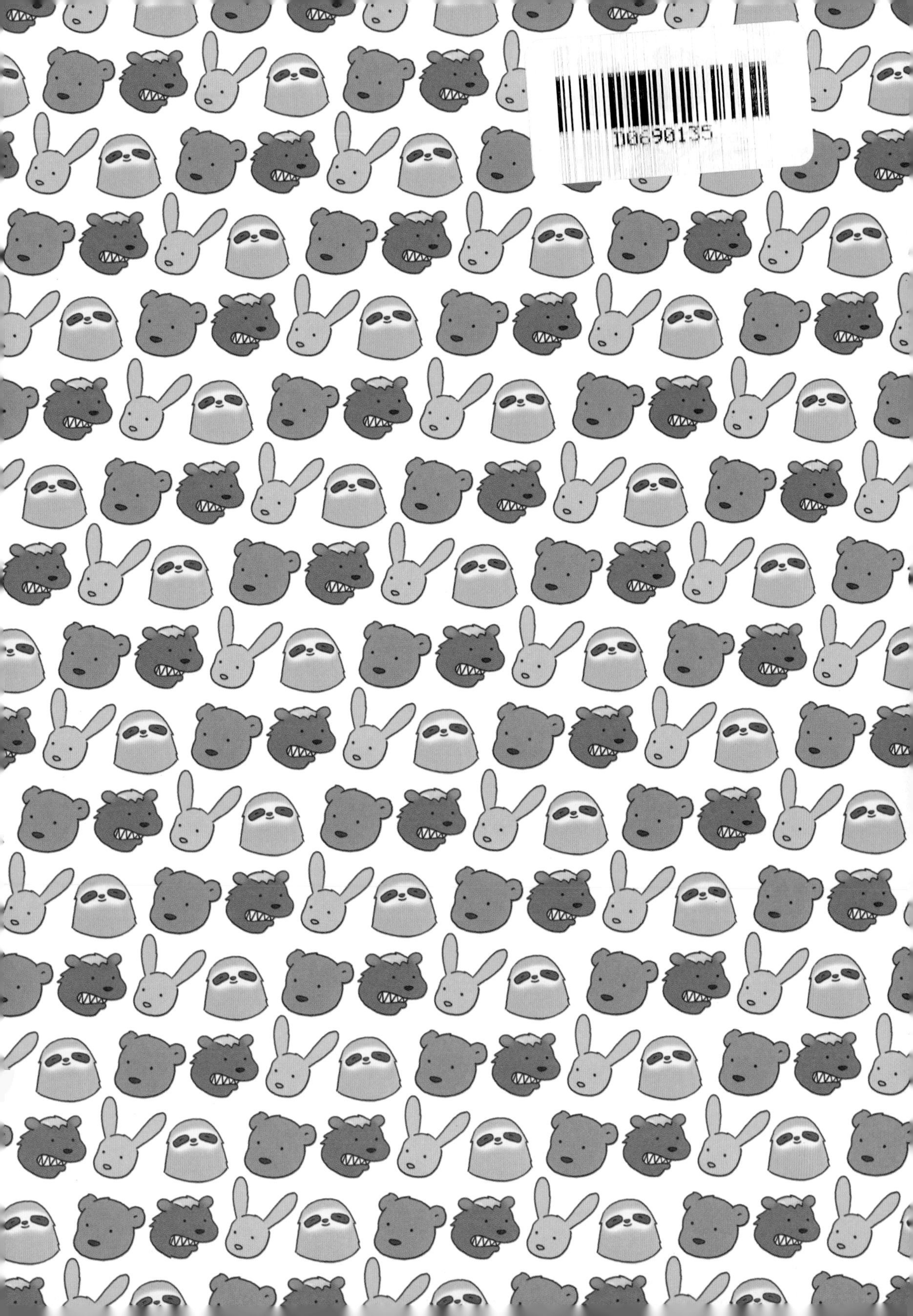

the
little world
of
liz climo

RUNNING PRESS
PHILADELPHIA · LONDON

for my
mom, dad,
sister, and
brother

© 2014 by Liz Climo
Published by Running Press,
A Member of the Perseus Books Group

Printed in China

Books published by Running Press are available at special discounts for bulk purchases in the United States by corporations, institutions, and other organizations. For more information, please contact the Special Markets Department at the Perseus Books Group, 2300 Chestnut Street, Suite 200, Philadelphia, PA 19103, or call (800) 810-4145, ext. 5000, or e-mail special.markets@perseusbooks.com.

ISBN 978-0-7624-5238-5
Library of Congress Control Number: 2014935279

E-book ISBN 978-0-7624-5546-1

12   11   10   9
Digit on the right indicates the number of this printing

Cover & interior design by Ashley Haag
Edited by Jennifer Kasius
Typography: Avenir and Draftsman Casual

Running Press Book Publishers
2300 Chestnut Street
Philadelphia, PA 19103-4371

Visit us on the web!
www.runningpress.com

Foreword

There is a time-honored adage that says, "To have a funny friend is to be rich in life." Actually, I just made that up. But it sounds like the kind of clichéd quote that typically kicks off book introductions. Original or not, I'm using it here because I believe it to be true. A funny friend can turn a night of shoddy service at a restaurant into a memorable meal, a boring road trip into a laugh-a-minute adventure, a bad movie into a so-bad-it's-good cult classic. Your funny friend takes the same mundane raw material life presents to all of us and somehow filters it through an idiosyncratic point of view, turning it into a potent and individual expression of humor. And you, as the friend, get to reap the benefits. Rich stuff indeed.

Liz Climo is one of the funniest friends I have. The kind of funny friend that always made me wish she could find a way to bottle up her particular brand of funny and share it with the whole world. Social networking coalesced our circle of friends over the last several years, like it did for just about everyone. Liz's posts are always consistently hilarious: short and sweet, never bragging or snide, yet overflowing with her uncommon wit and most of all, her unique humor. I once told her that Facebook should pay her to be a professional status updater.

And then Liz started drawing these comics and posting them online. I knew from the get-go she had figured out a brilliant way to bottle up her comedy. Her short and sweet text posts were transformed into charming illustrations, with no wasted lines, no extraneous background elements, only what is needed to tell the joke, pure and simple. So it was no surprise that Liz's comics resonated way beyond our little network of friends to delight tens of thousands of people across borders, oceans, and language barriers. Now the world can reap the benefits of having Liz Climo as its very own funny friend.

Bryan Konietzko
Co-creator of *Avatar: The Last Airbender*
and *The Legend of Korra*

Intrduction

Hi, I'm Liz!

Thanks for buying this book—that was so nice of you! Maybe you bought it because you like the drawings. Or maybe because you like the jokes inside. Or maybe you don't like either of those things but you just needed a doorstop or something. Either way, I am extremely grateful. The very notion that I would have a book that might be used as a doorstop is still a bit shocking. I never expected these characters to show up anywhere except the backs of bar napkins or on paper placemats at restaurants. And now, here they are—in this fancy little book, in your fancy little hands (or holding your door open).

   I grew up loving to read and draw comics. When I was a child visiting my grandparents' house, I'd sit in the corner by myself reading their *Far Side* desk calendar in its entirety. I'd read it over and over, each time we'd visit, even though it never changed. I just loved it so much. At my mother's encouragement, I would write and illustrate my own stories, which always started at the back cover and read from right to left. (It was easier that way, because I'm left-handed, and also because I was a little weirdo.) I'd try to be darkly funny like the characters in Matt Groening's *Life in Hell,* or create beautiful illustrations like the ones in my *Calvin and Hobbes* books, but I would never quite achieve either of those things. Regardless, I drew my little heart out and dreamed of a day when I'd grow up to be an artist who drew her very own cartoons. I feel so lucky that I actually get to do that now, but I definitely encountered some obstacles along the way.

   I have had the privilege of knowing a lot of extremely talented artists, who both inspired me and made me incredibly insecure. I struggled with drawing too "cartoony" in high school (my art teacher's exact words, and she was absolutely right). In college, I worked tirelessly toward a degree in Animation & Illustration, and was heartbroken when the admissions office rejected my portfolio. I caught a lucky break soon after, when I got a job working as an animator on *The Simpsons*, which was an absolute dream come true. I was incredibly underqualified, but I worked hard and somehow managed not to get fired. After ten years of working in animation, I had seen the incredible talent there is in the industry, and it scared the bejeezus out of me. I had learned to draw the Simpsons just fine, but when it came to my own work, I was terrified my colleagues might laugh at my crude little cartoon drawings. Luckily, I married someone who was encouraging enough to convince me to keep drawing them—and bossy enough to make me post them on the Internet. He helped me get over all of that nonsense and start feeling proud of my work.

When I began posting my comics, I was still sort of figuring out who these characters were and what they meant to me. I watched them develop and come to life, completely exposed to the big bad Internet. I began to pay close attention to the things people around me said and the way people reacted to things. As I drew more comics, the characters' personalities began to mirror those in my daily life. The dinosaurs became my friends when they play with their children. The mother sloth and koala became my own mother, the way she would speak to me when I was a little girl. The clumsy bear became me, the sarcastic rabbit became my husband, and bullied characters represented my memories of being teased in high school. I began to really love and care about the characters because they represented everything that was dear to me in my own life.

So here they are, a whole book of my ridiculous comics for you to enjoy. I hope they make you laugh and smile, or even just feel a little bit better than you did before you started reading.

Liz Climo

love and friendship

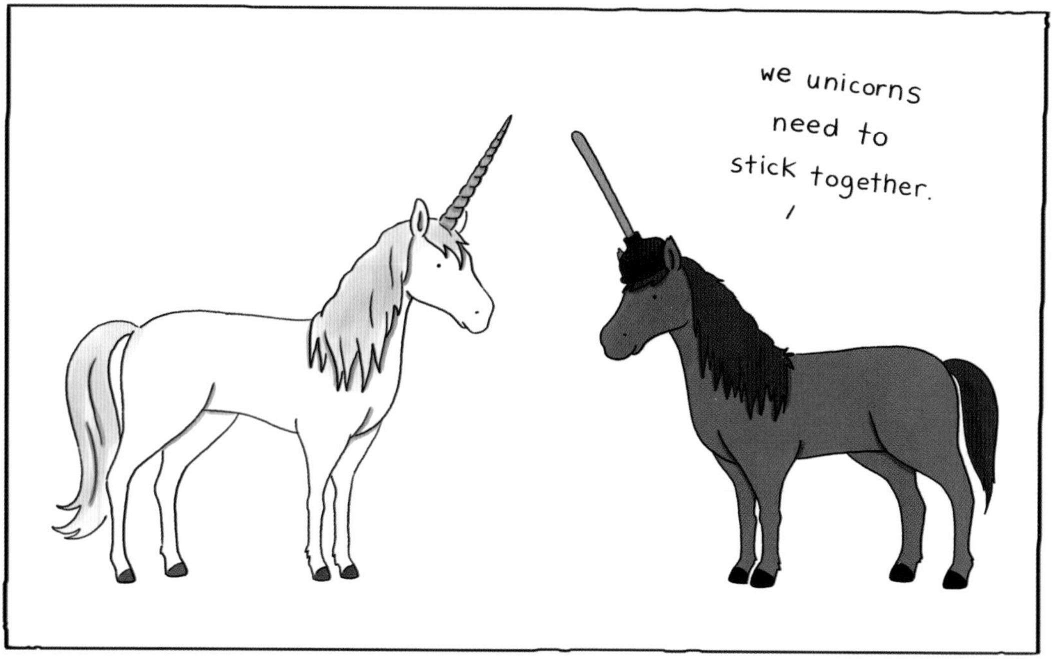
we unicorns need to stick together.

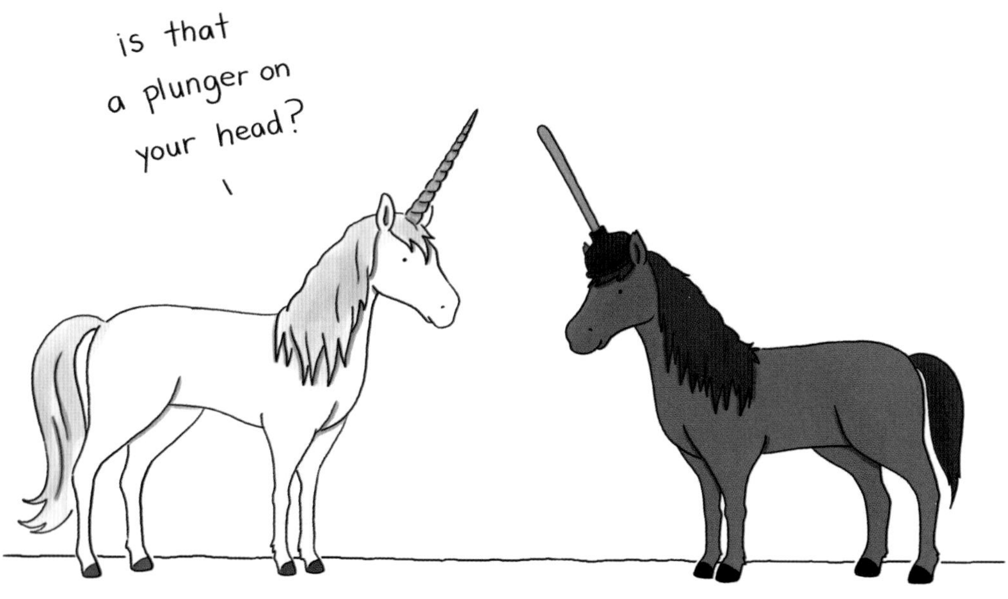
is that a plunger on your head?

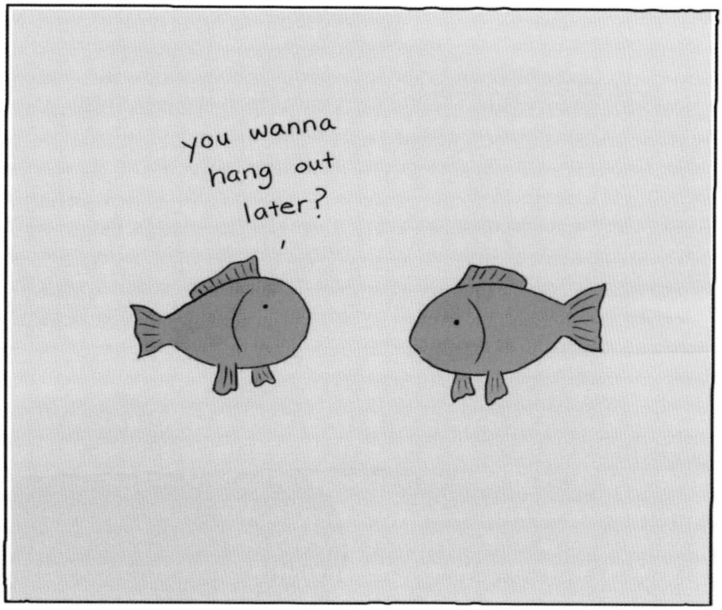
you wanna hang out later?

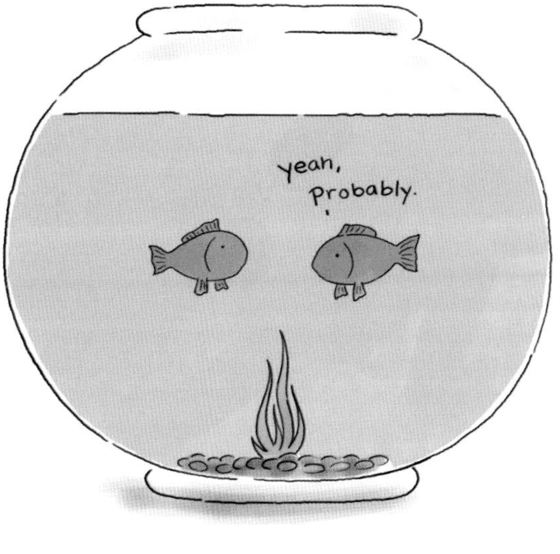
yeah, Probably.

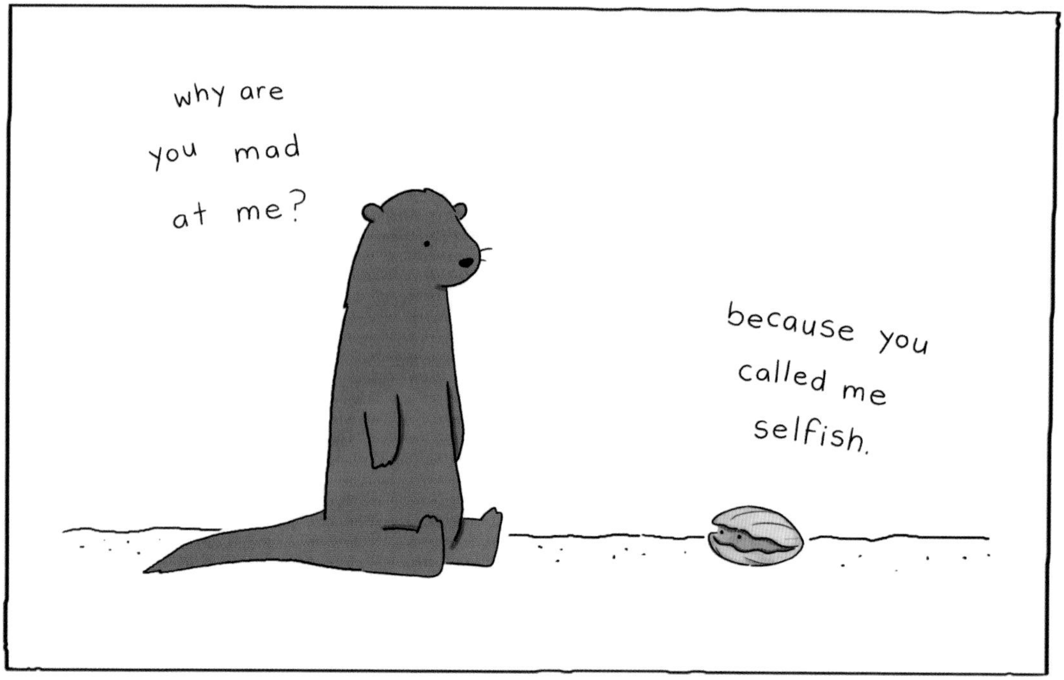
why are you mad at me?
because you called me selfish.

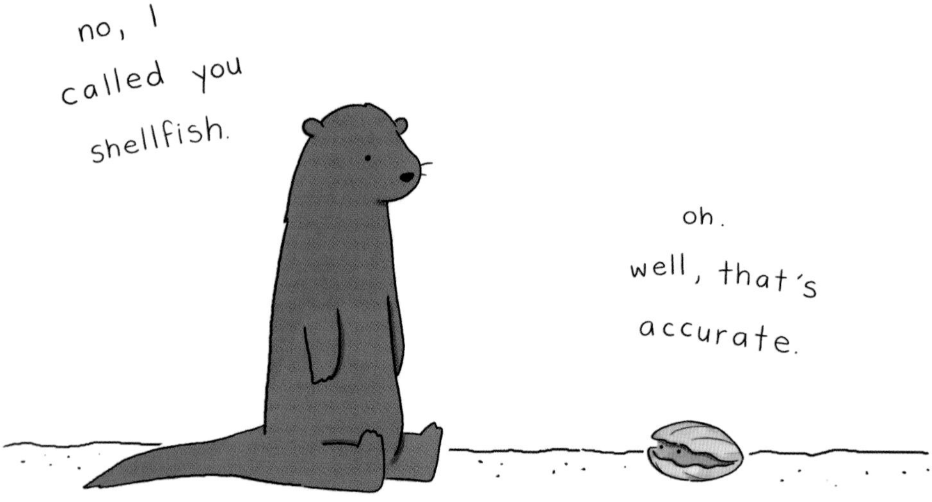
no, I called you shellfish.
oh.
well, that's accurate.

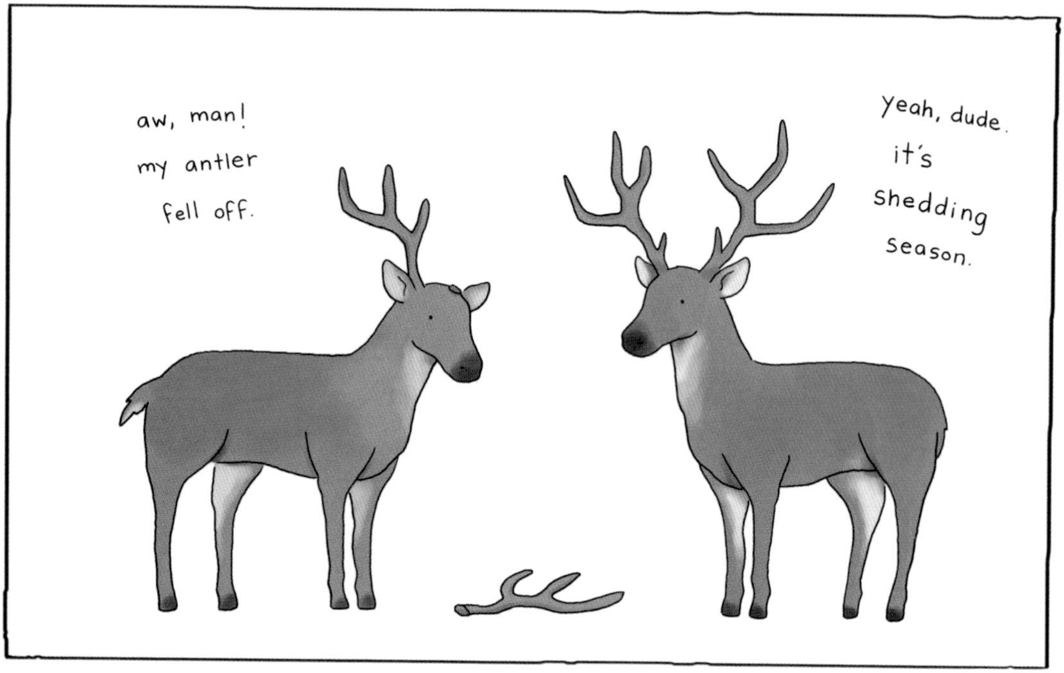
aw, man! my antler fell off.
yeah, dude. it's shedding season.

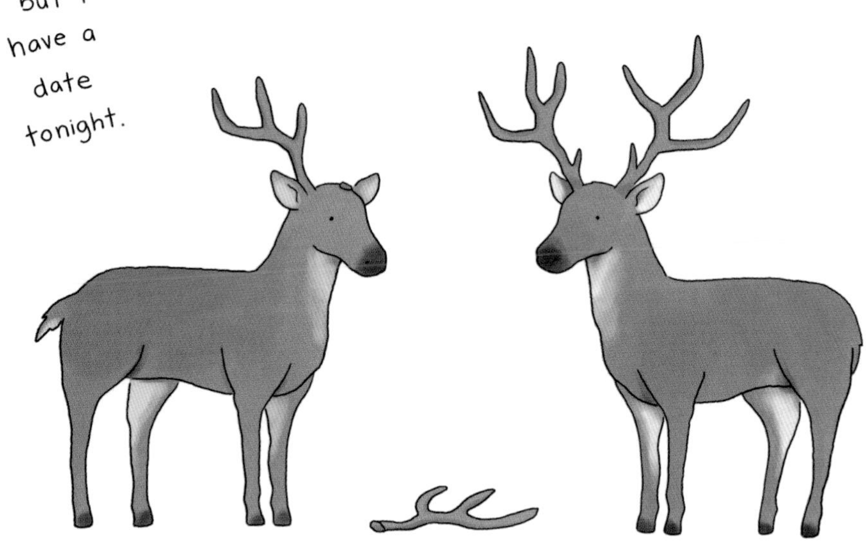
but I have a date tonight.

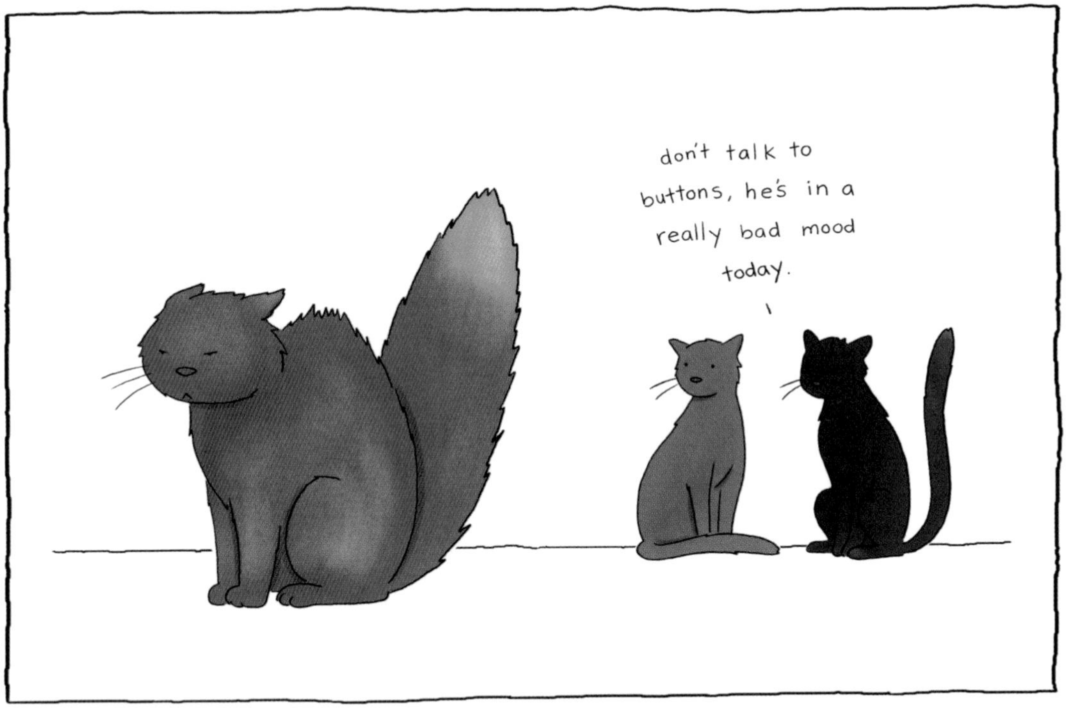
don't talk to buttons, he's in a really bad mood today.

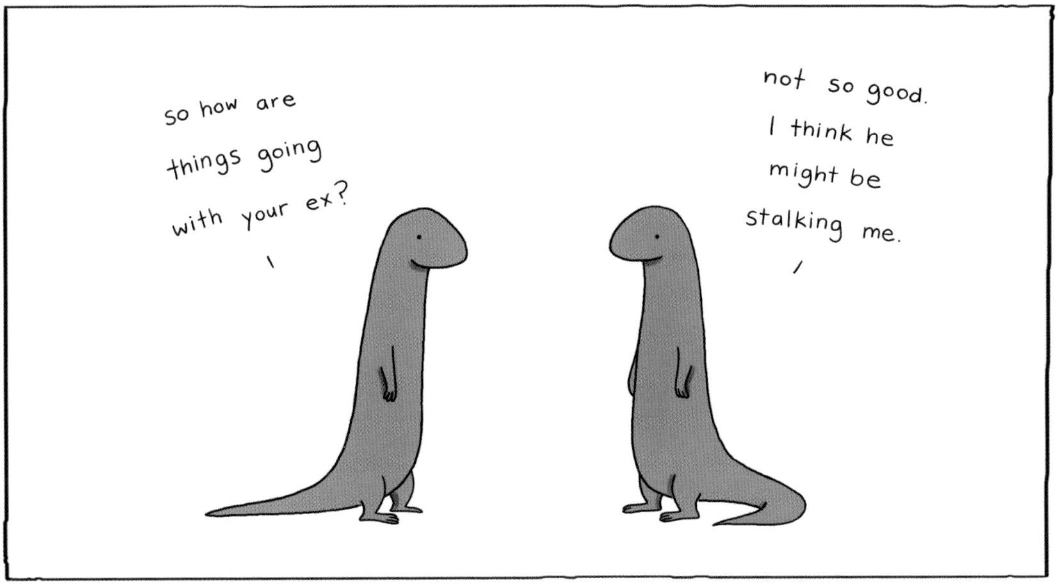
so how are things going with your ex?
not so good. I think he might be stalking me.

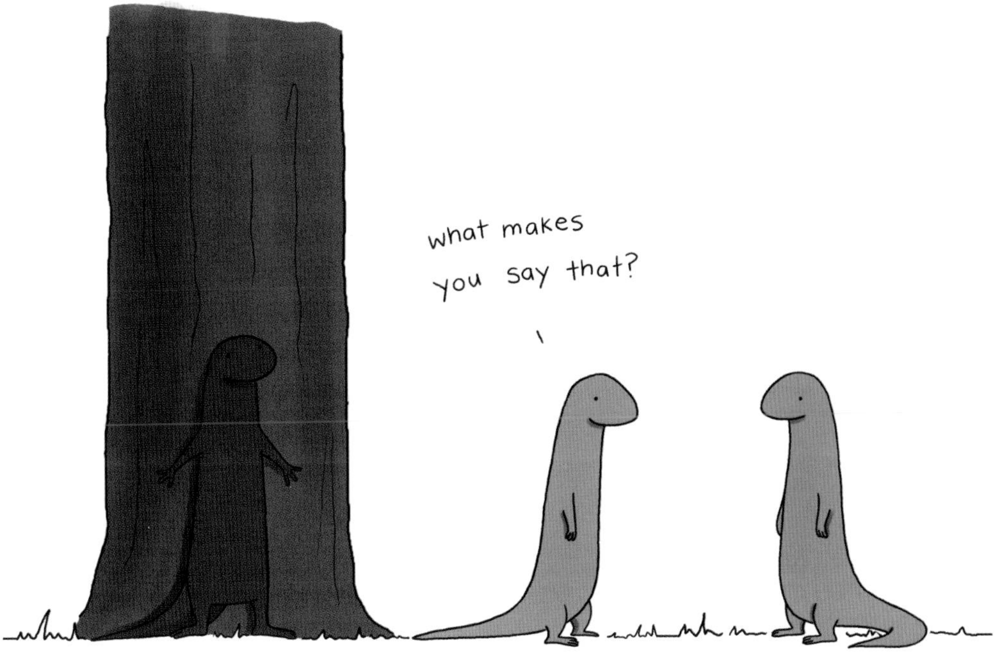
what makes you say that?

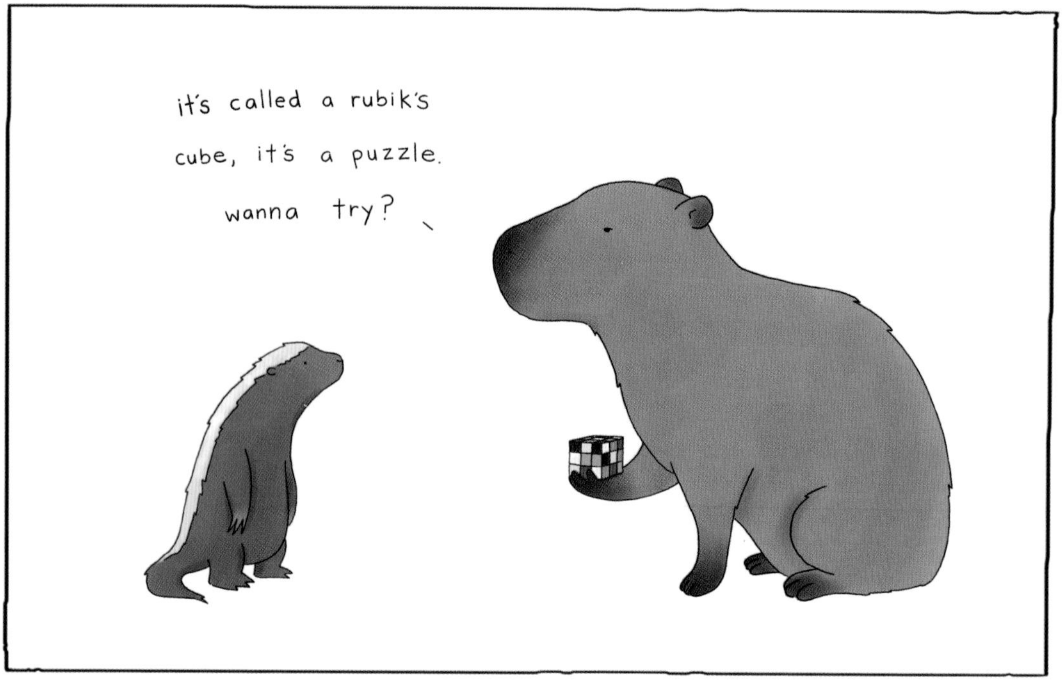
it's called a rubik's
cube, it's a puzzle.
wanna try?

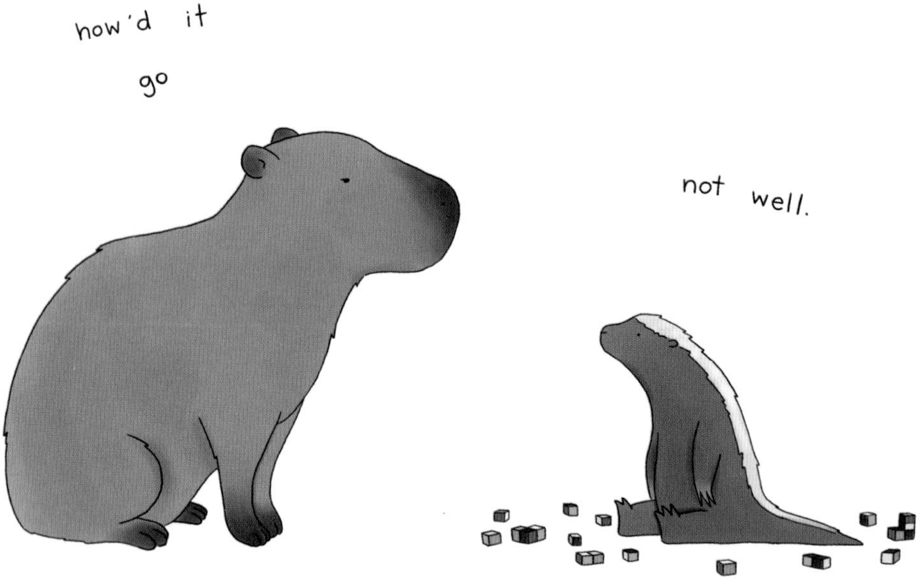
how'd it
go
not well.

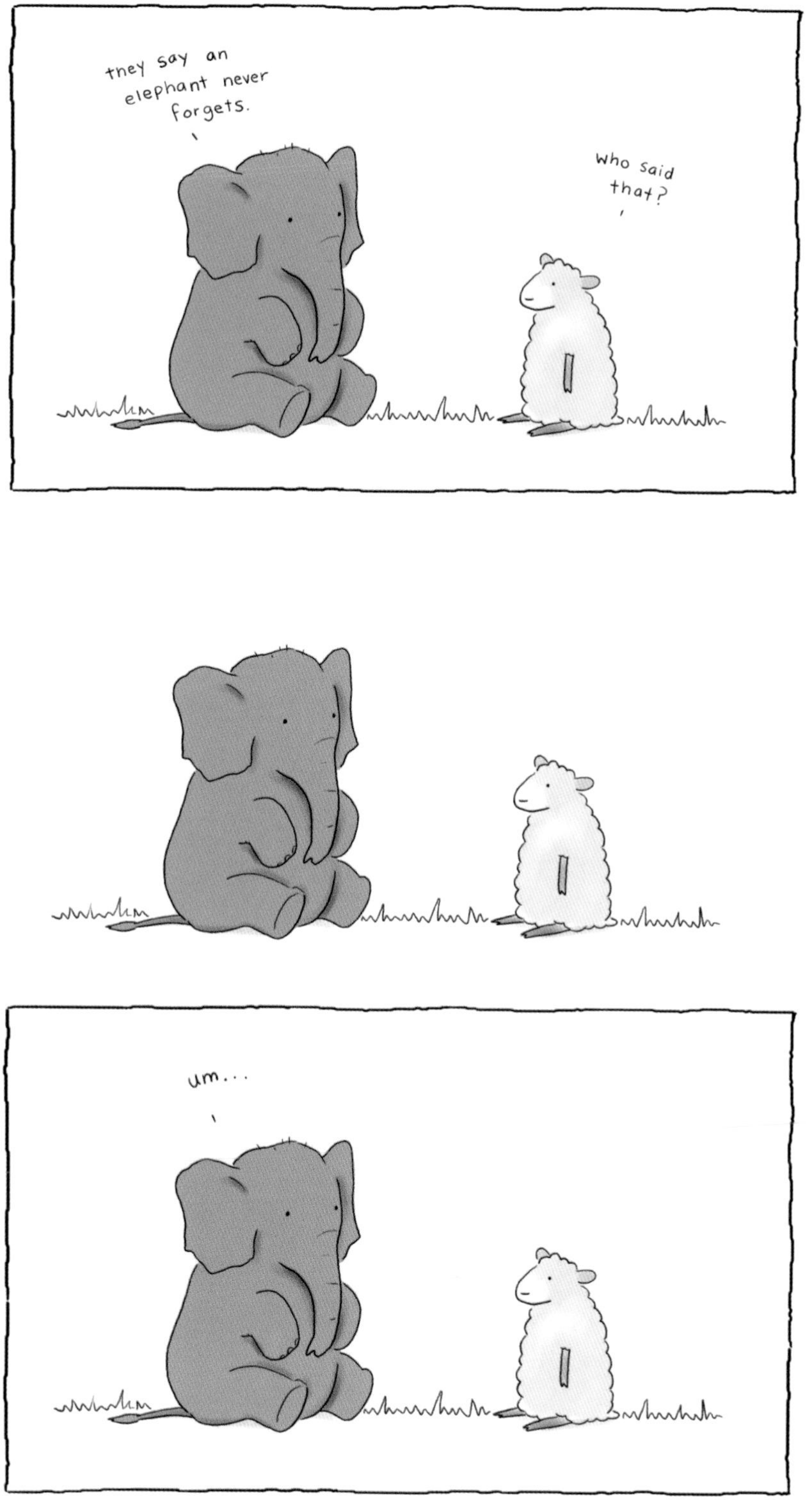
they say an elephant never forgets.
who said that?
um...

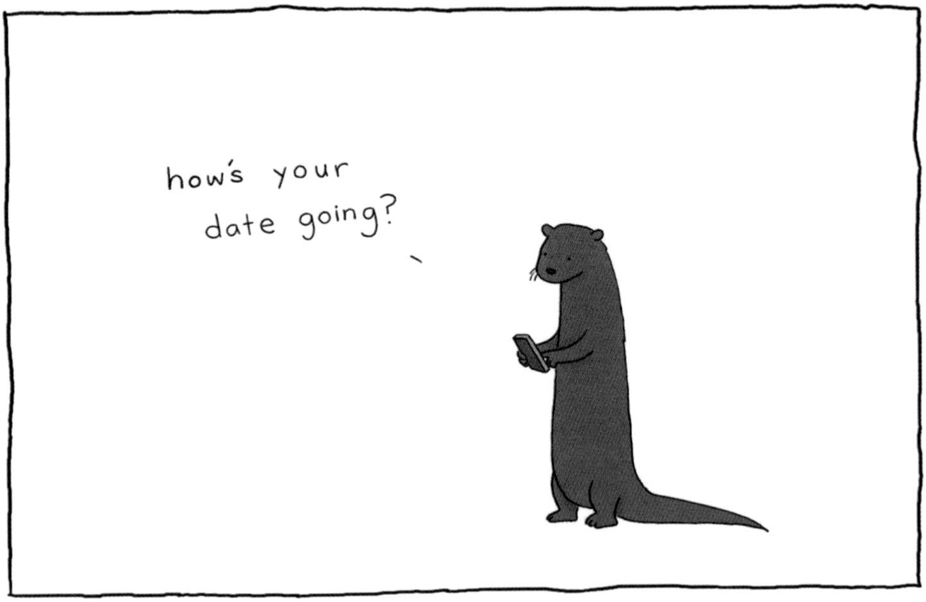
how's your
date going?

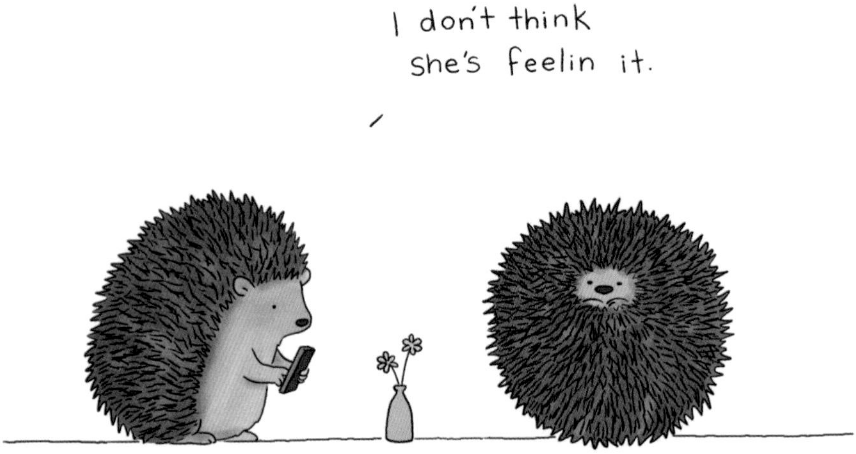
I don't think
she's feelin it.

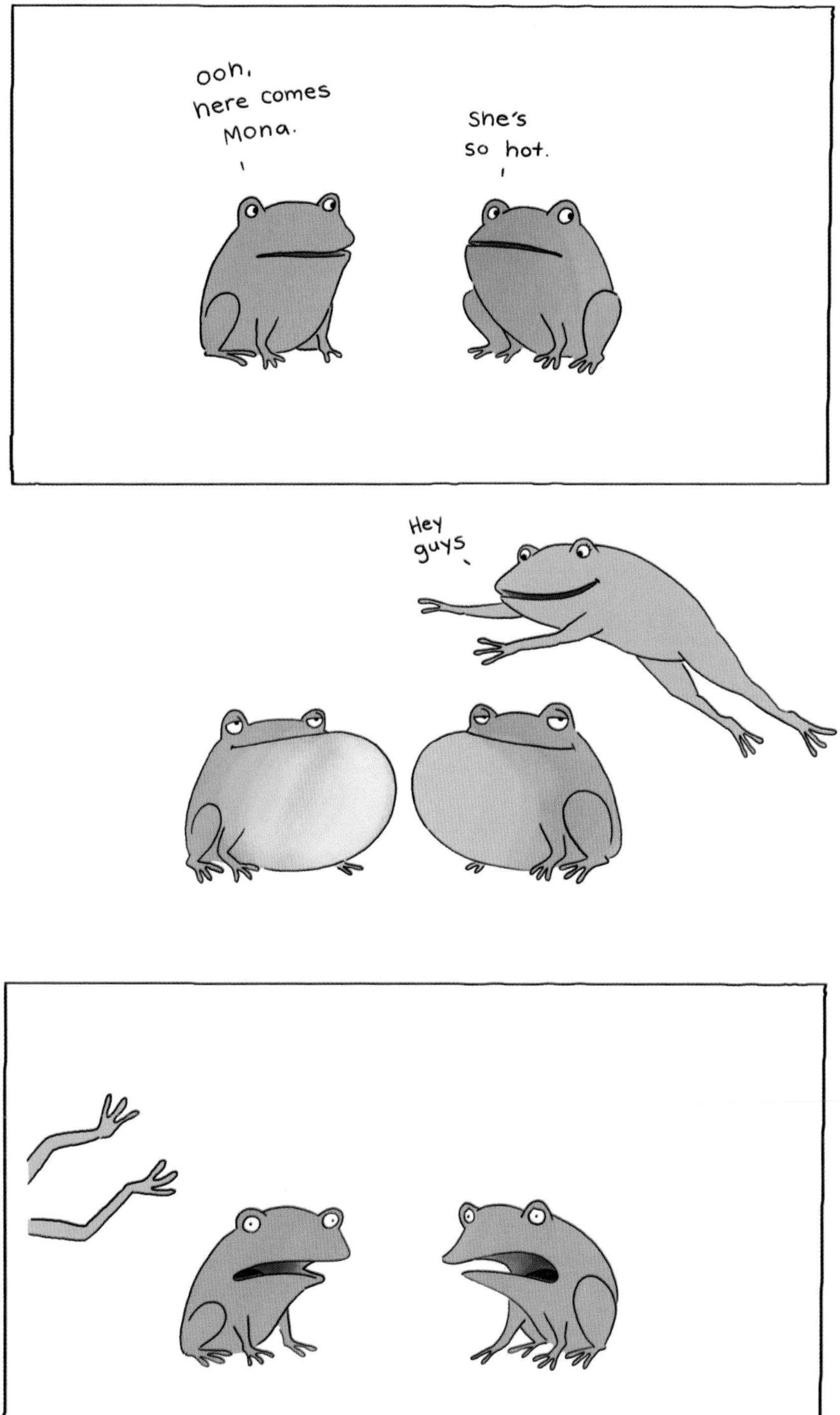
ooh, here comes Mona.
She's so hot.
Hey guys

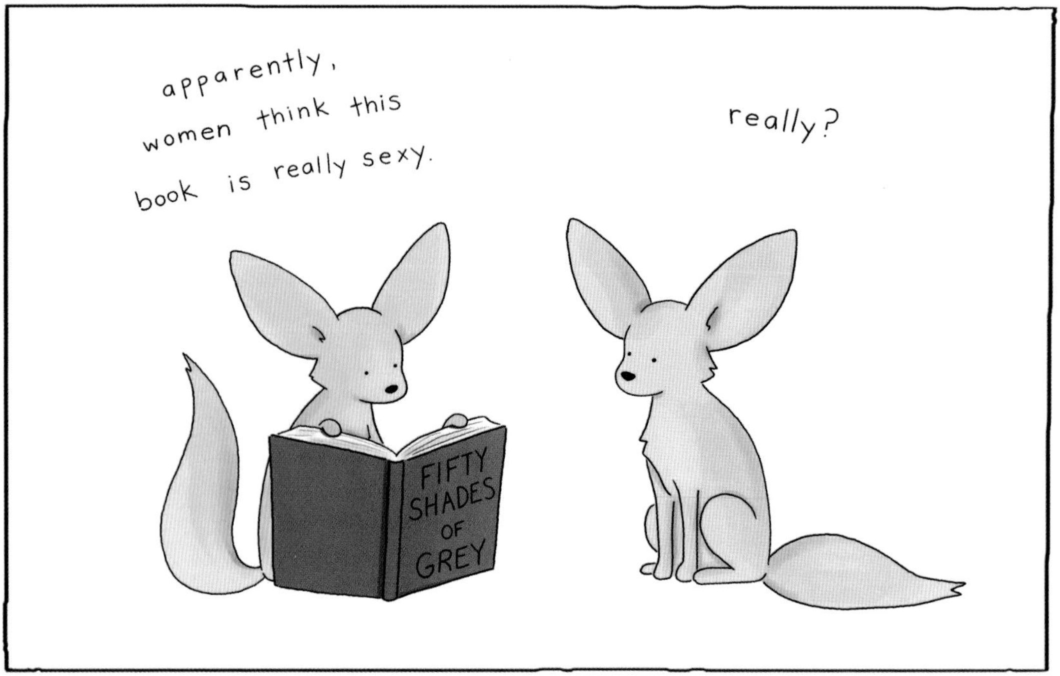
apparently, women think this book is really sexy.
really?
FIFTY SHADES OF GREY

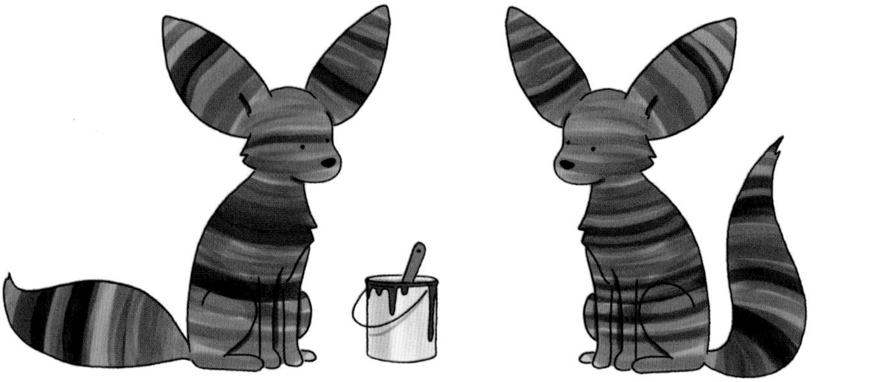

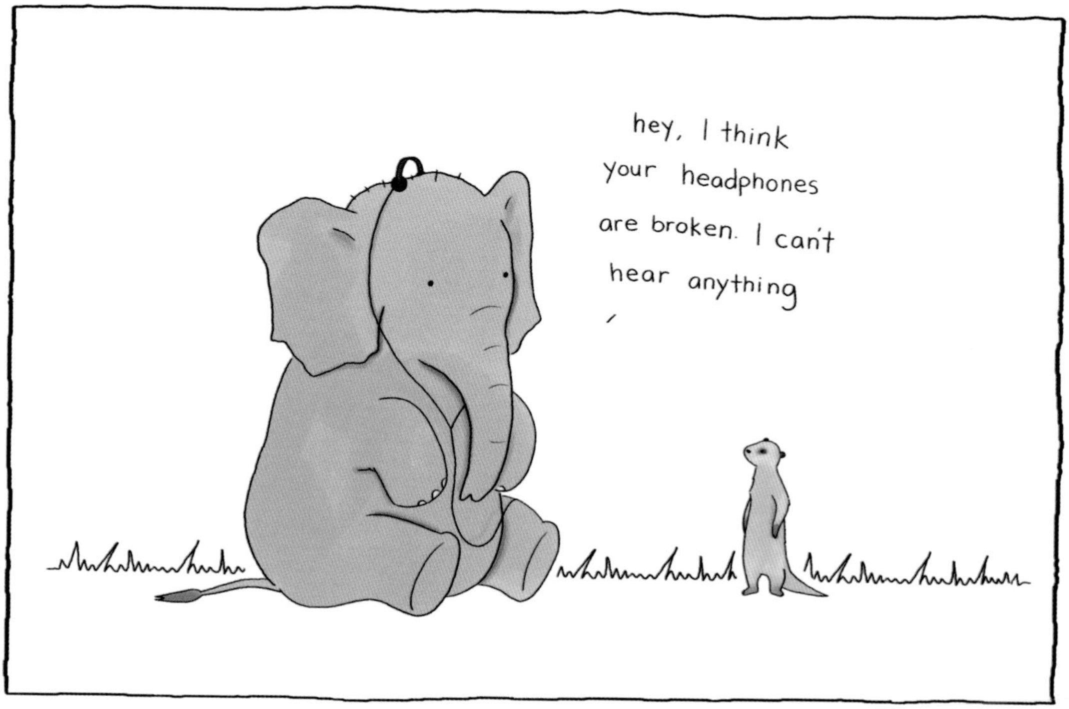
hey, I think your headphones are broken. I can't hear anything

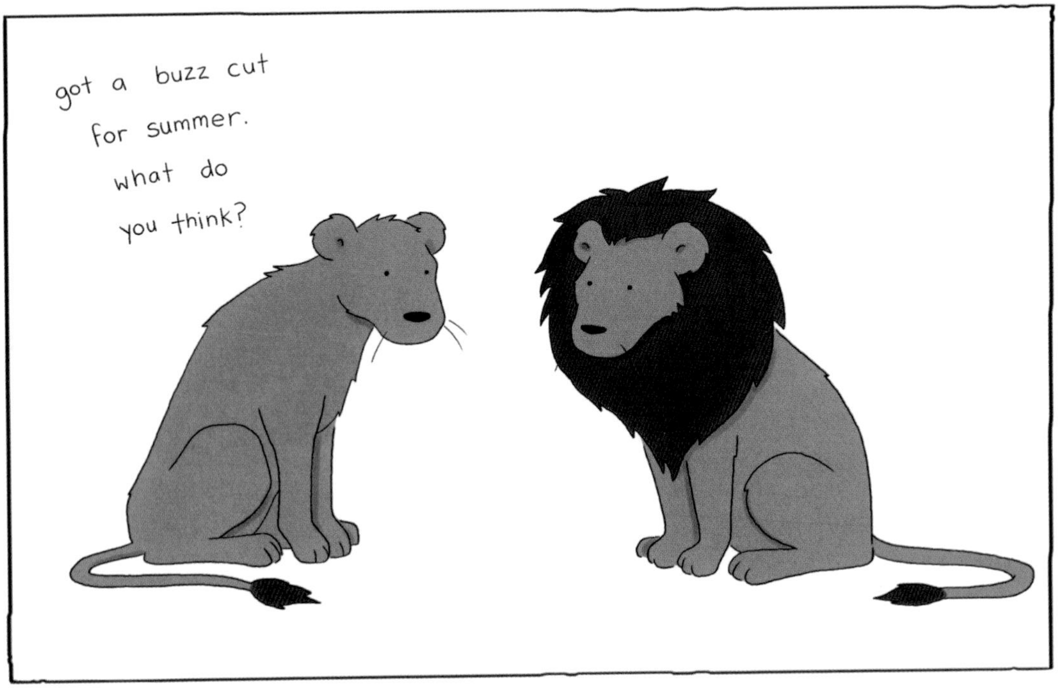
got a buzz cut for summer. what do you think?

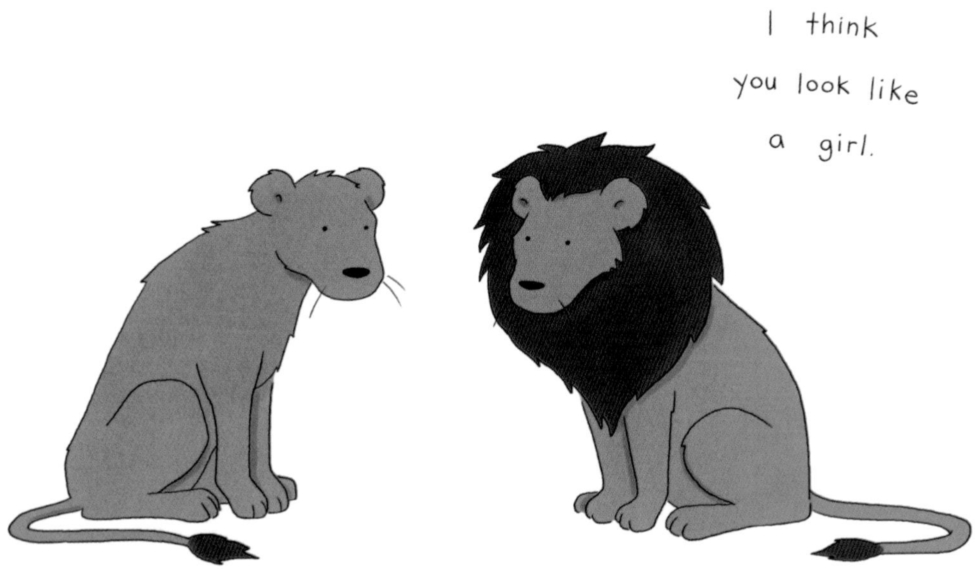
I think you look like a girl.

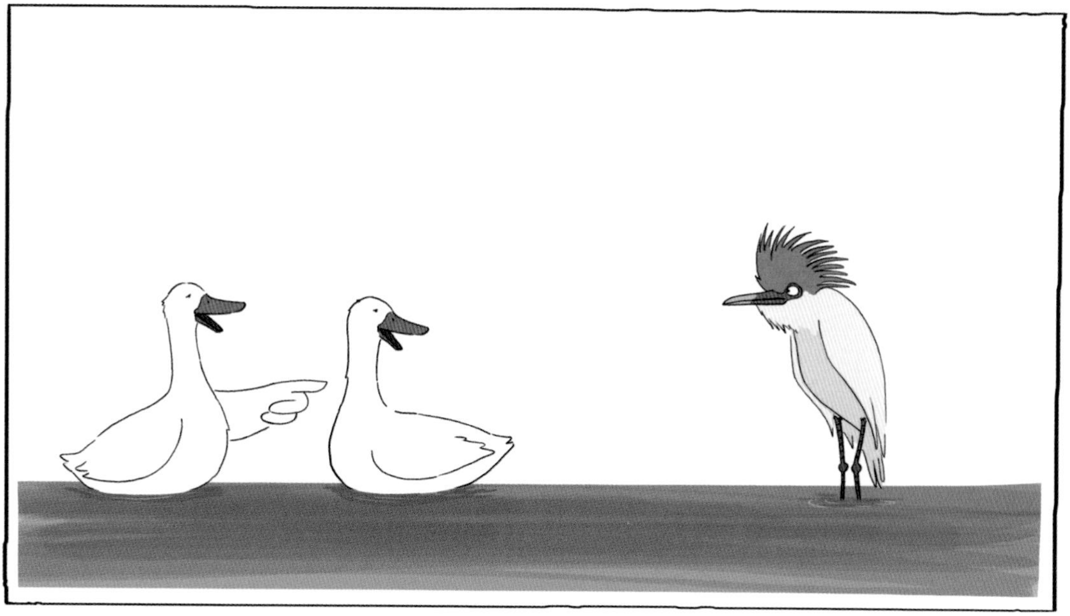

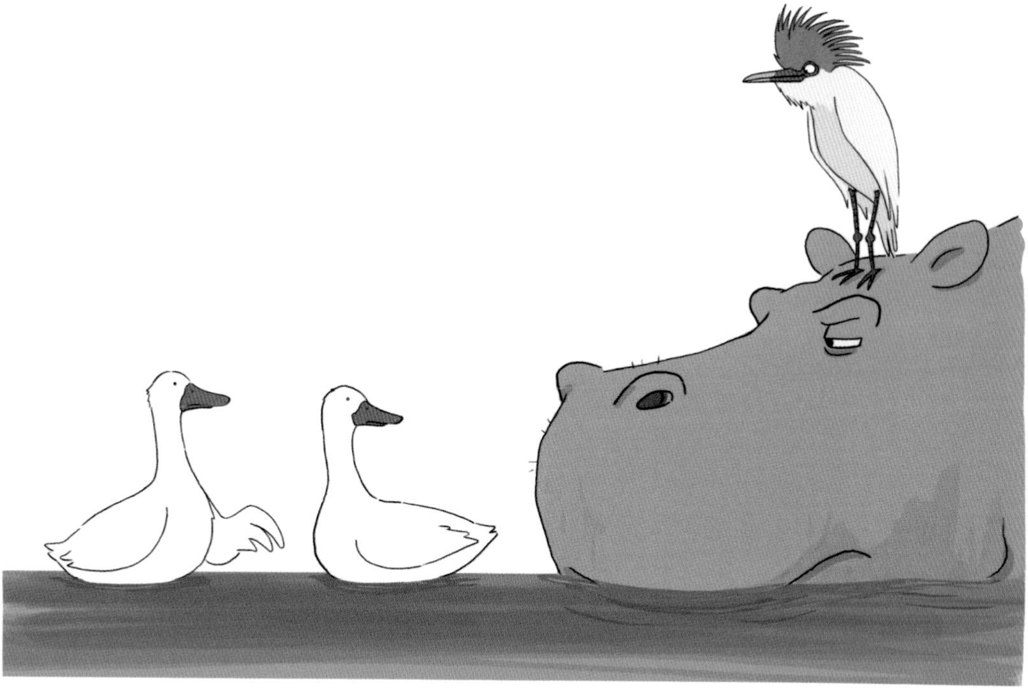

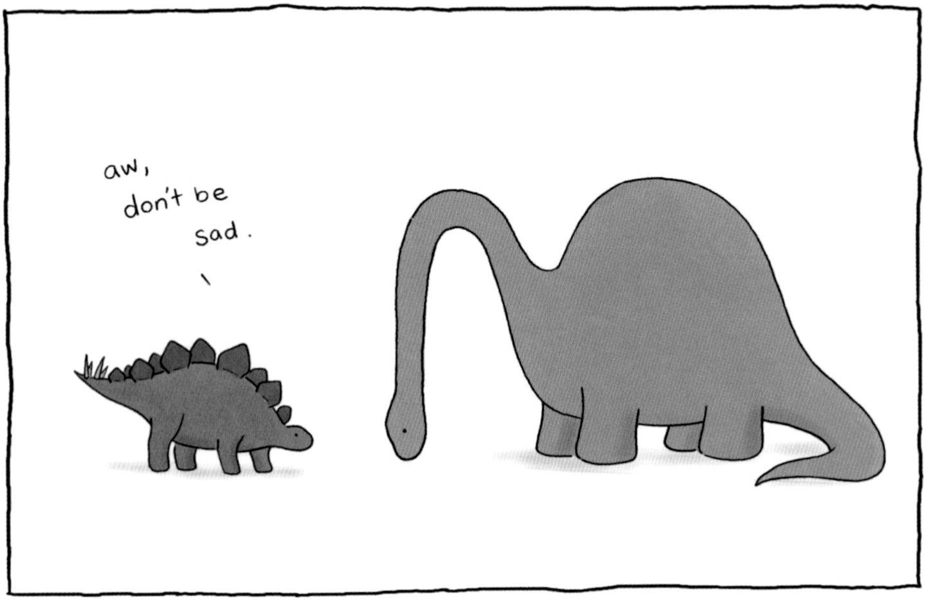
aw, don't be sad.

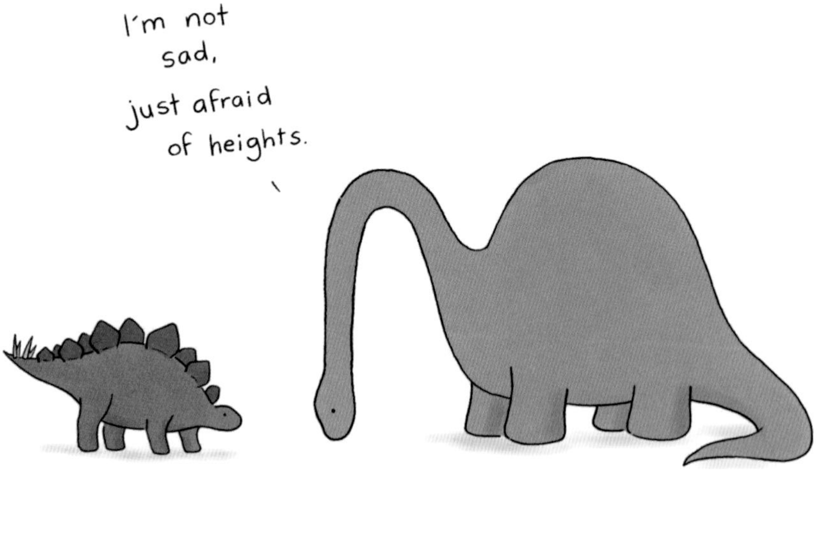
I'm not sad, just afraid of heights.

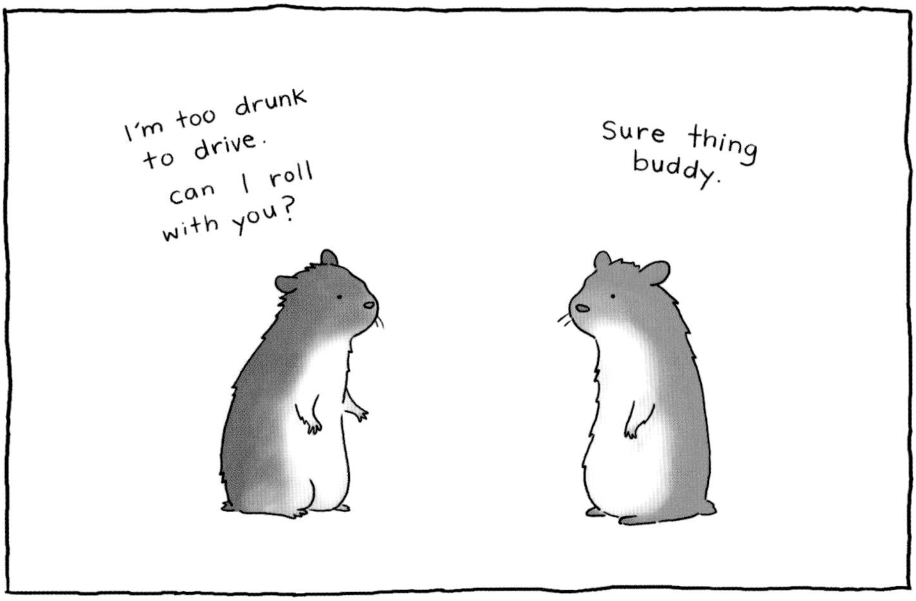
I'm too drunk to drive. can I roll with you?
Sure thing buddy.

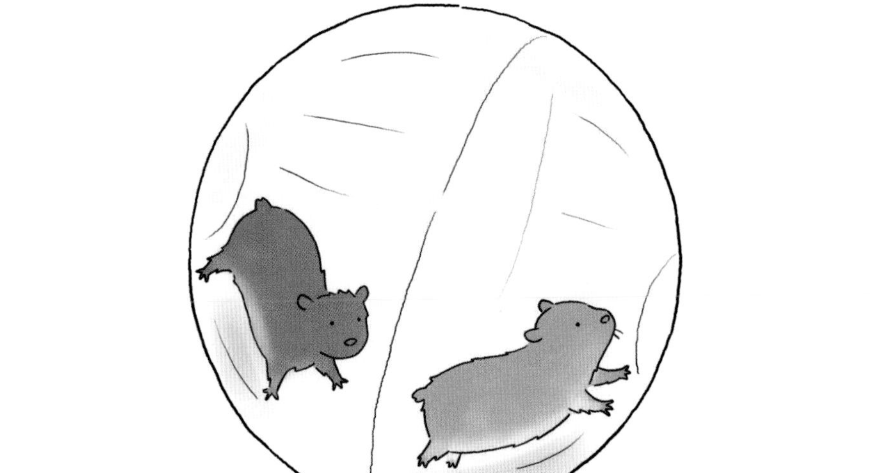

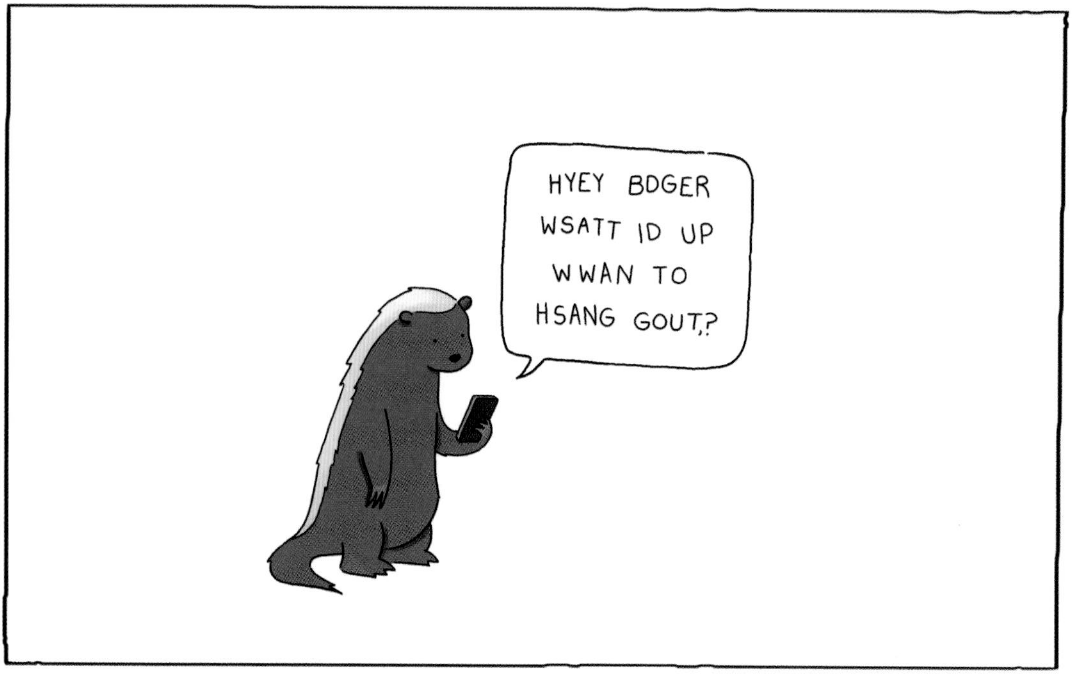
HYEY BDGER WSATT ID UP WWAN TO HSANG GOUT,?

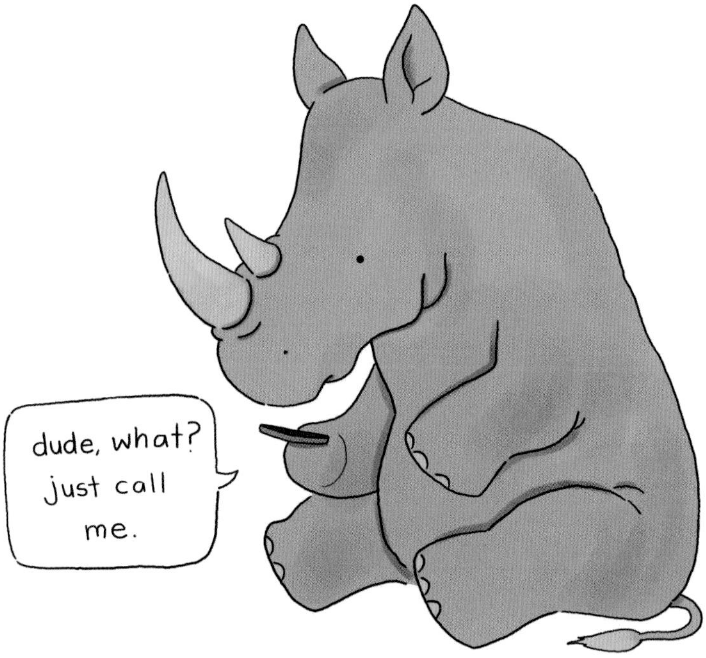
dude, what? just call me.

could you hurry
it up?
you're really boring
when you
hibernate.

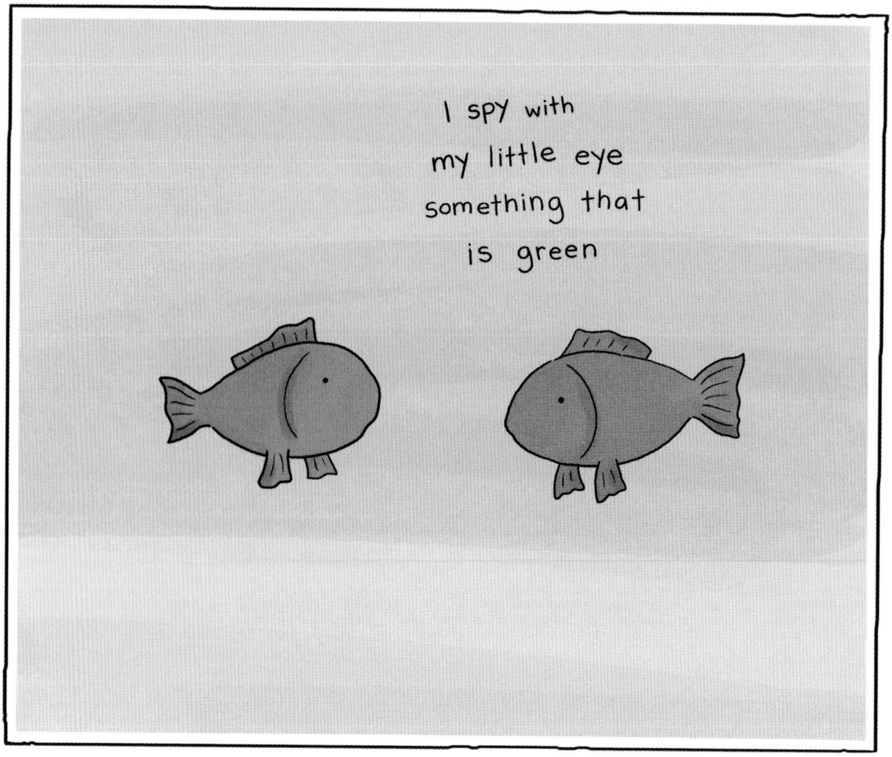
I spy with
my little eye
something that
is green

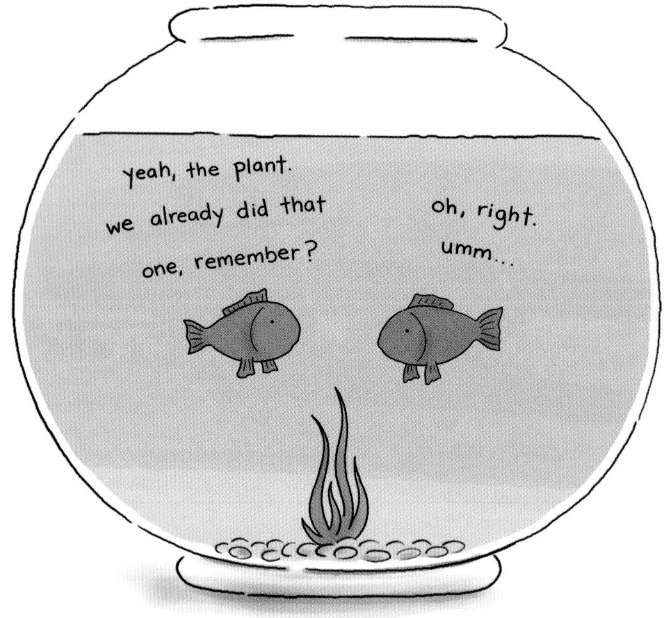
yeah, the plant.
we already did that
one, remember?
oh, right.
umm...

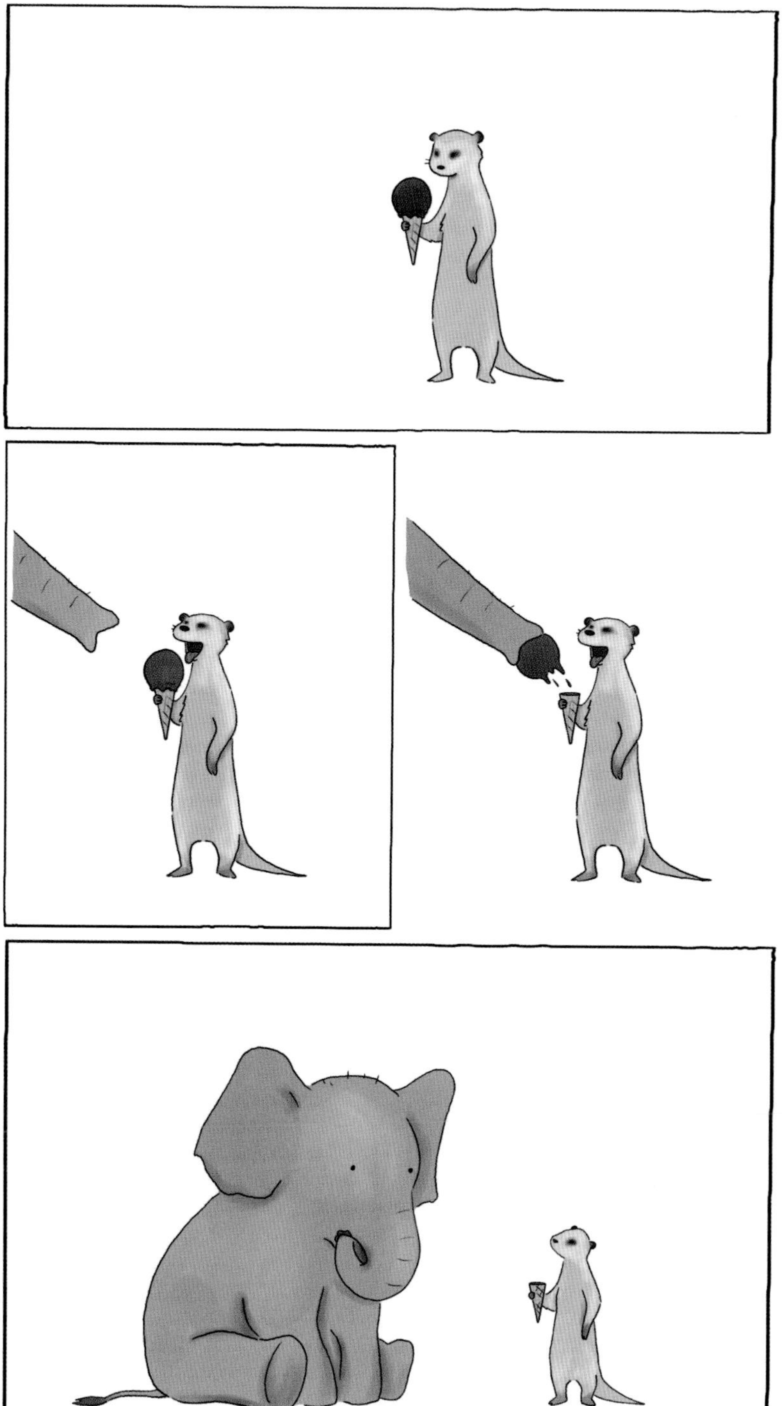

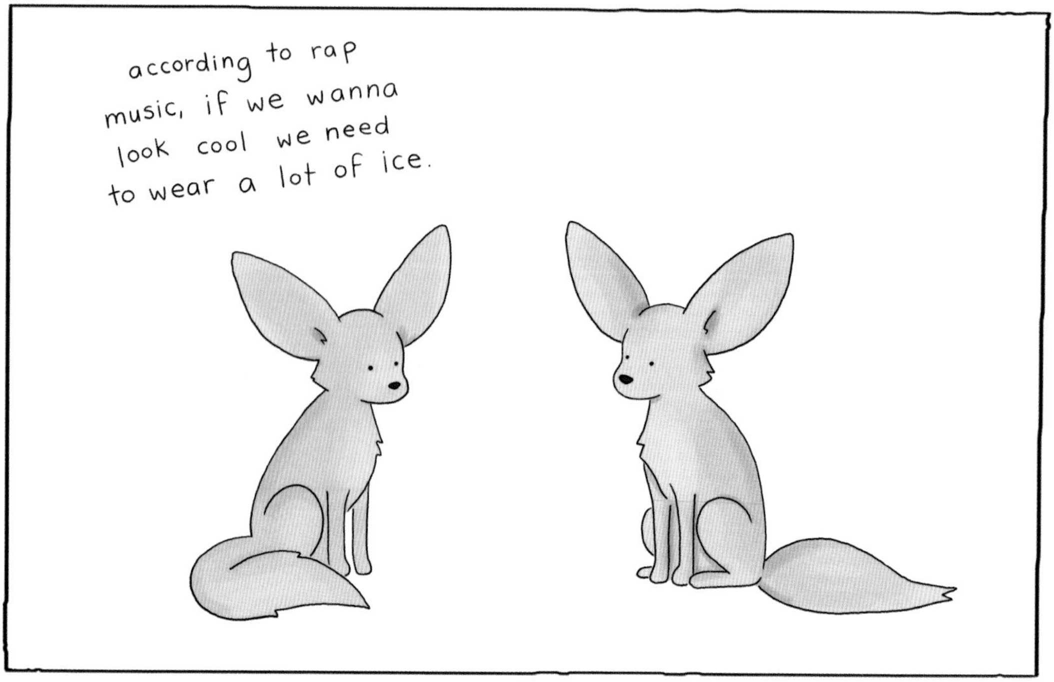
according to rap music, if we wanna look cool we need to wear a lot of ice.

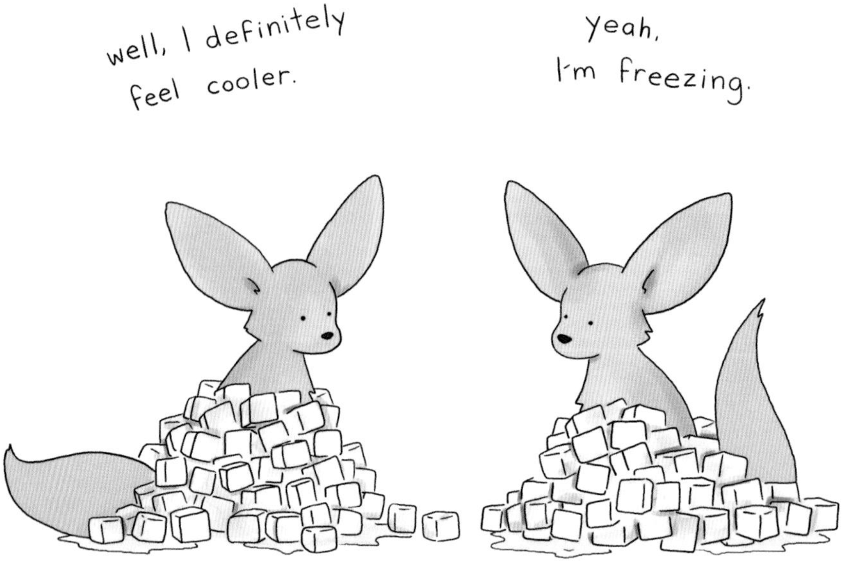
well, I definitely feel cooler.
yeah, I'm freezing.

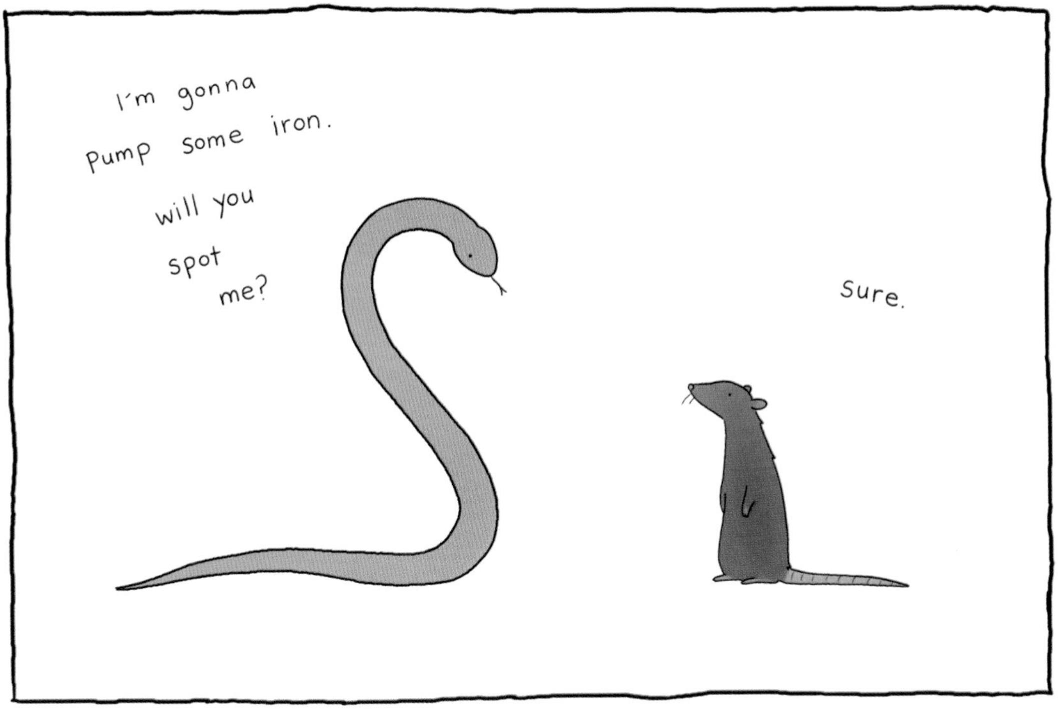
I'm gonna pump some iron.
will you spot me?
sure.

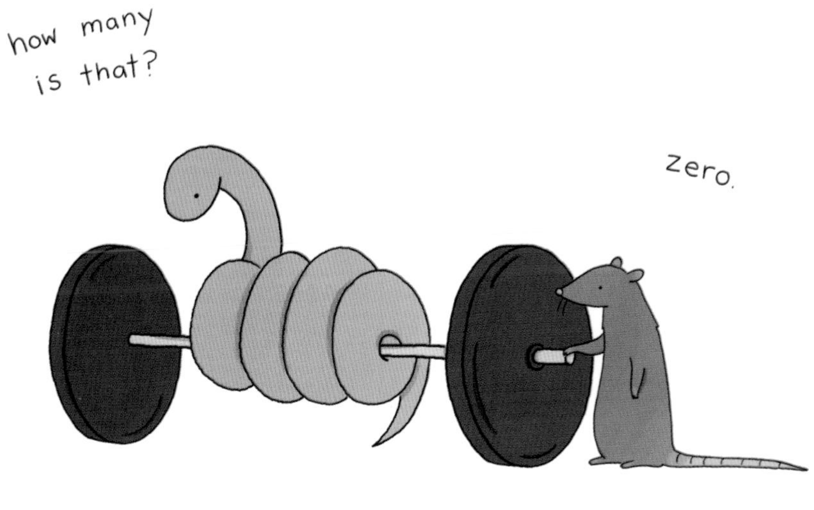
how many is that?
zero.

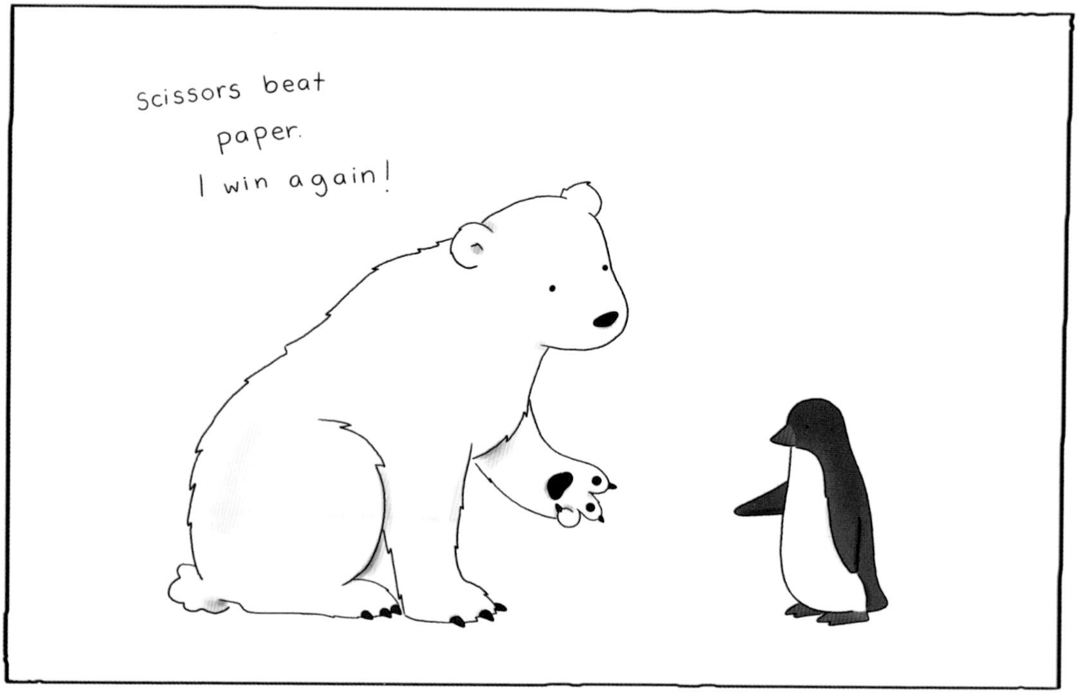
Scissors beat
paper.
I win again!

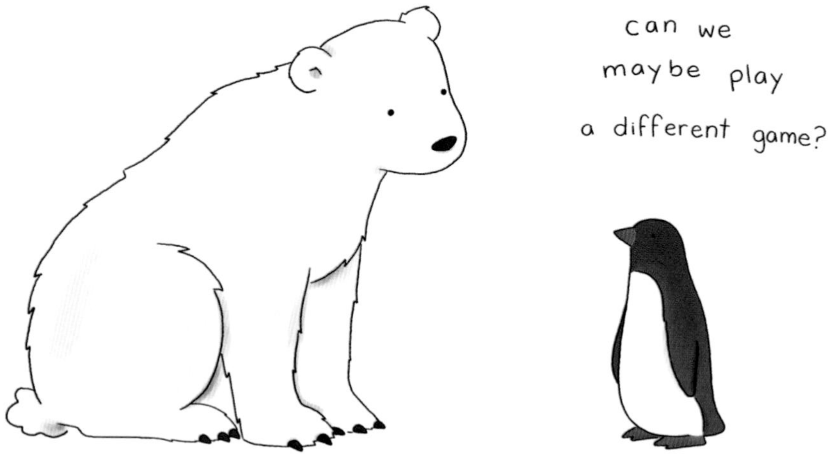
can we
maybe play
a different game?

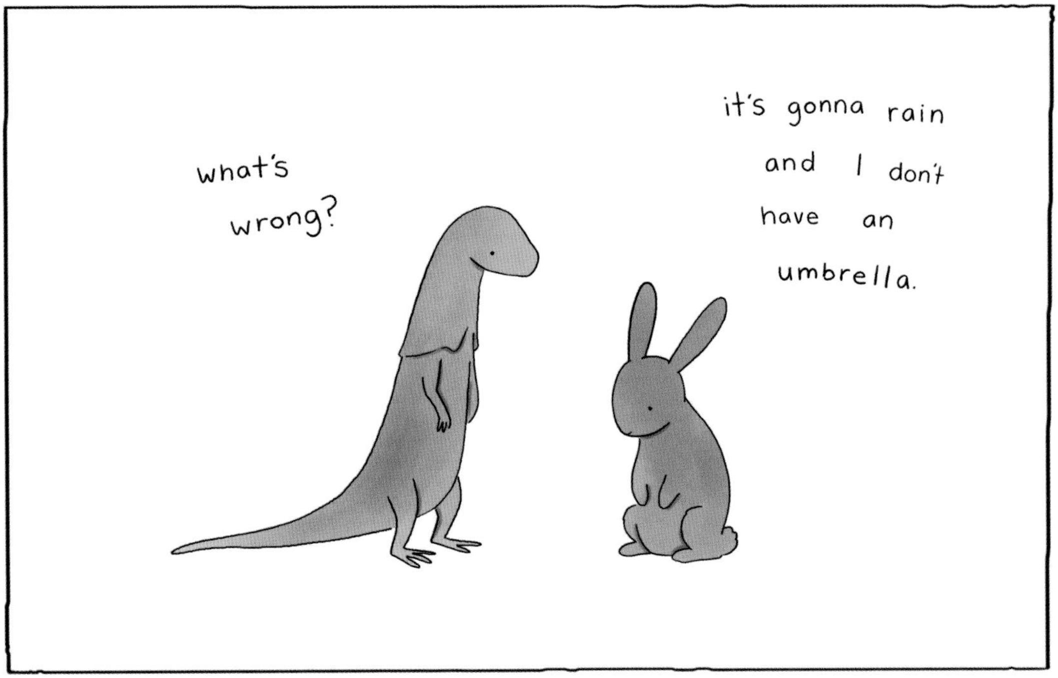
what's wrong?
it's gonna rain and I don't have an umbrella.

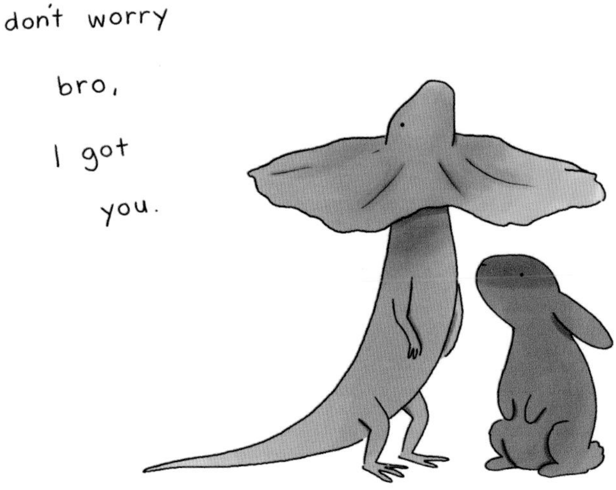
don't worry bro, I got you.

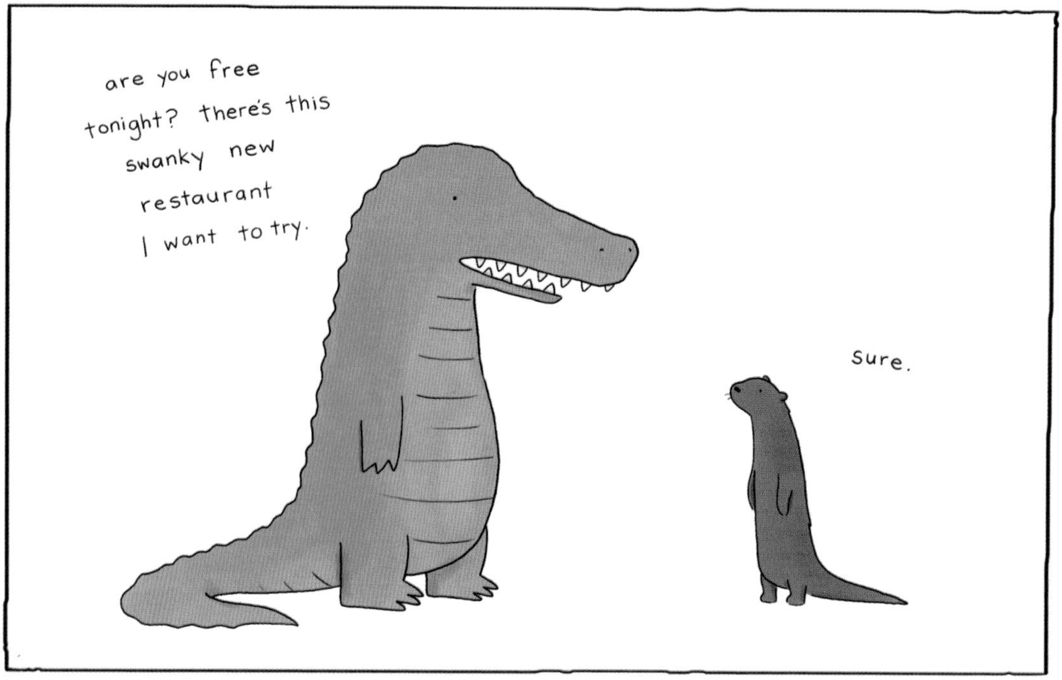
are you free tonight? there's this swanky new restaurant I want to try.
sure.

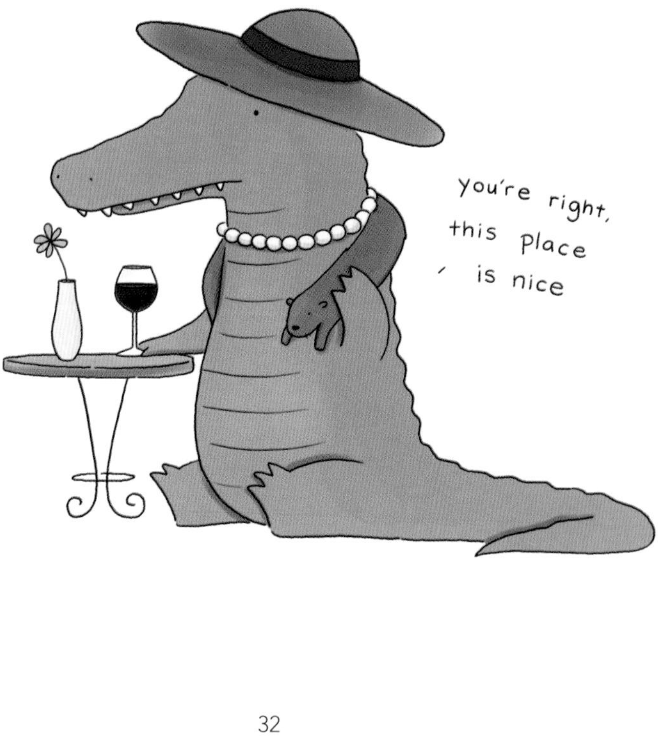
you're right, this place is nice

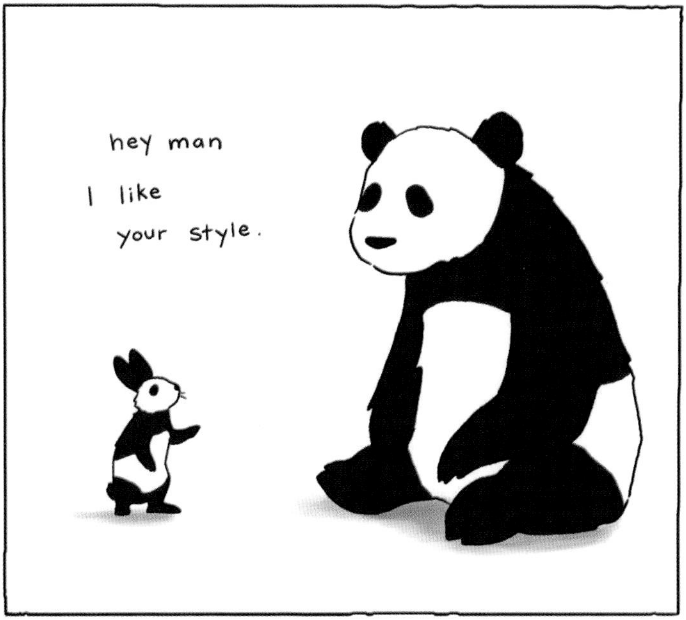
hey man
I like
your style.

oh no!

oops, I
must have fallen
asleep while
I was eating
my salad.

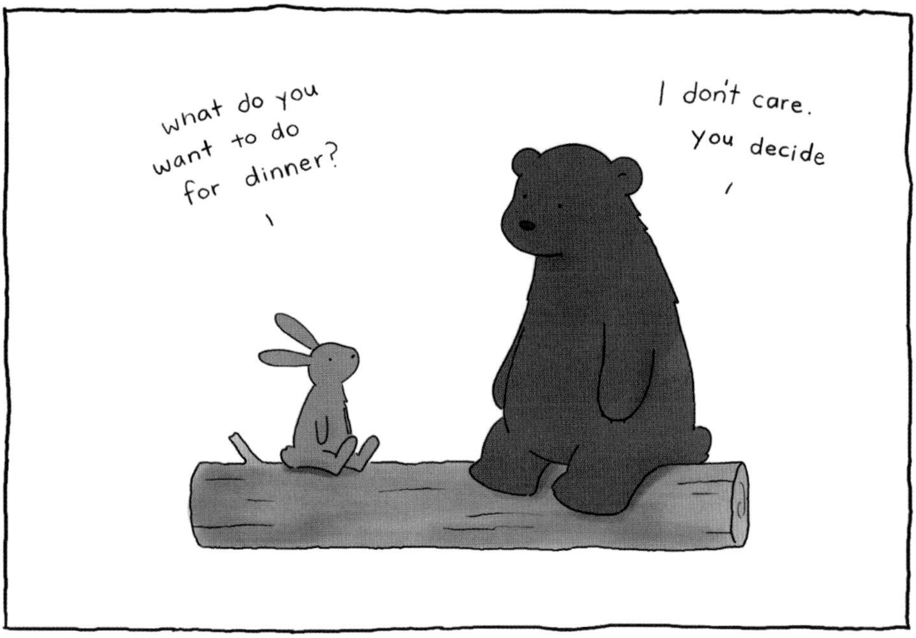
what do you want to do for dinner?
I don't care. you decide

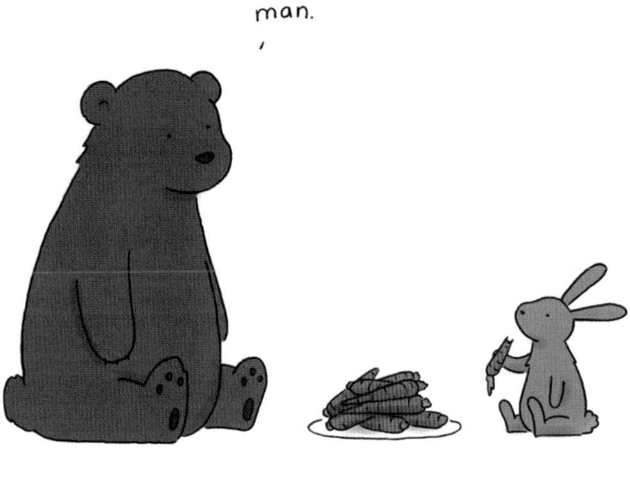
man.

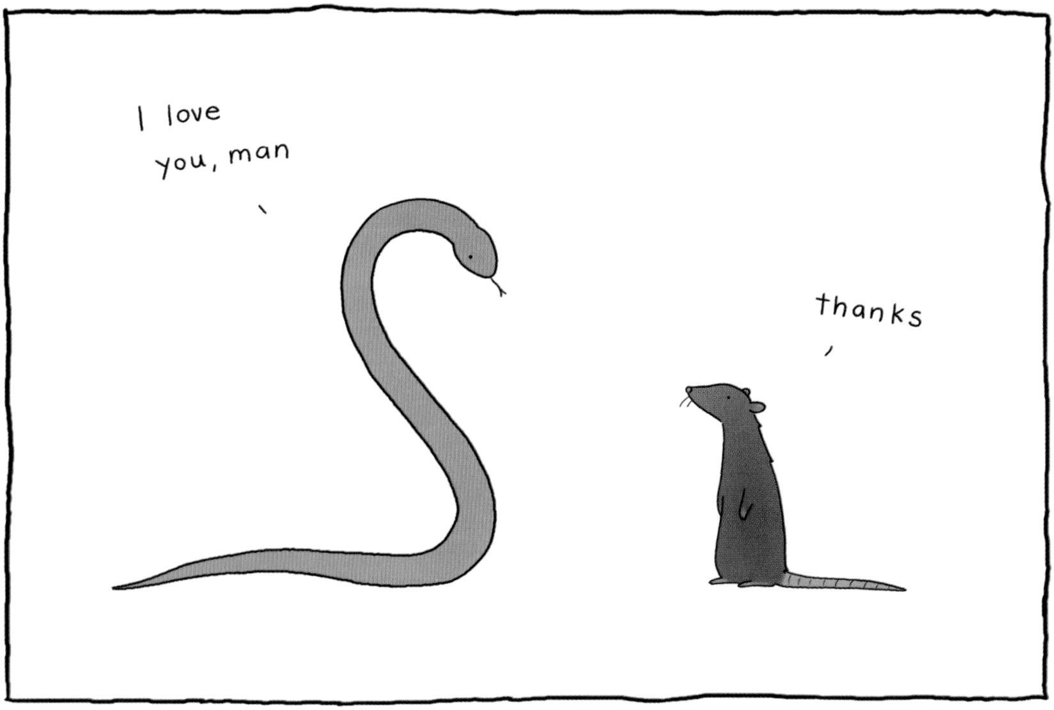
I love you, man
thanks

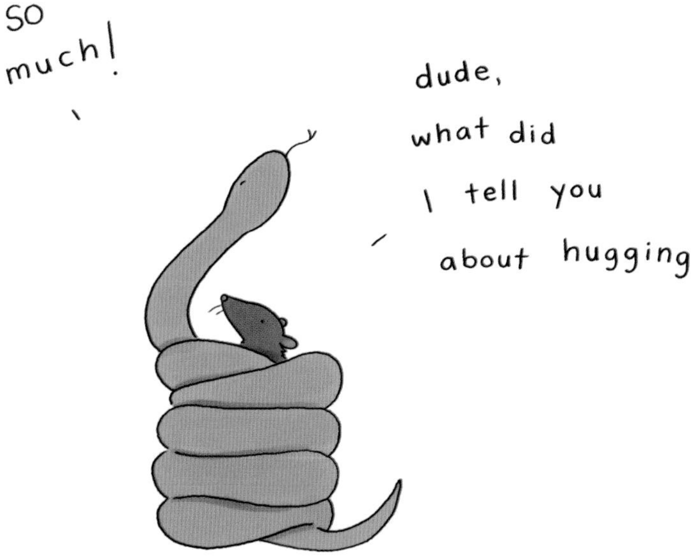
SO much!
dude, what did I tell you about hugging

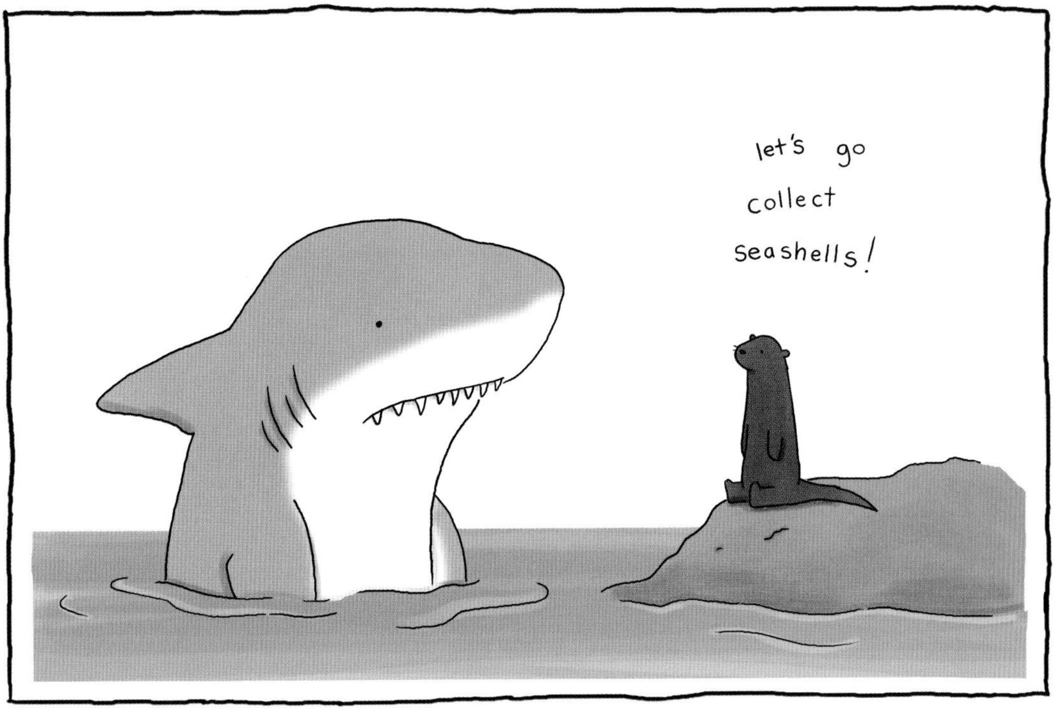
let's go collect seashells!

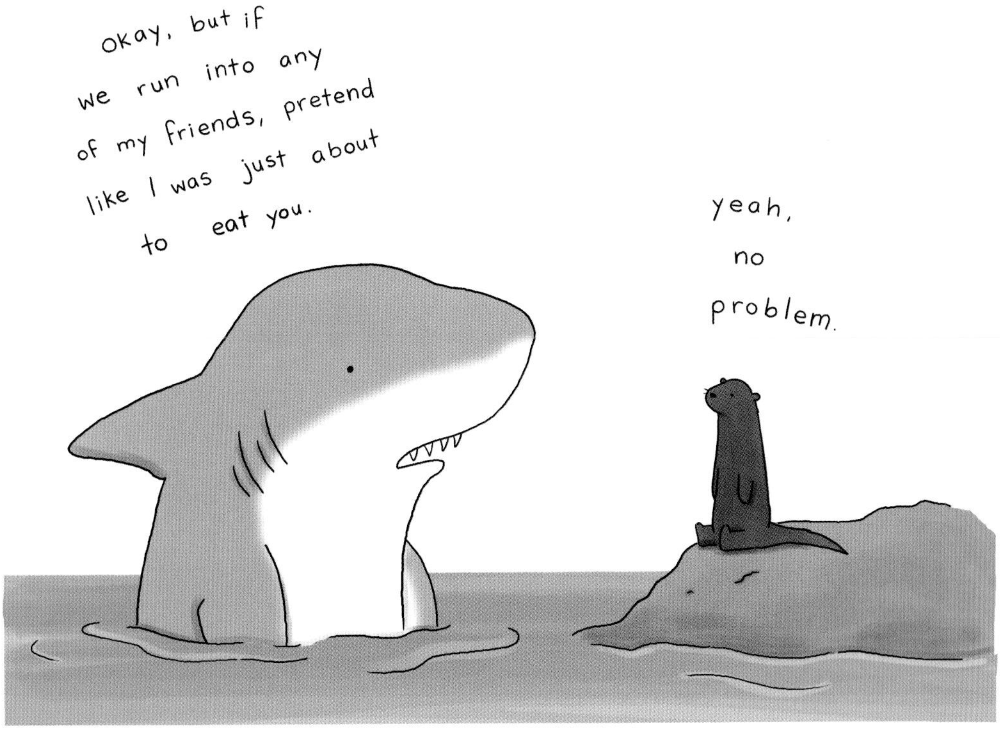
okay, but if we run into any of my friends, pretend like I was just about to eat you.
yeah, no problem.

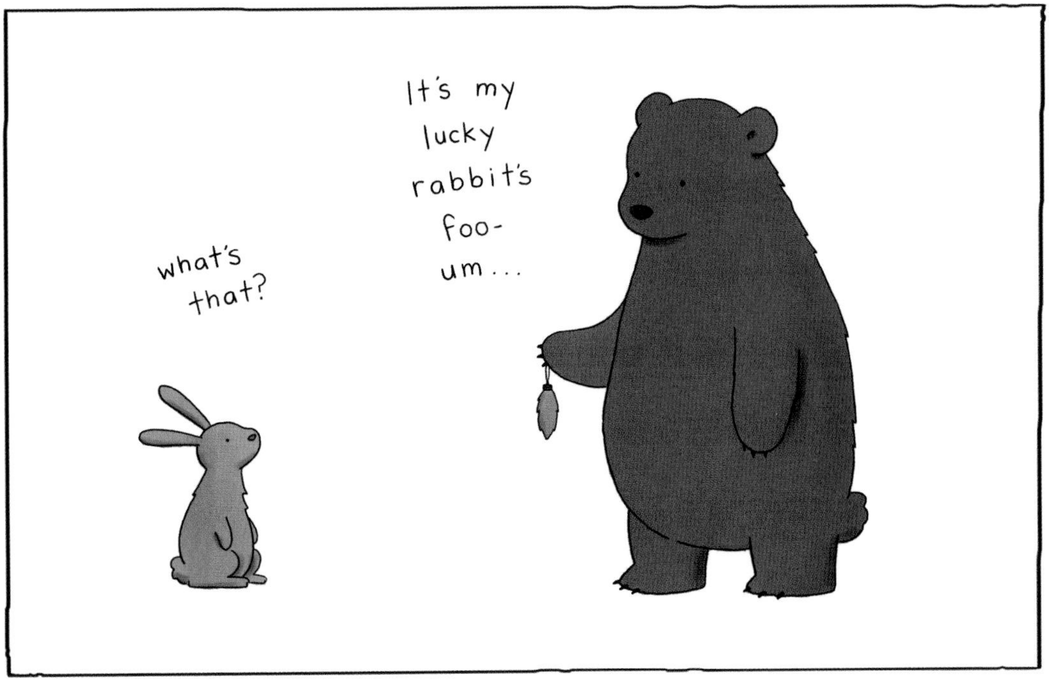
what's that?
It's my lucky rabbit's foo- um...

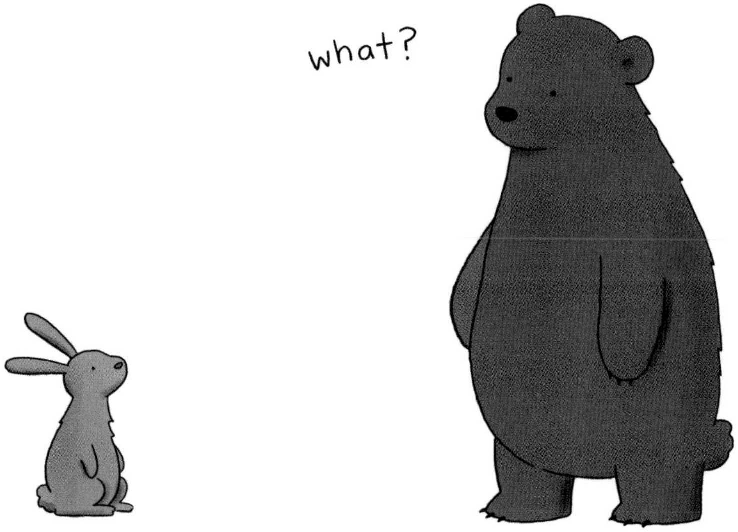
what?

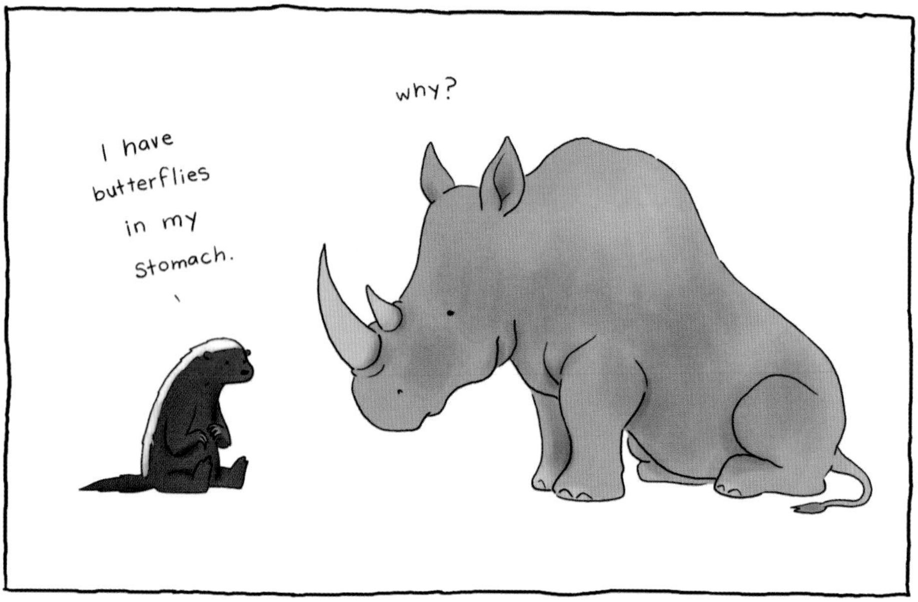
I have butterflies in my stomach.
why?

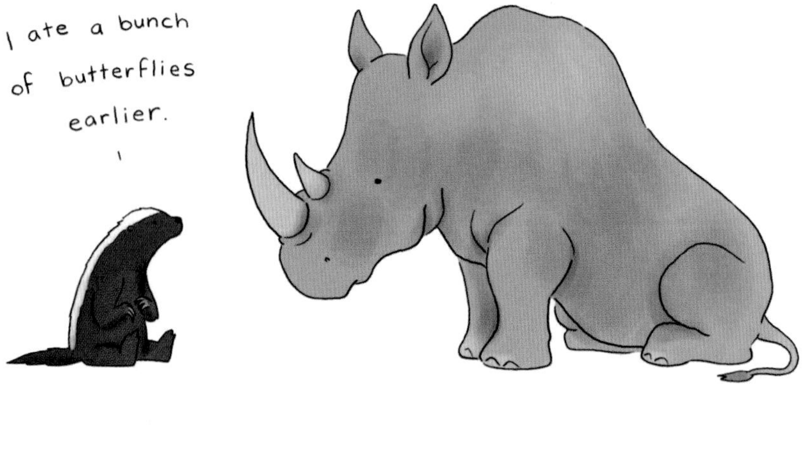
I ate a bunch of butterflies earlier.

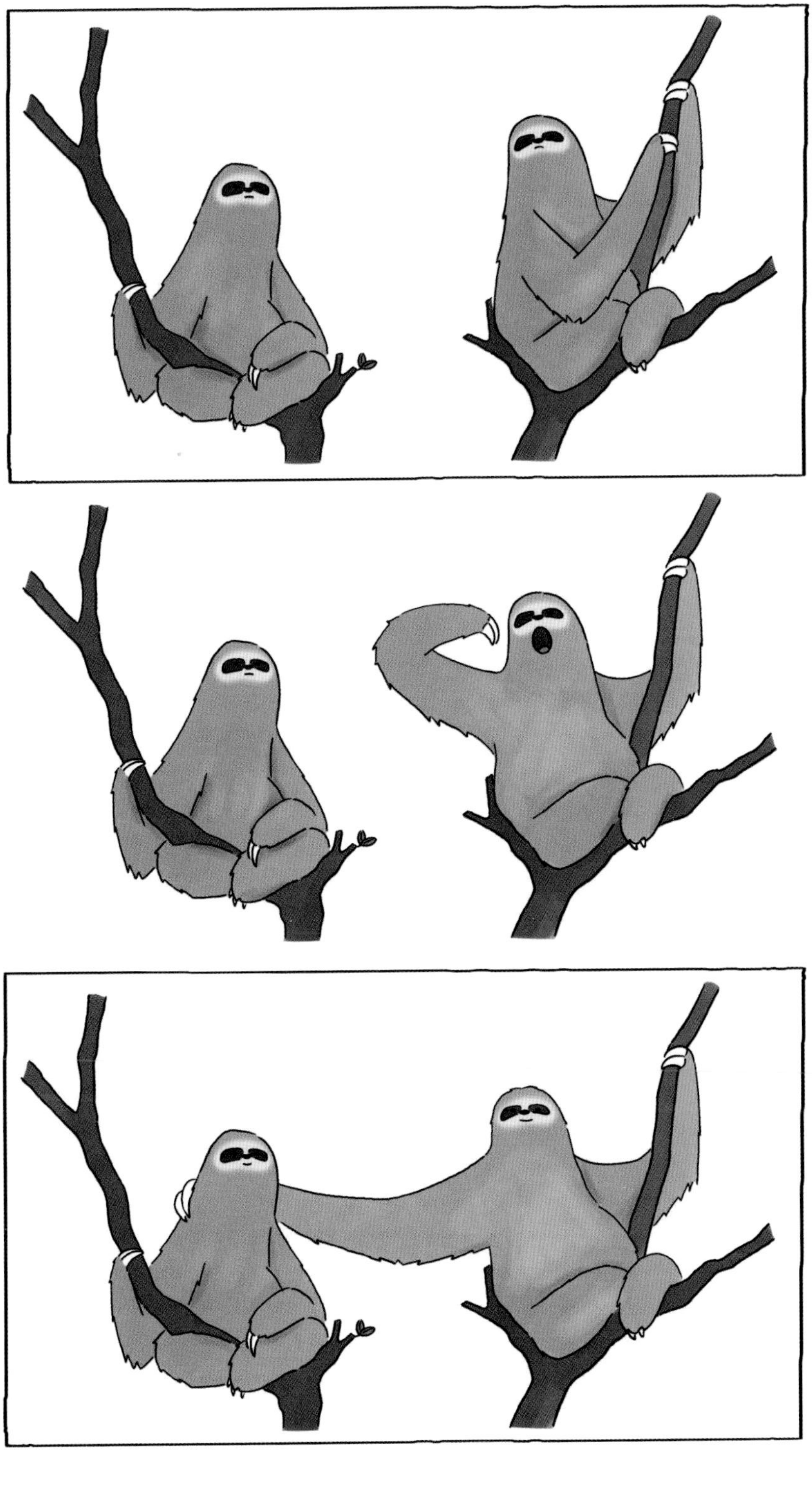

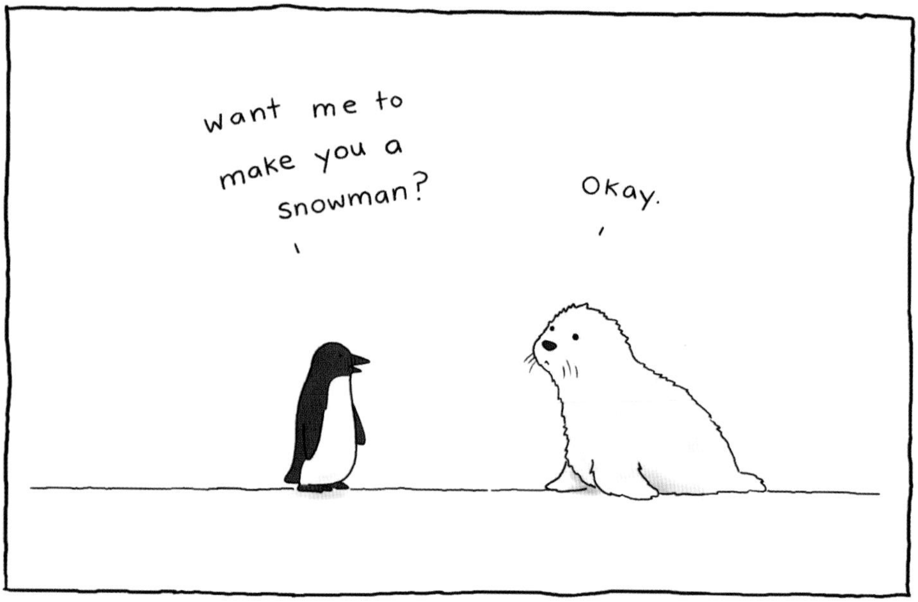
Want me to make you a snowman?
Okay.

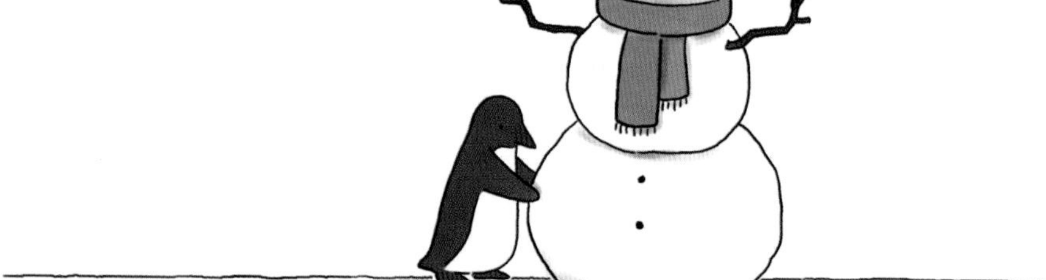

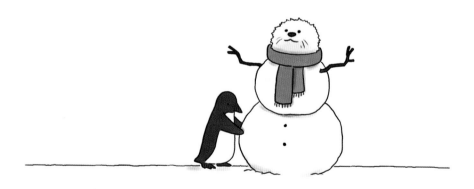

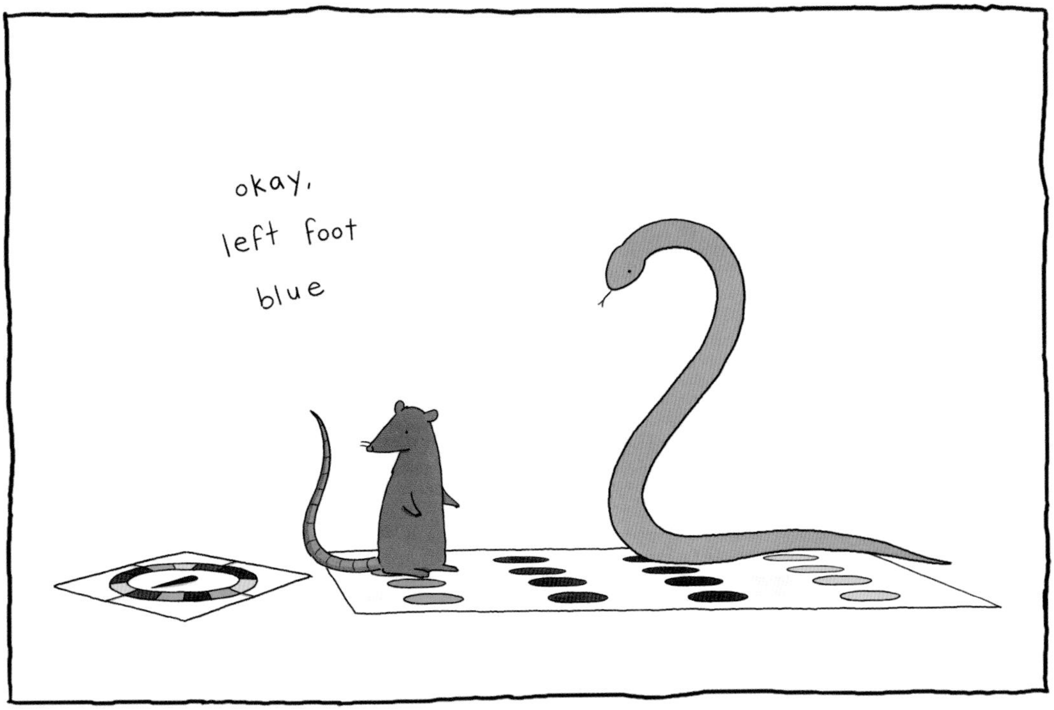
okay,
left foot
blue

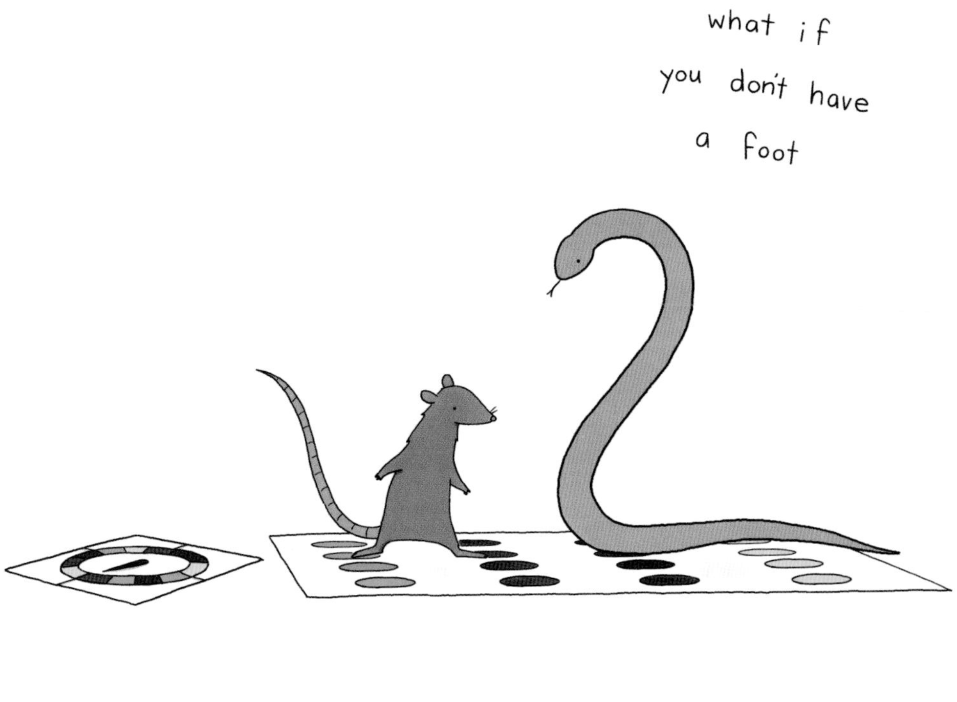
what if
you don't have
a foot

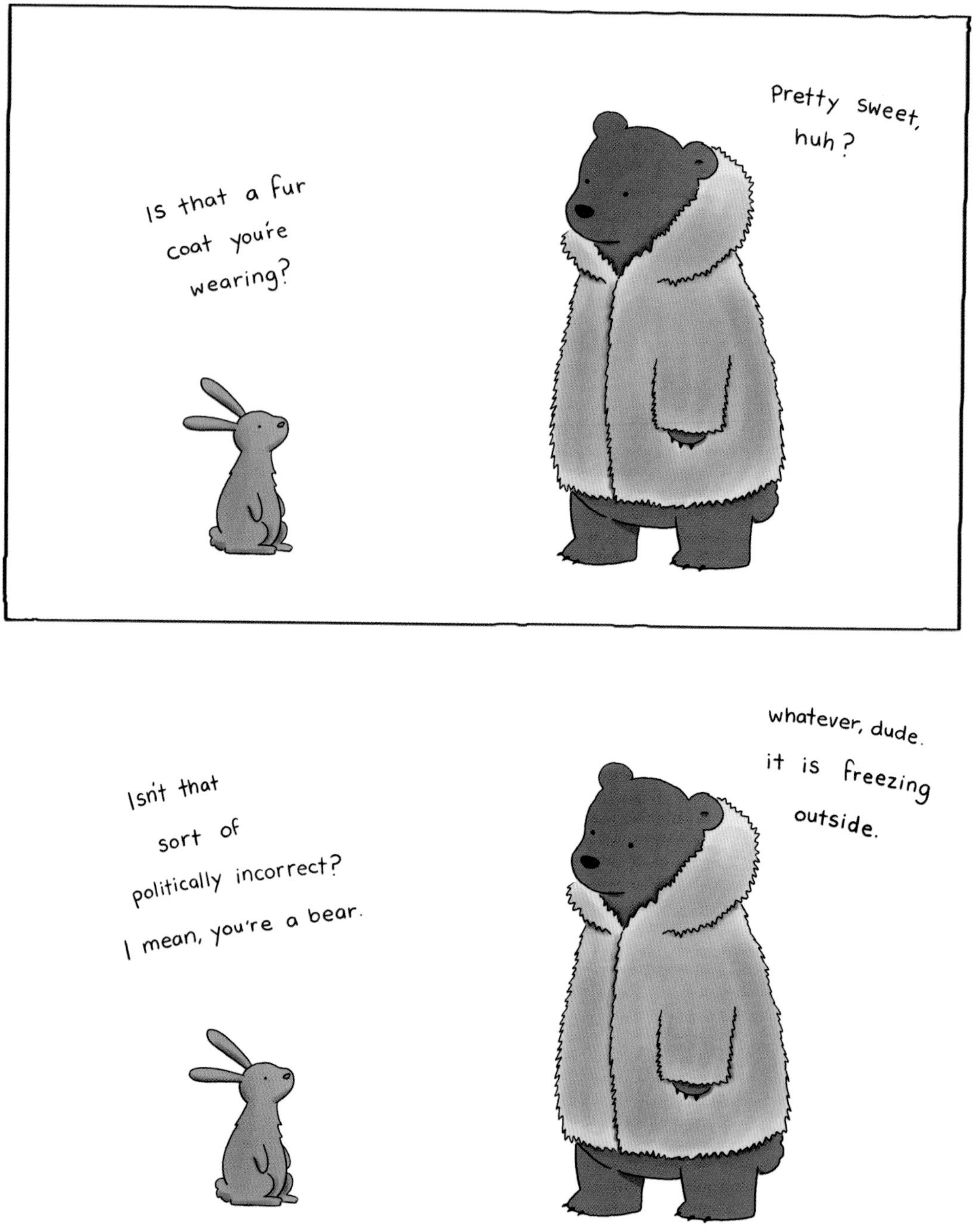
Is that a fur coat you're wearing?
Pretty sweet, huh?
Isn't that sort of politically incorrect? I mean, you're a bear.
whatever, dude. it is freezing outside.

holidays
and
celebrations

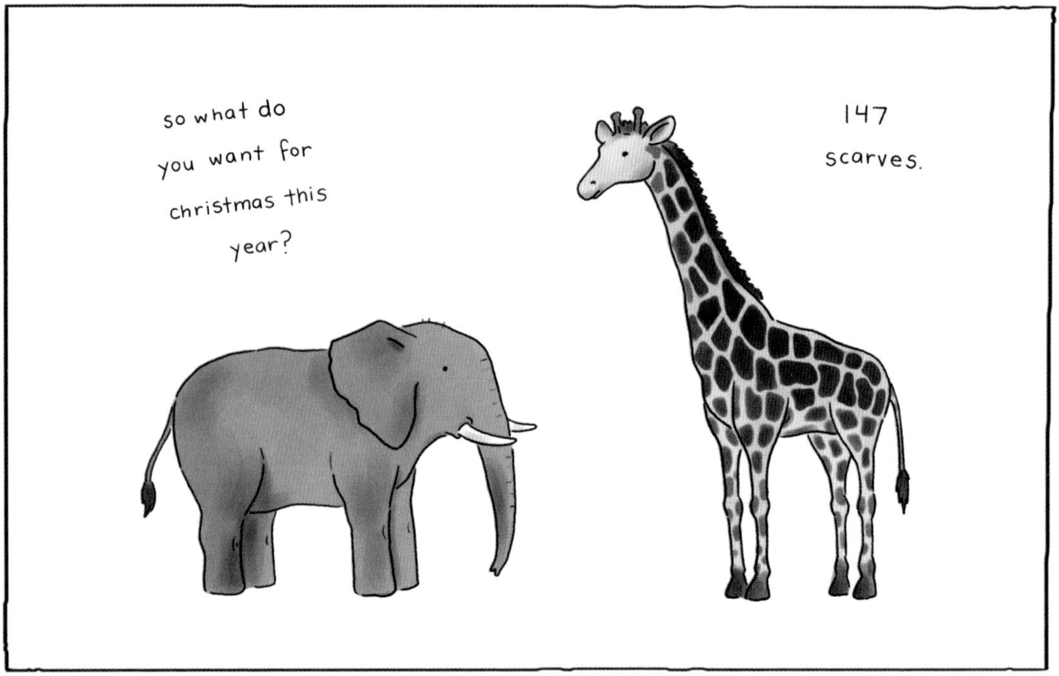
so what do
you want for
christmas this
year?
147
scarves.

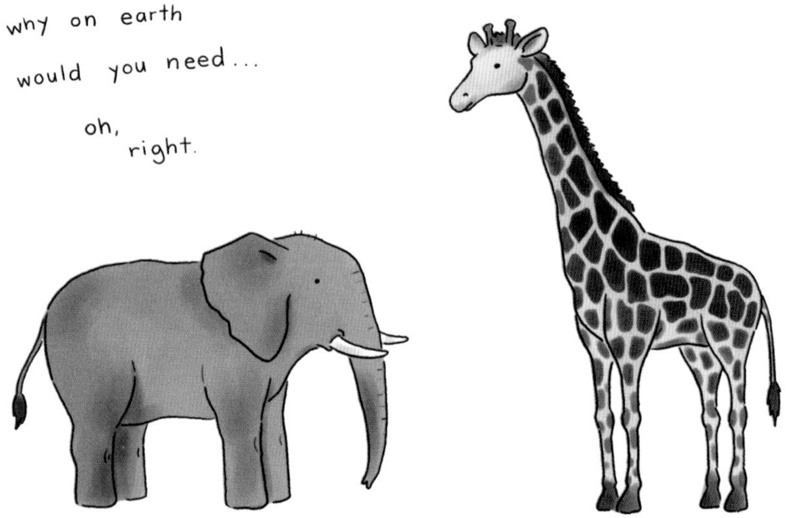
why on earth
would you need...
oh,
right.

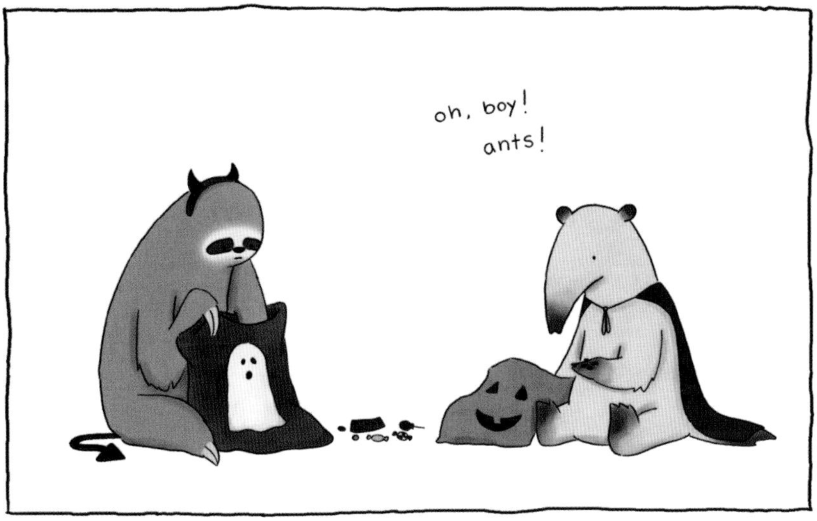
oh, boy!
ants!

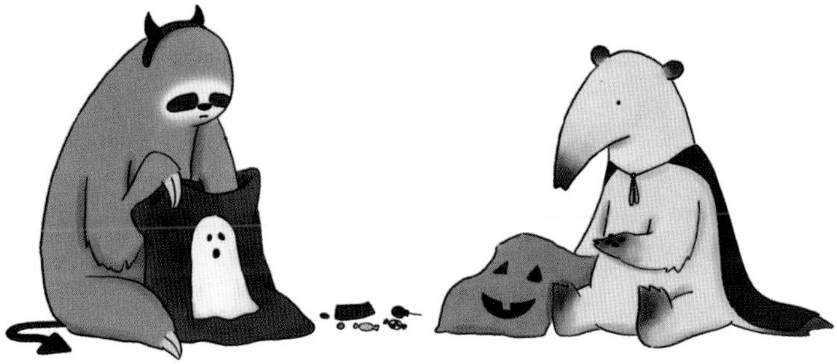
those are
raisins.
oh.
gross.

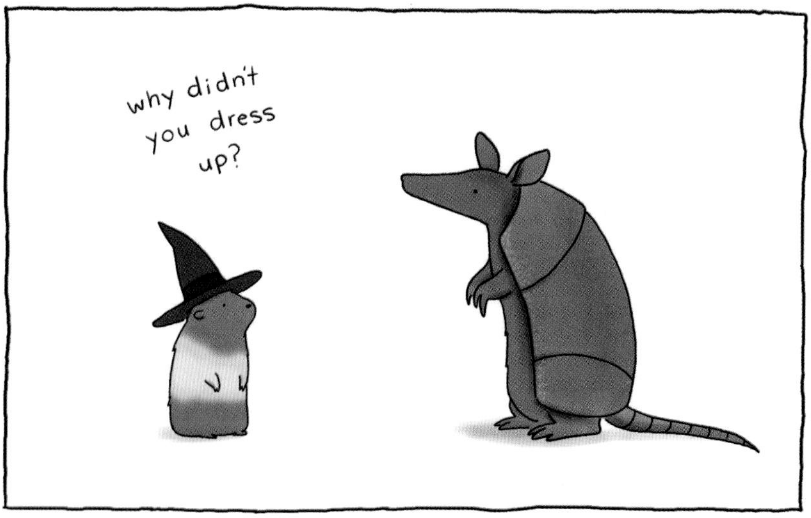
why didn't you dress up?

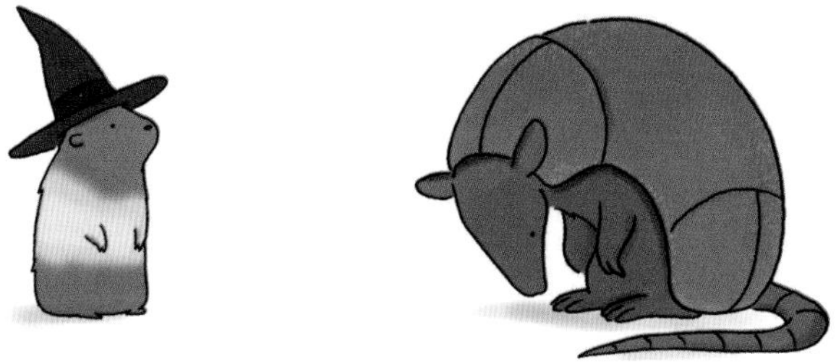

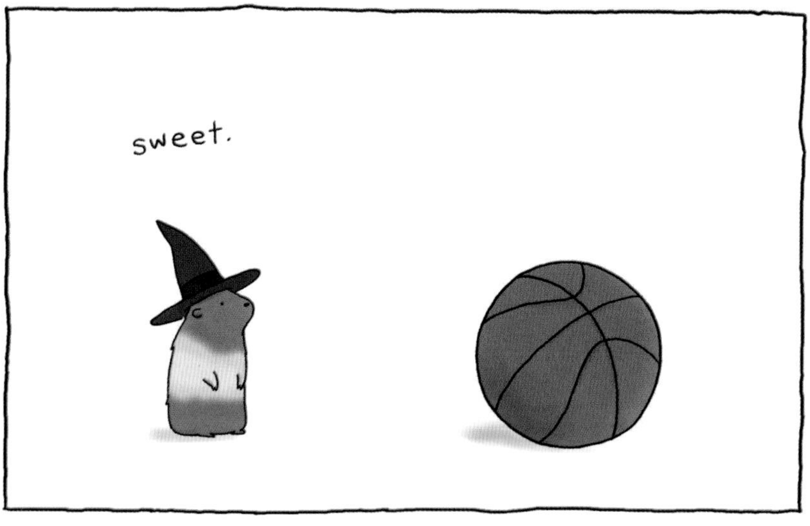
sweet.

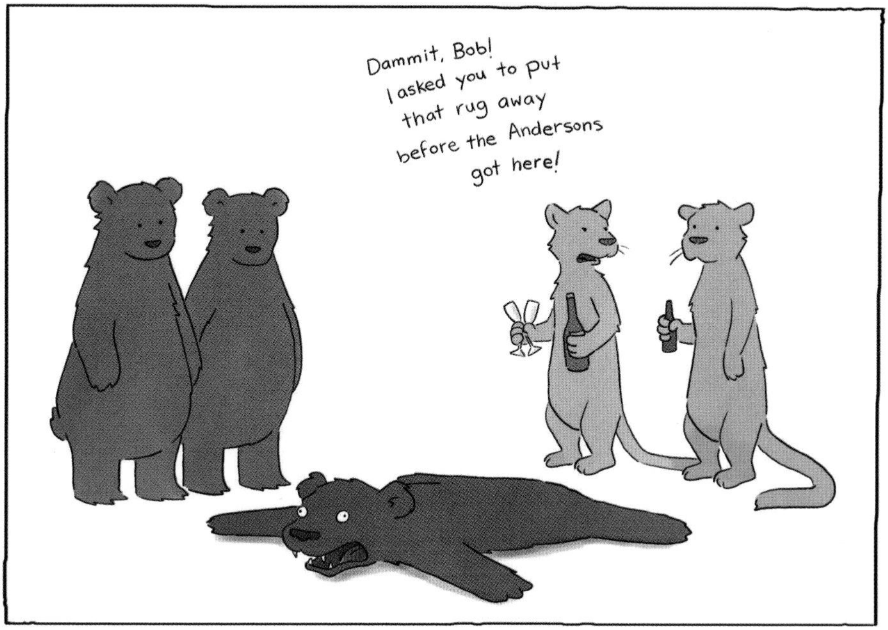
Dammit, Bob!
I asked you to put
that rug away
before the Andersons
got here!

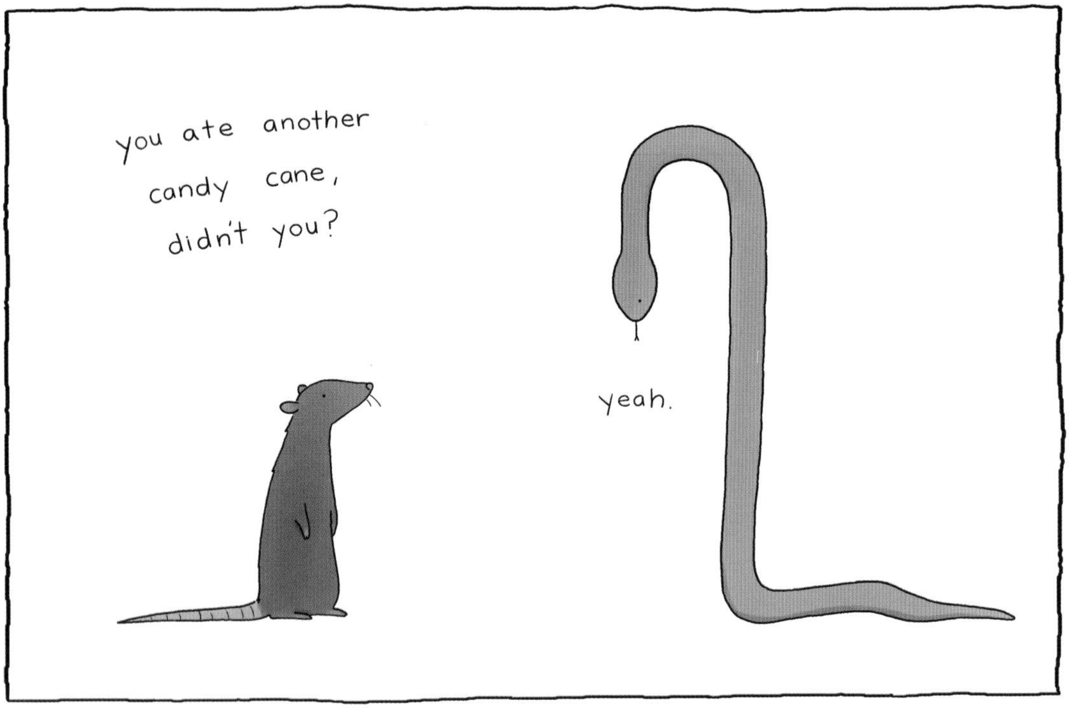
you ate another
candy cane,
didn't you?
yeah.

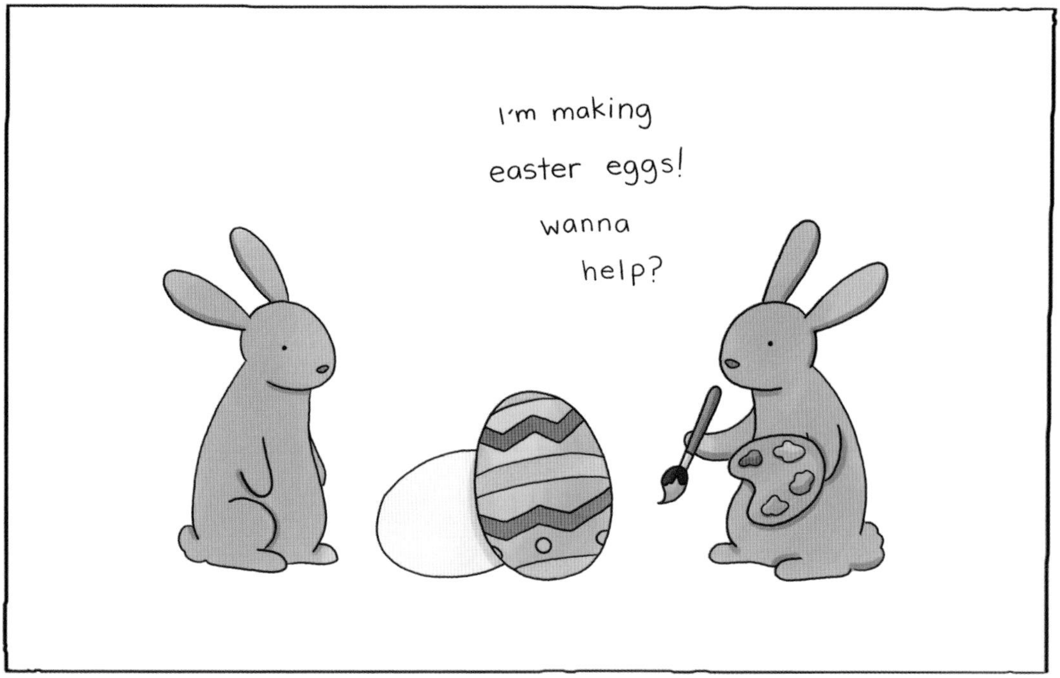
I'm making
easter eggs!
wanna
help?

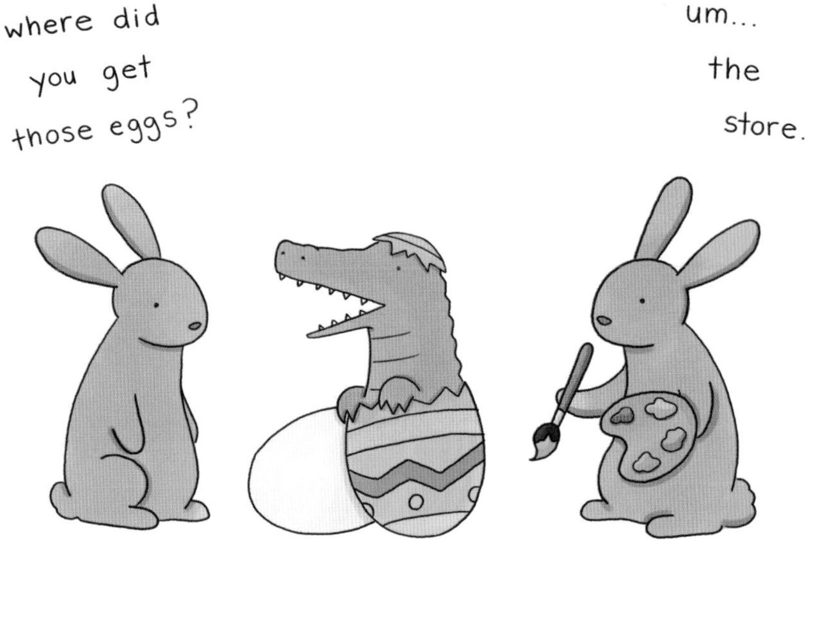
where did
you get
those eggs?
um...
the
store.

no, see-
this is a black
bear costume.
I'm a grizzly

It's still
Pretty
confusing
dude.

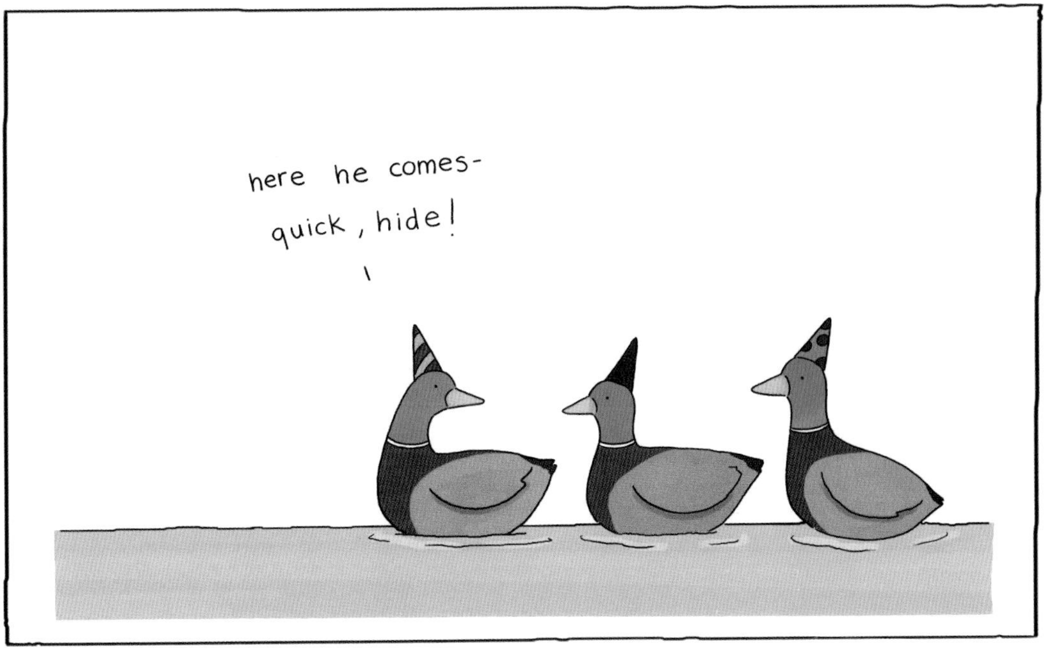
here he comes-
quick, hide!

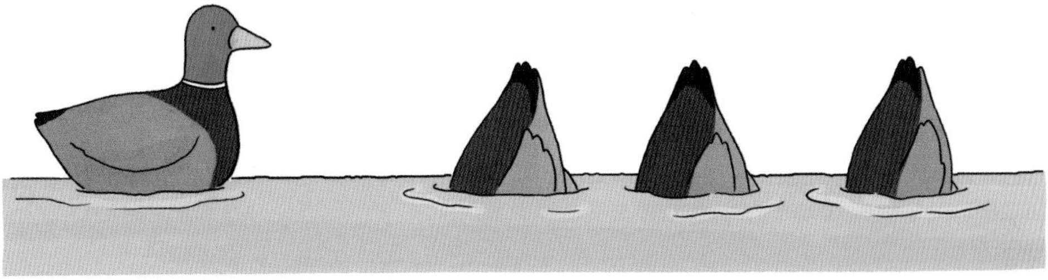

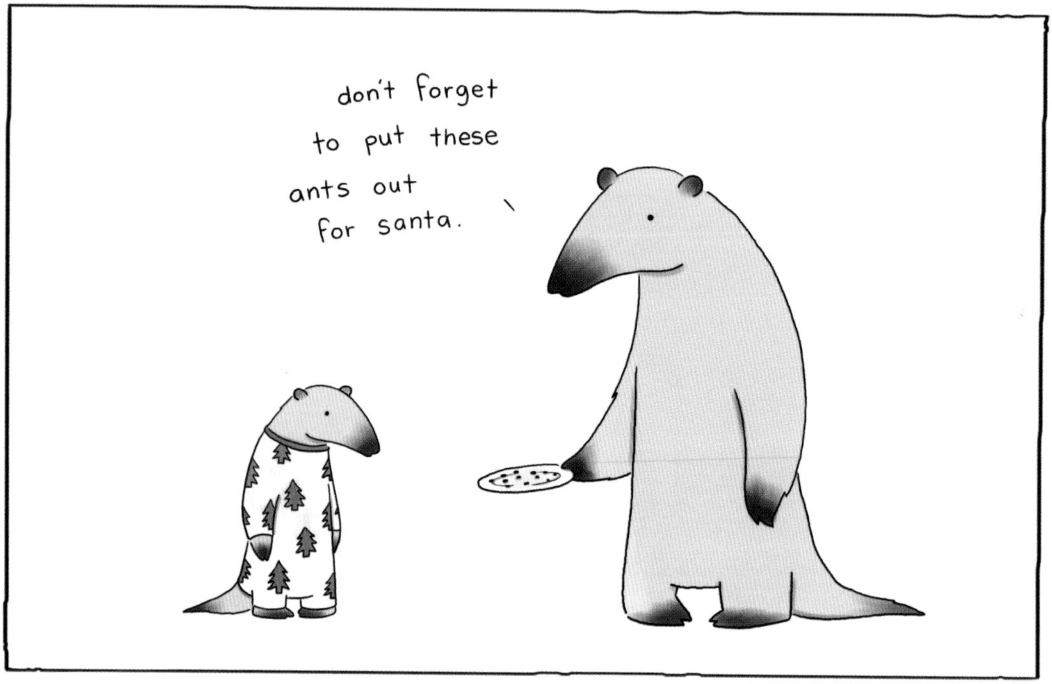
don't forget to put these ants out for santa.

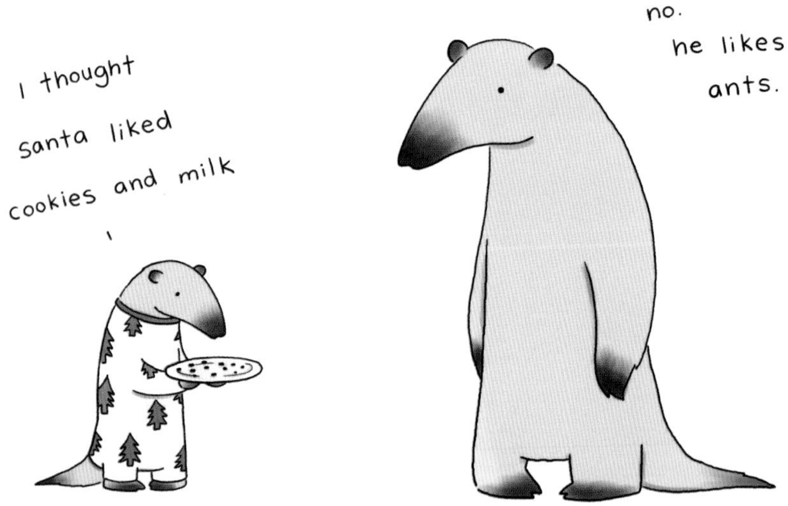
I thought santa liked cookies and milk
no. he likes ants.

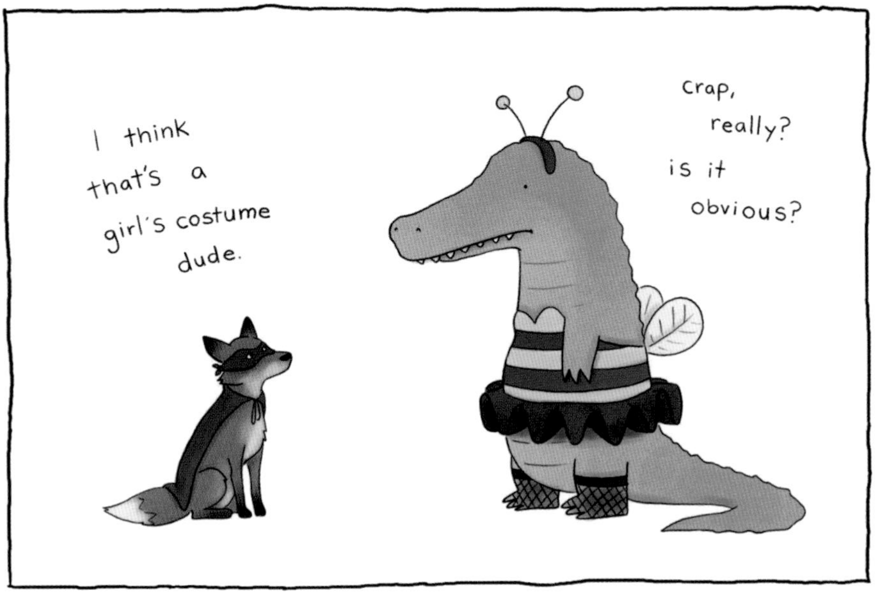
I think that's a girl's costume dude.
crap, really? is it obvious?

I don't
understand
your costume.

I'm a
ghost.

I think you're
supposed to use
a white sheet,
not one with little
dinosaurs all
over it.

but that's
all I
had

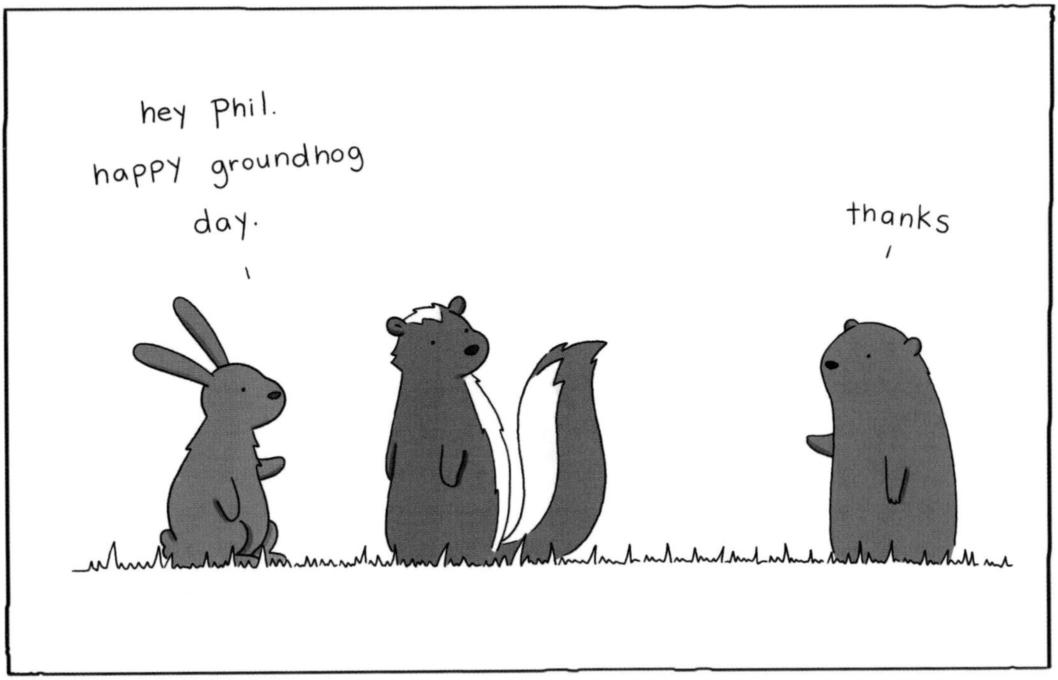
hey Phil. happy groundhog day.
thanks

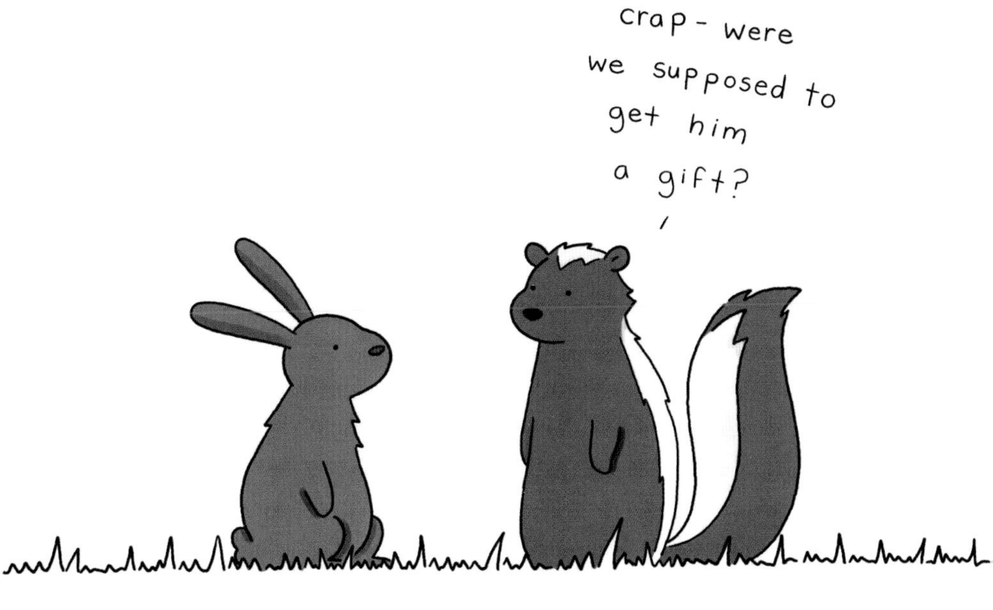
crap - were we supposed to get him a gift?

here he comes!
everybody
hide!

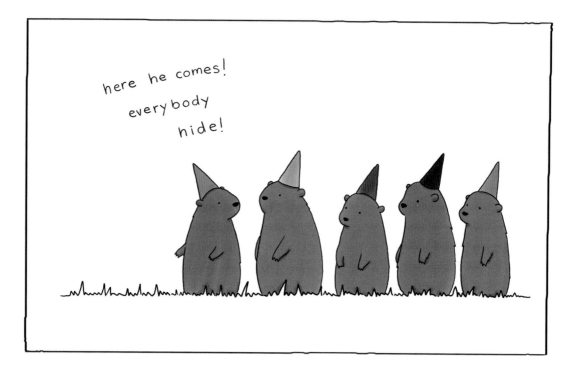

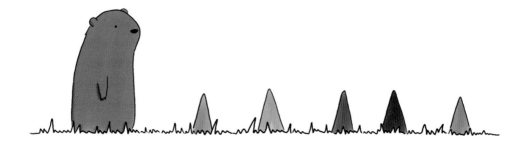

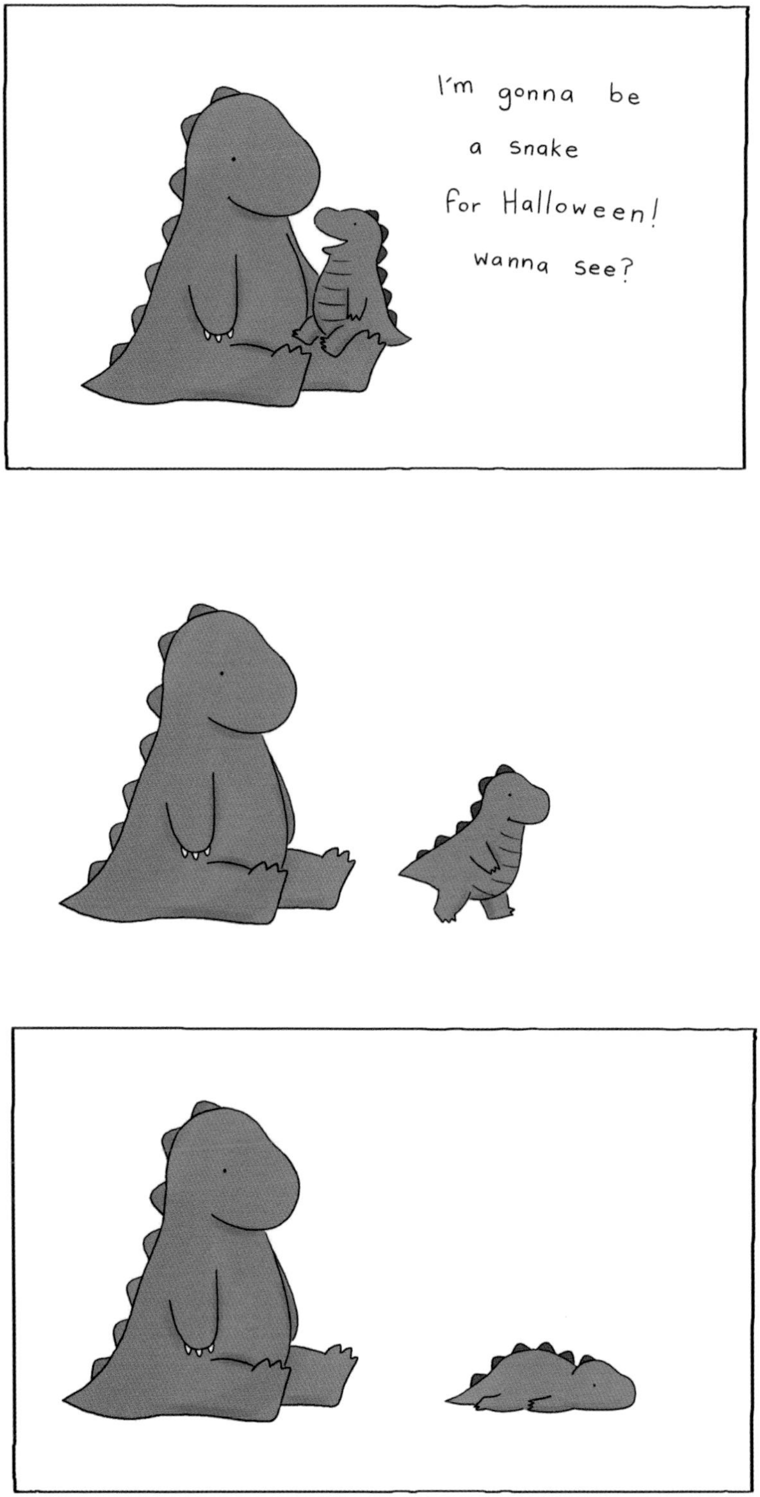
I'm gonna be a snake for Halloween! wanna see?

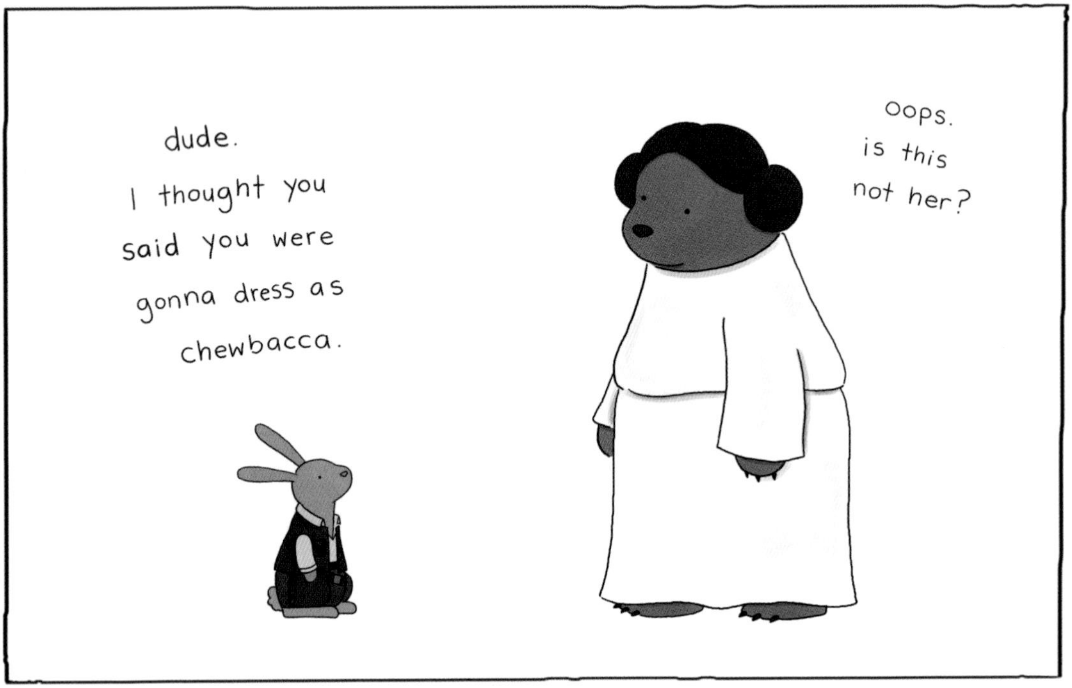
dude.
I thought you
said you were
gonna dress as
chewbacca.
oops.
is this
not her?

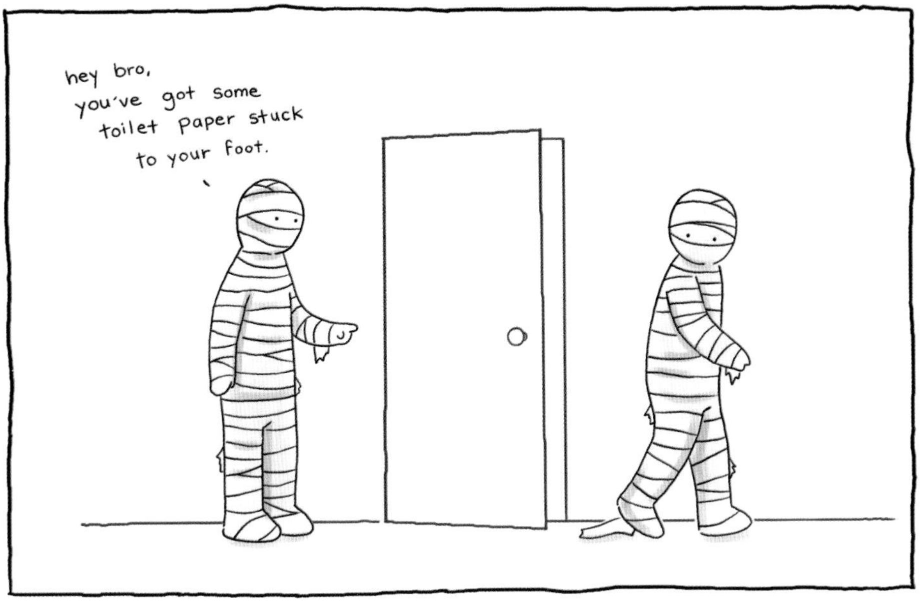
hey bro,
you've got some
toilet paper stuck
to your foot.

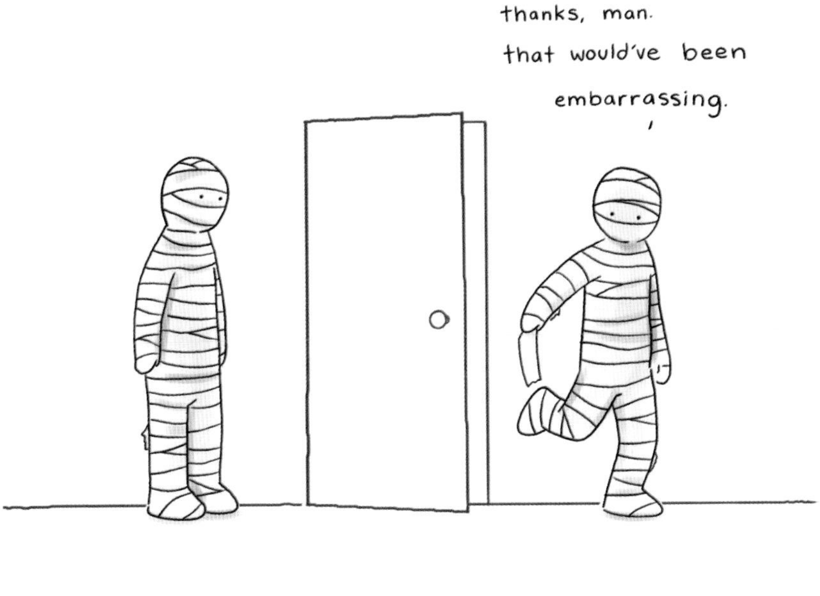
thanks, man.
that would've been
embarrassing.

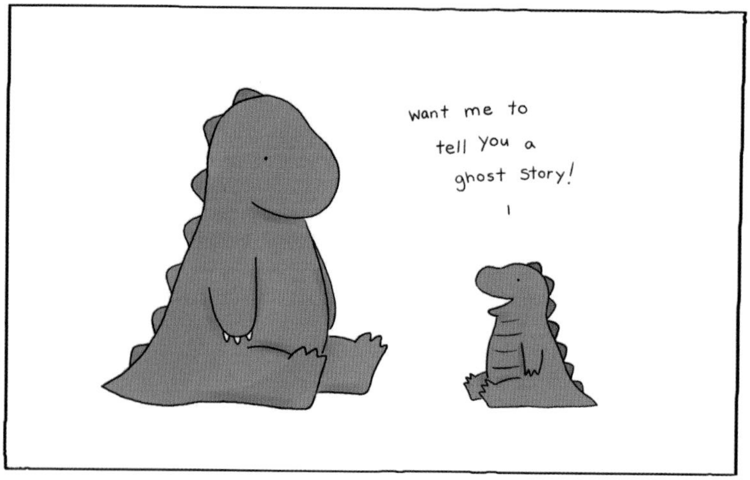
want me to tell you a ghost story!

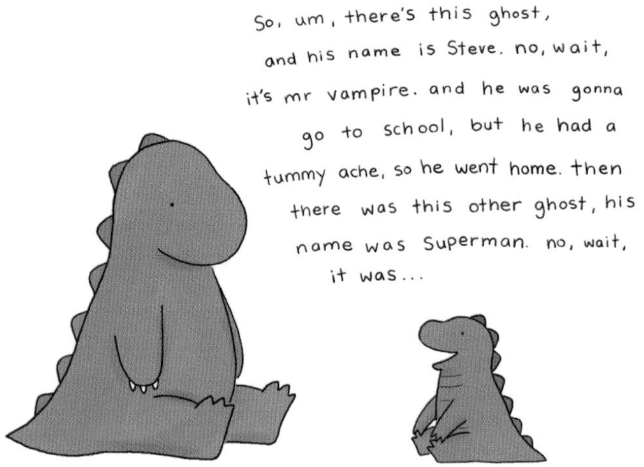
So, um, there's this ghost, and his name is Steve. no, wait, it's mr vampire. and he was gonna go to school, but he had a tummy ache, so he went home. then there was this other ghost, his name was Superman. no, wait, it was...

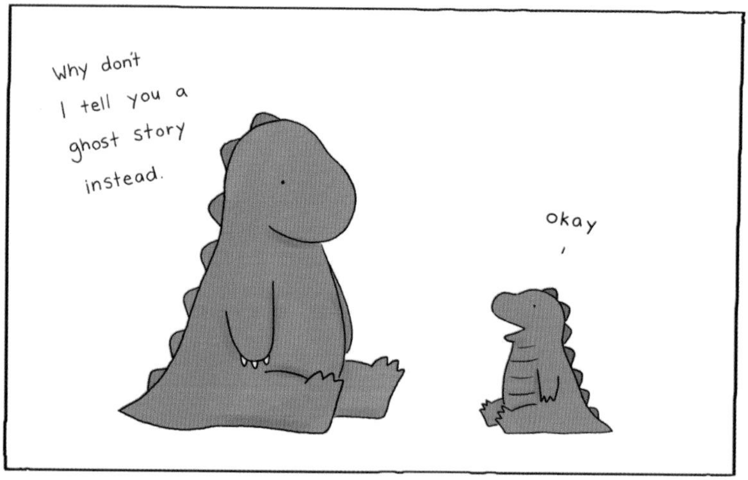
Why don't I tell you a ghost story instead.
okay

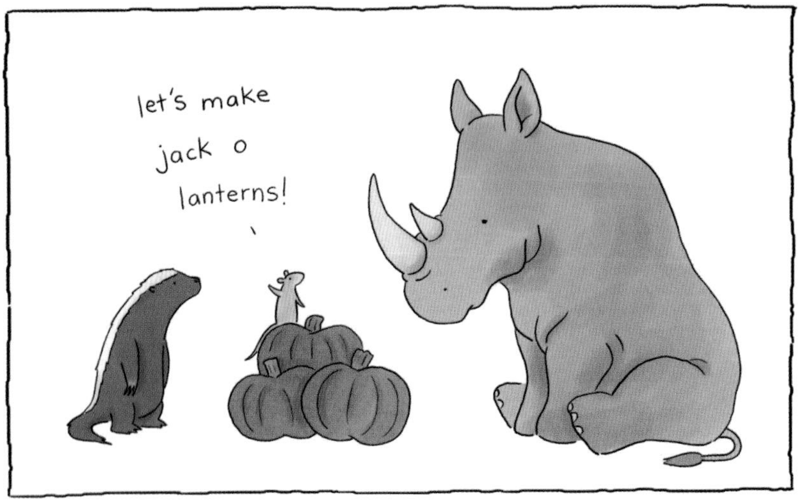
let's make jack o lanterns!

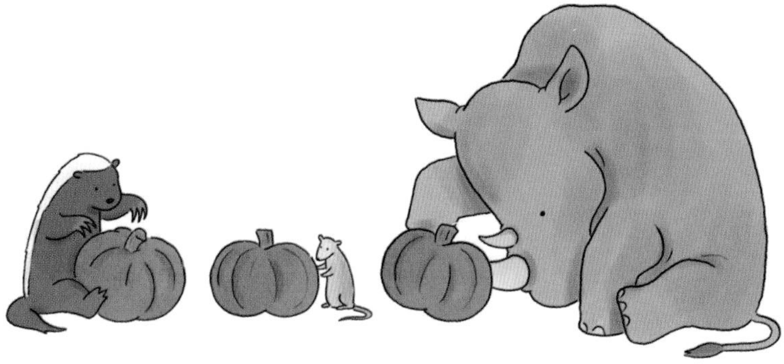

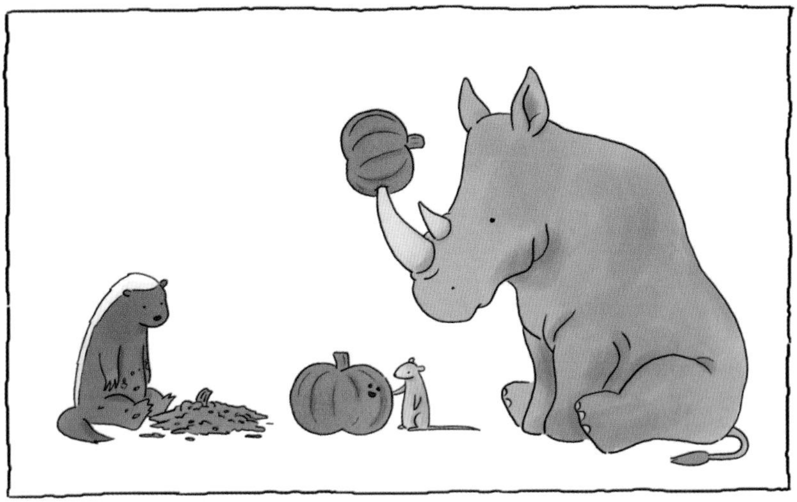

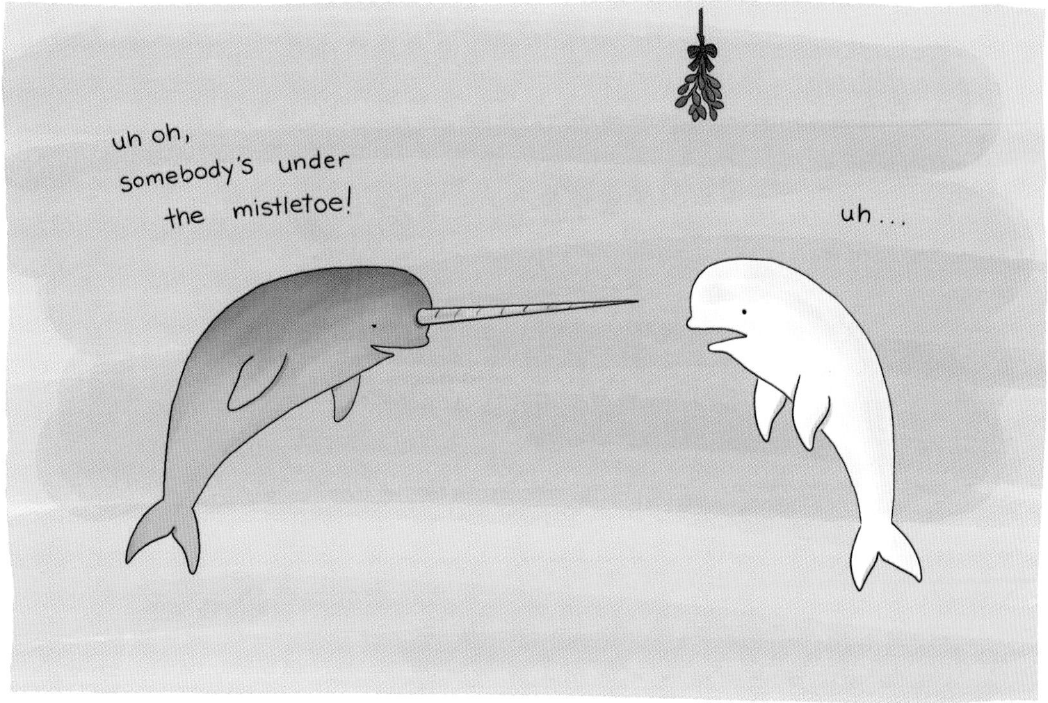
uh oh,
somebody's under
the mistletoe!
uh...

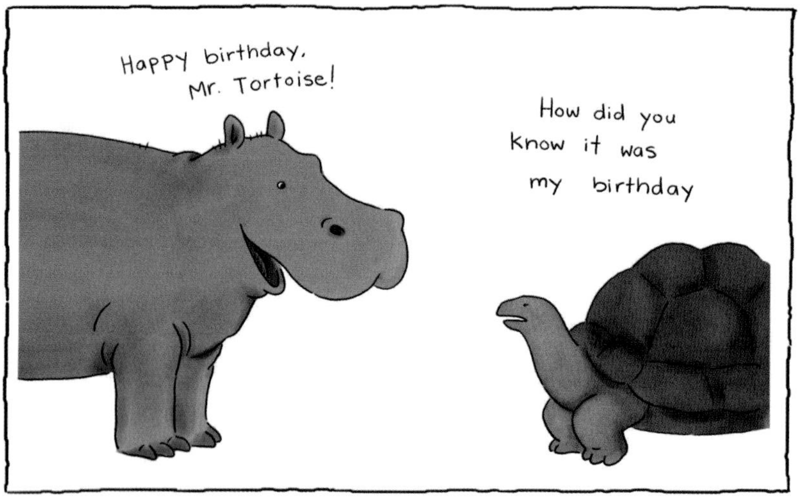
Happy birthday, Mr. Tortoise!
How did you know it was my birthday

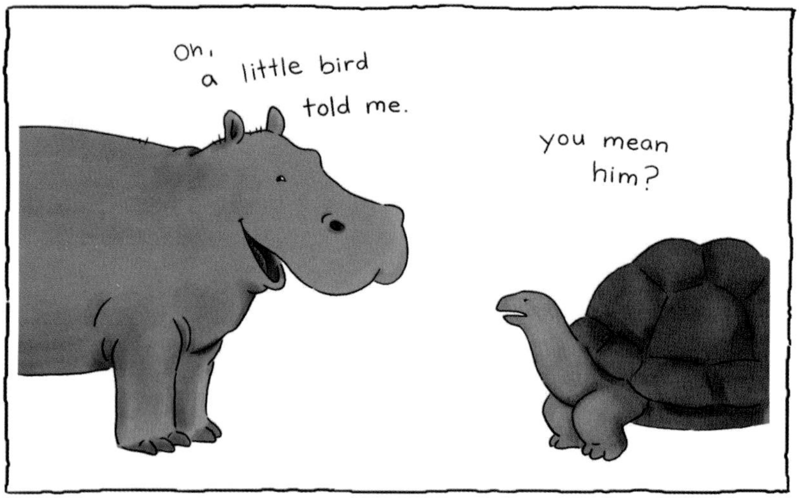
Oh, a little bird told me.
you mean him?

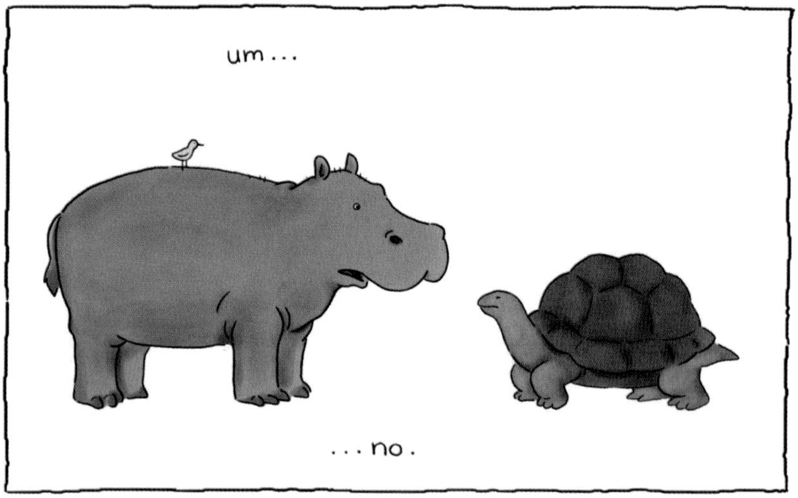
um...
...no.

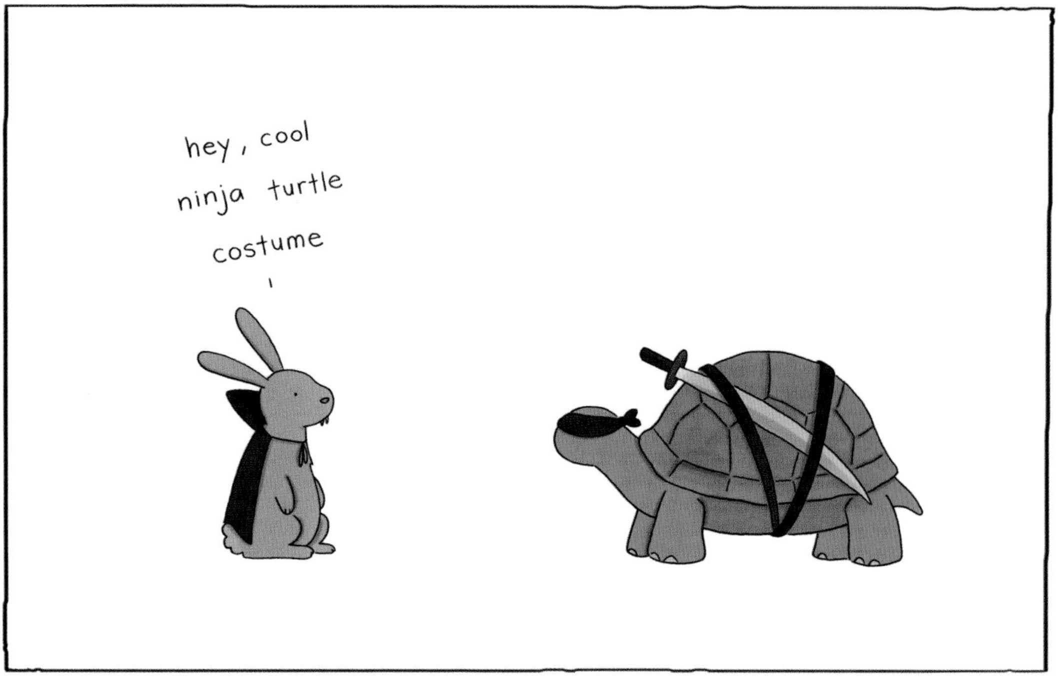
hey, cool ninja turtle costume

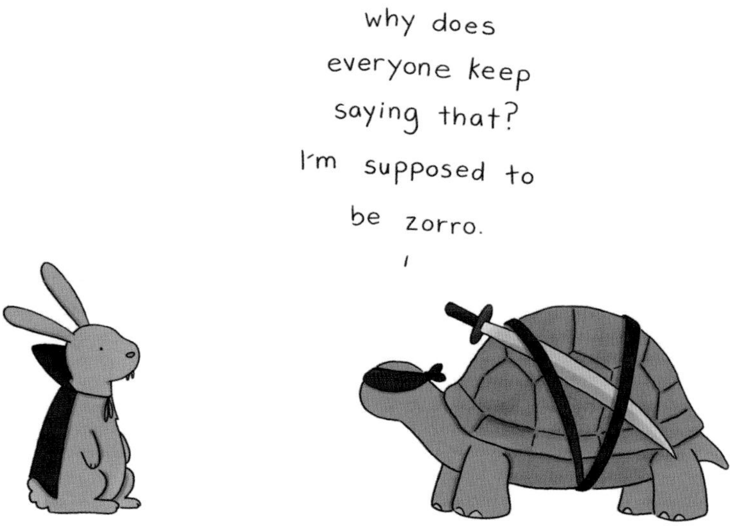
why does everyone keep saying that? I'm supposed to be zorro.

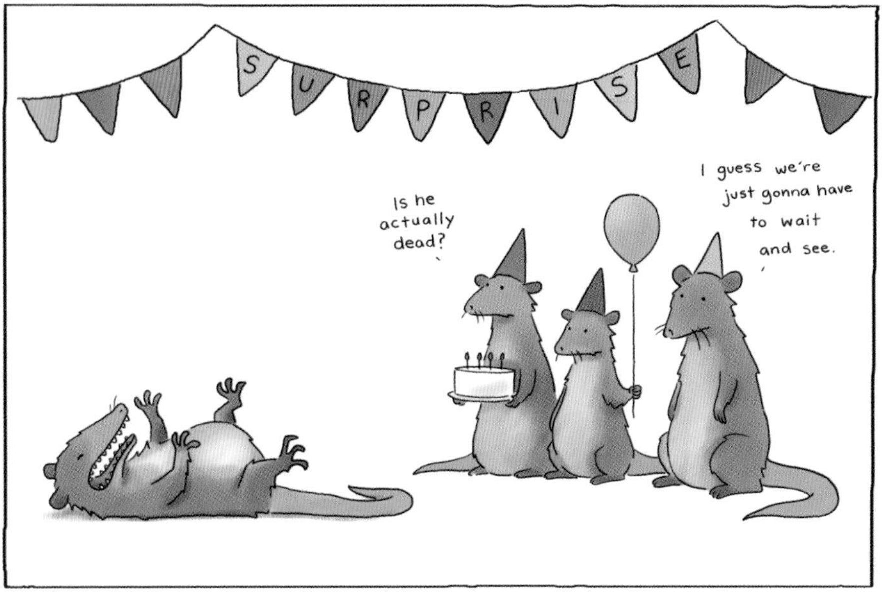
SURPRISE
Is he actually dead?
I guess we're just gonna have to wait and see.

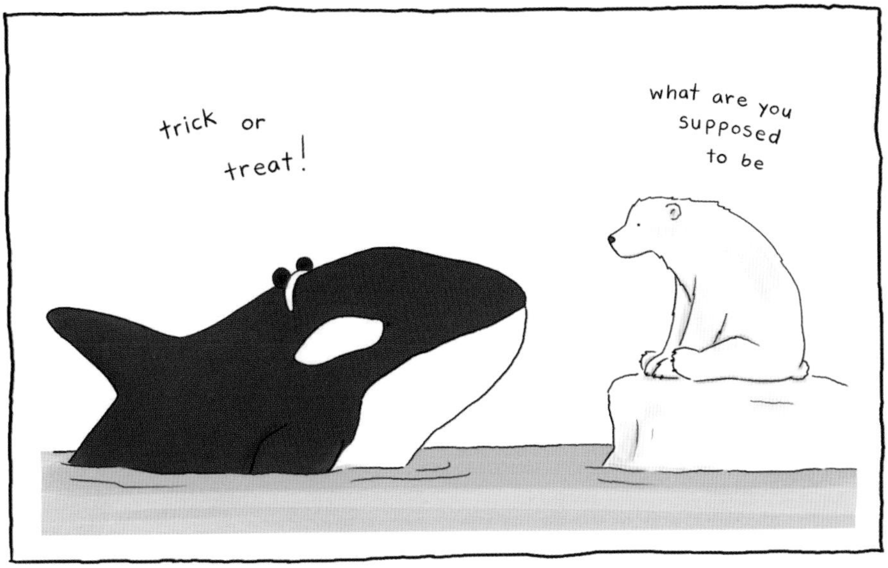
trick or treat!
what are you supposed to be

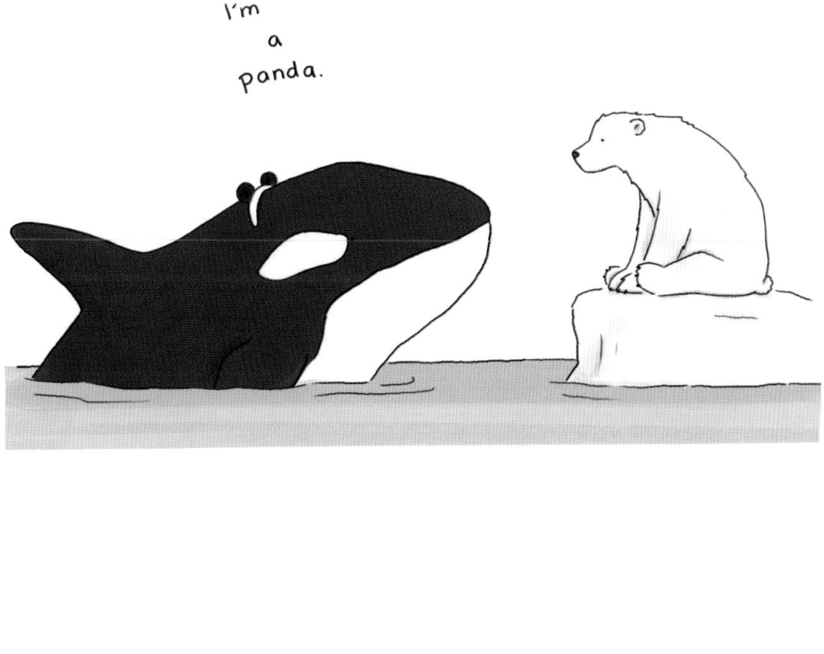
I'm a panda.

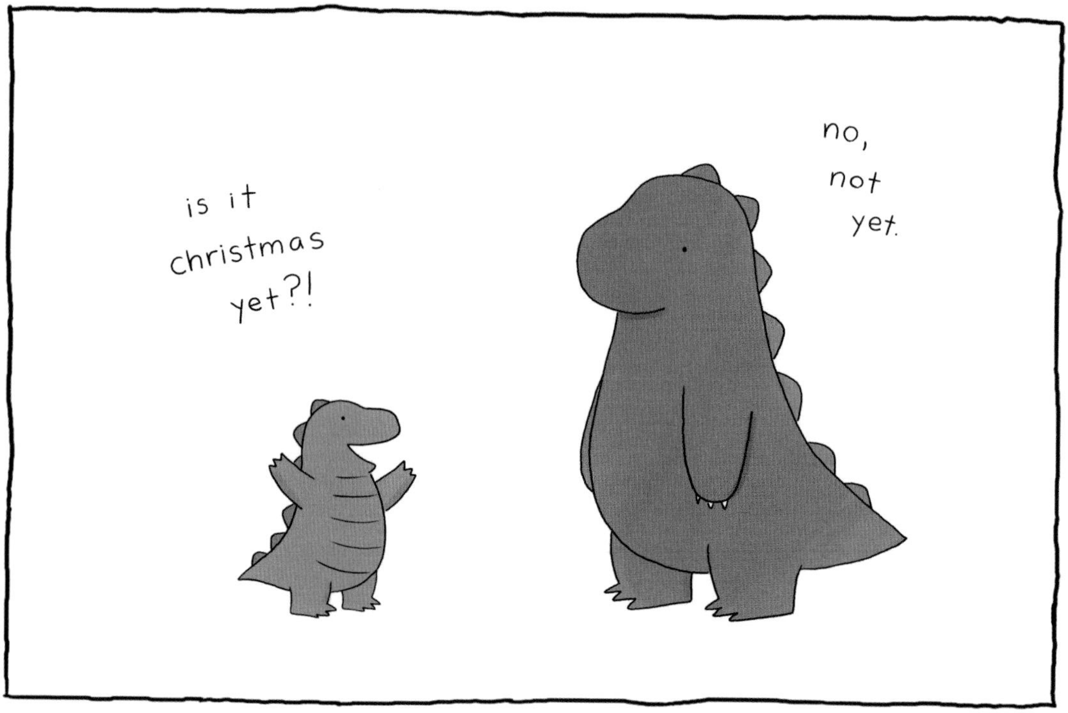
is it christmas yet?!
no, not yet.

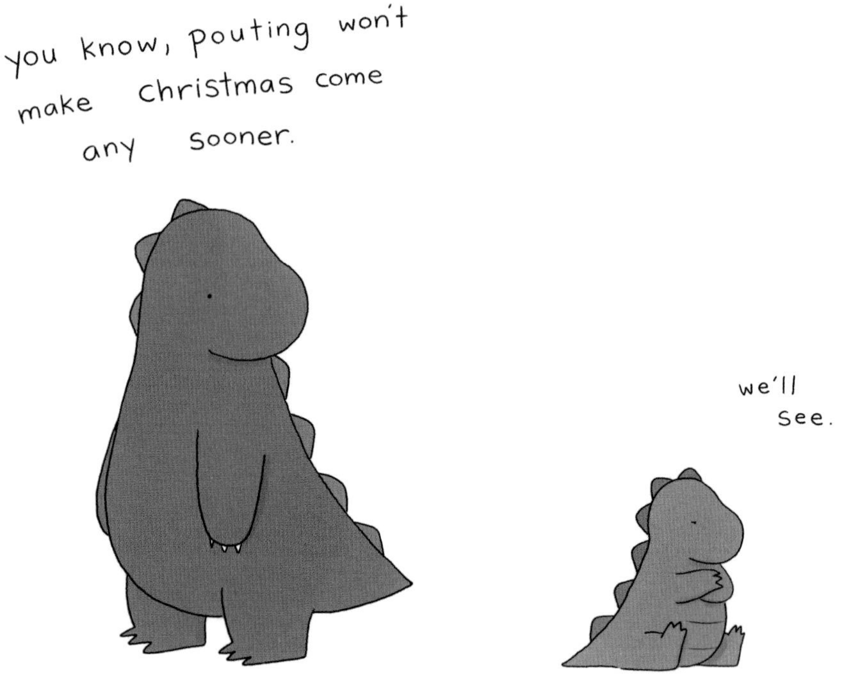
you know, pouting won't make christmas come any sooner.
we'll see.

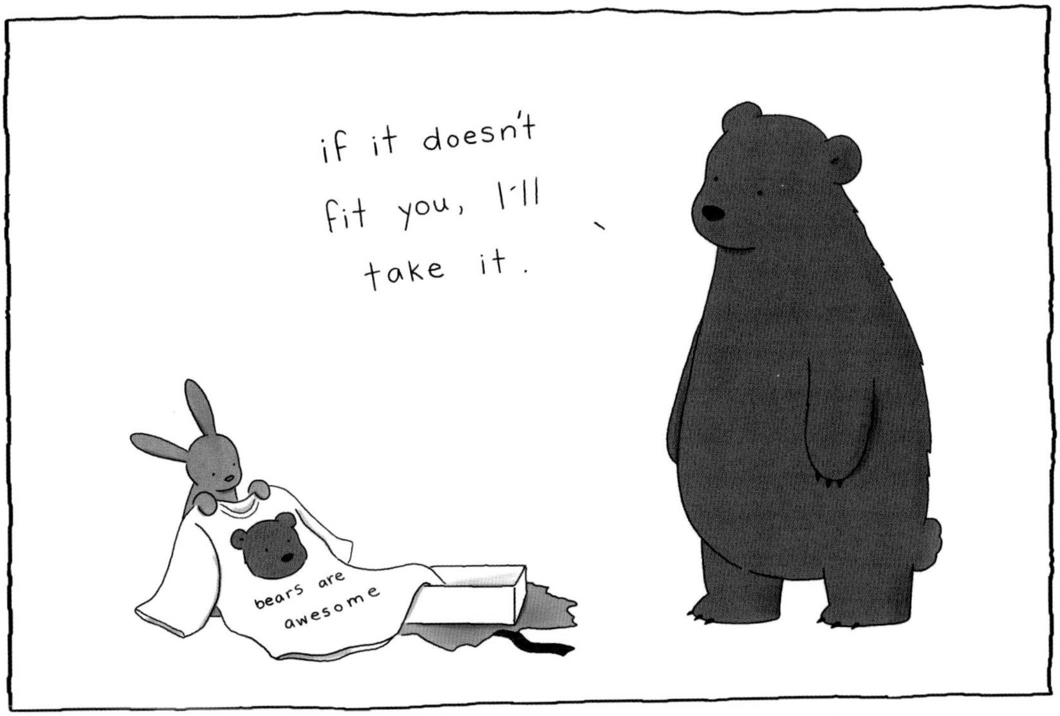
if it doesn't fit you, I'll take it.
bears are awesome

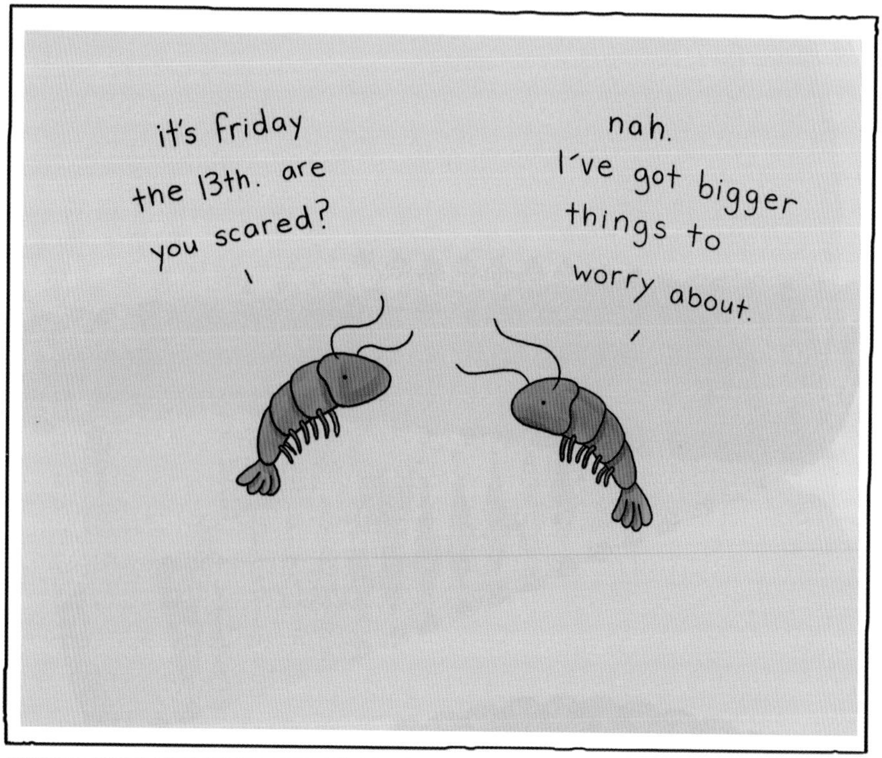
it's friday the 13th. are you scared?
nah. I've got bigger things to worry about.

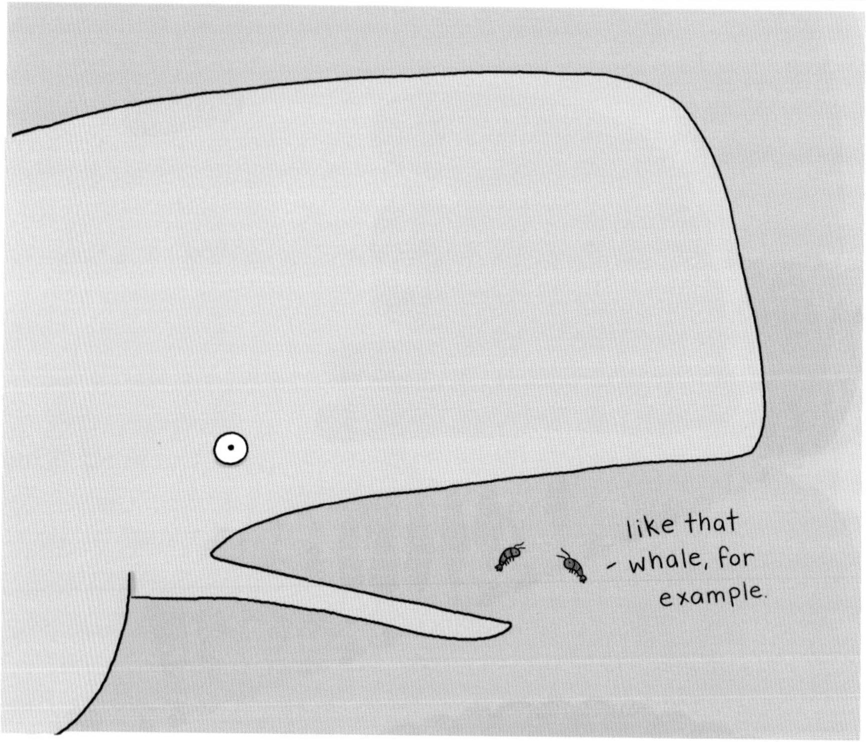
like that whale, for example.

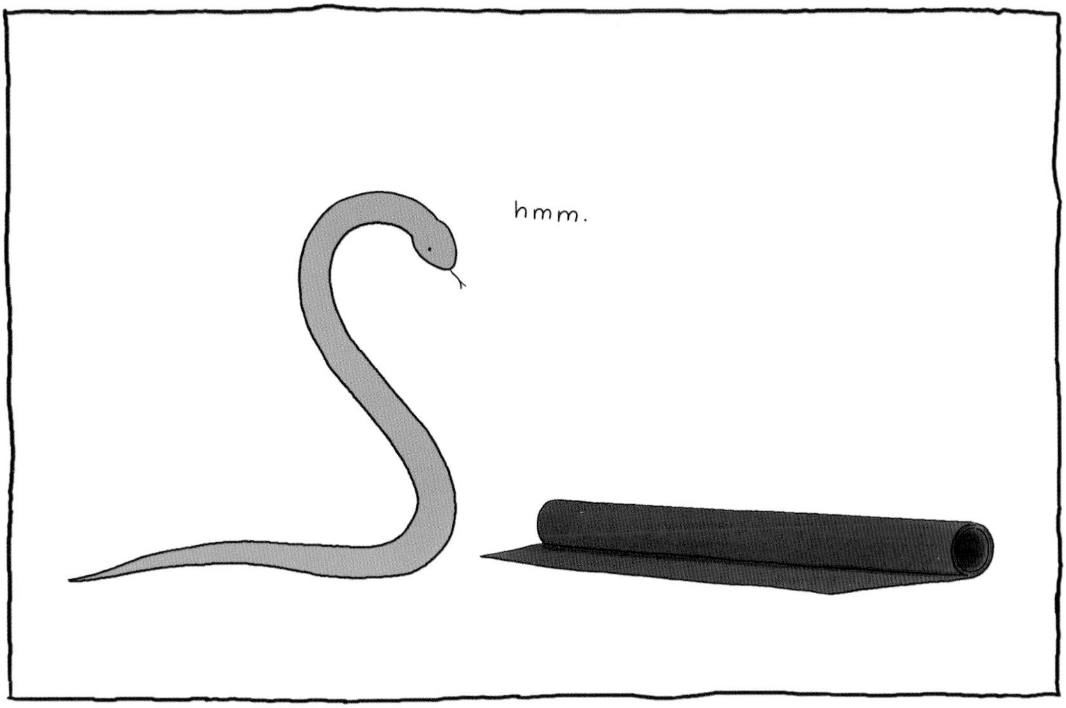
hmm.

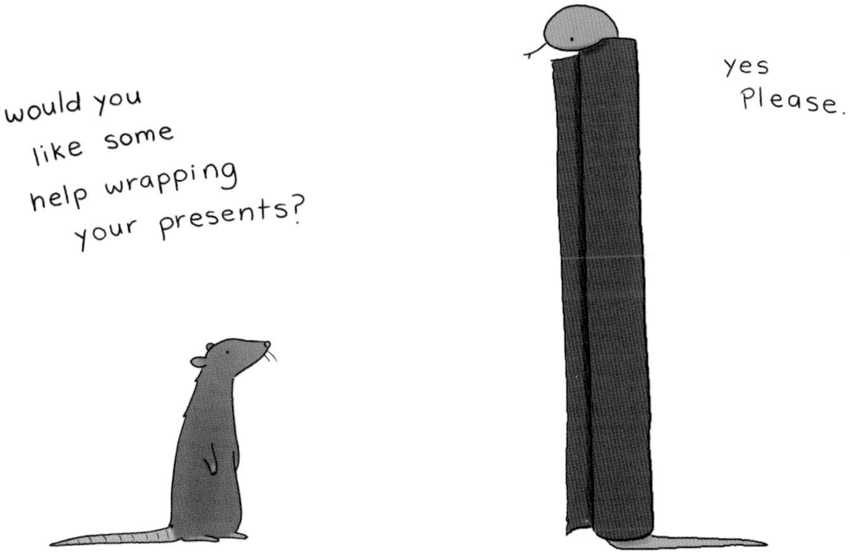
would you
like some
help wrapping
your presents?
yes
Please.

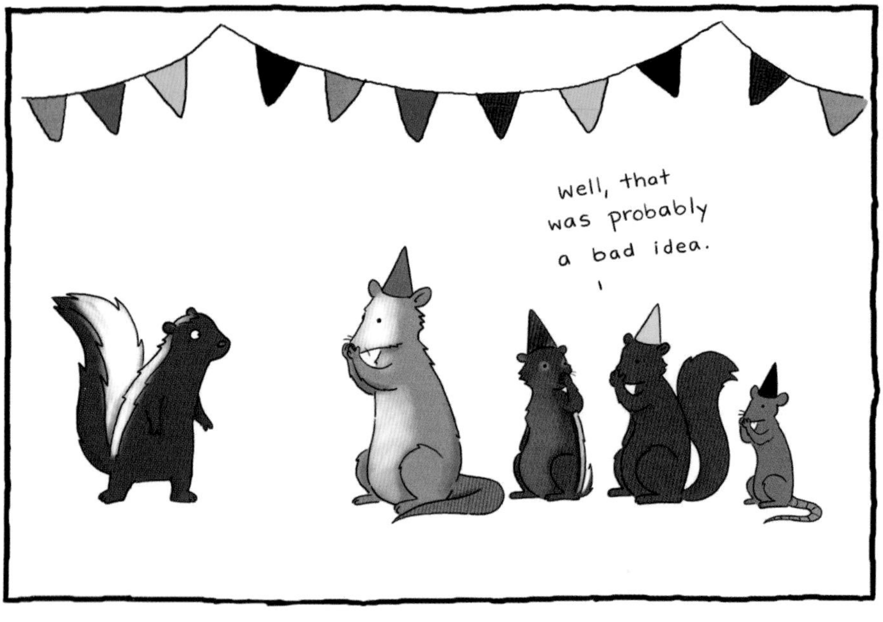
Well, that
was probably
a bad idea.

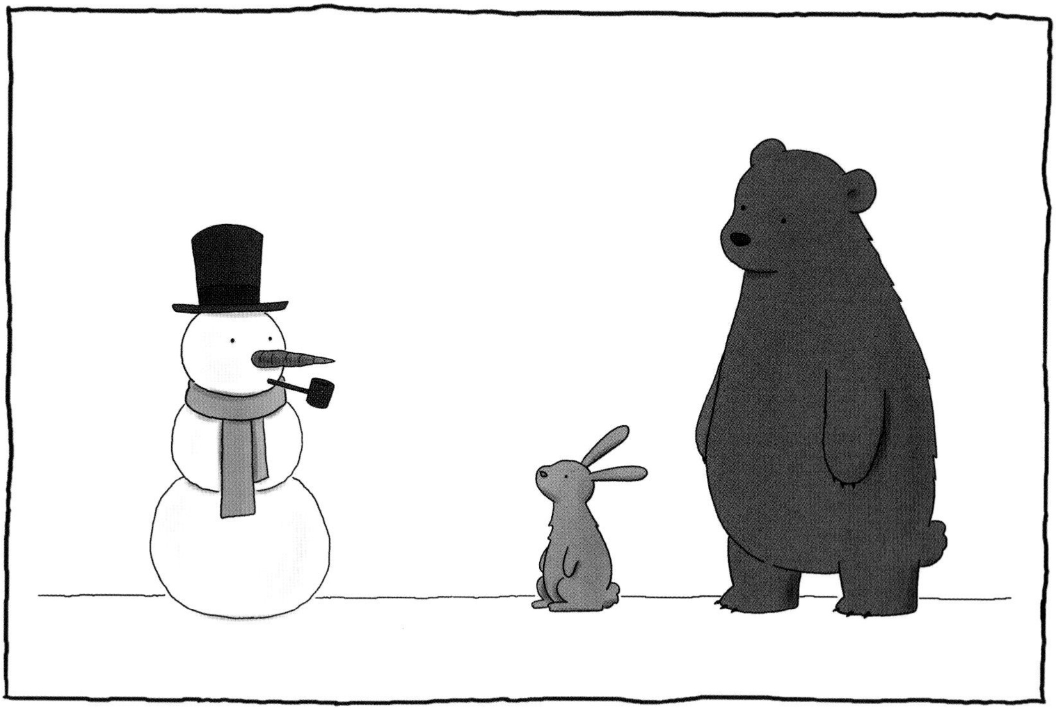

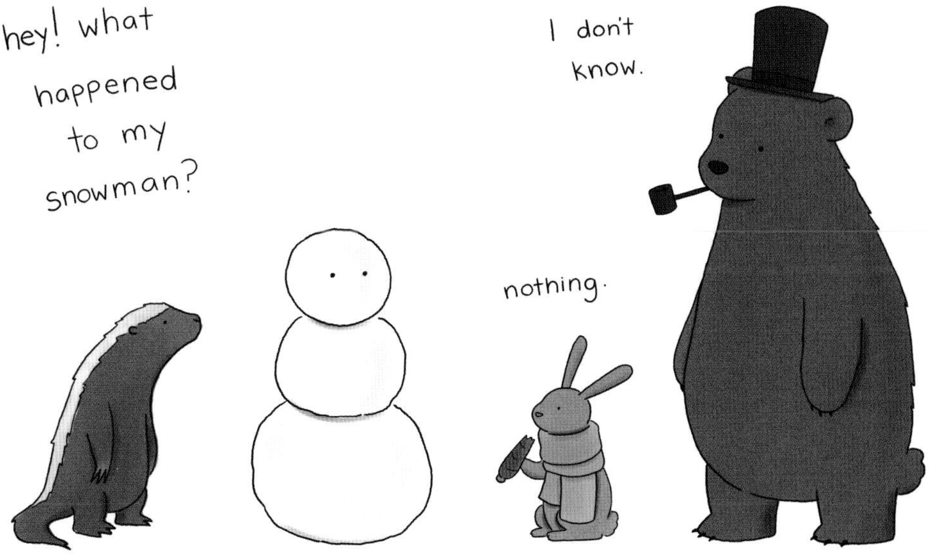
hey! what happened to my snowman?
I don't know.
nothing.

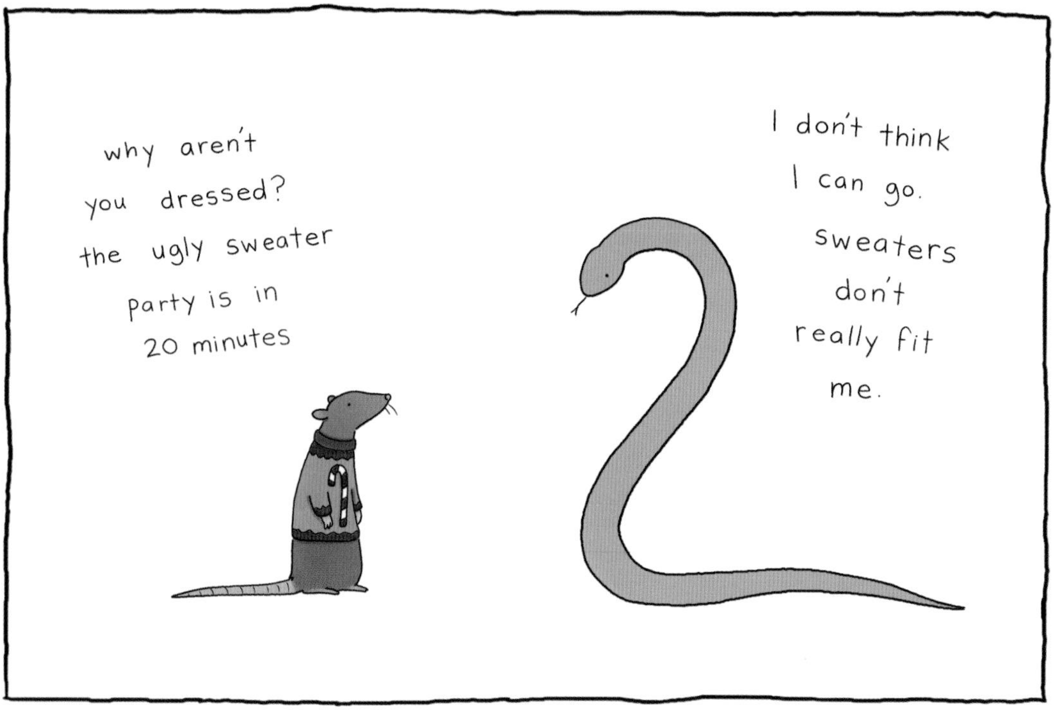
why aren't you dressed? the ugly sweater party is in 20 minutes
I don't think I can go. sweaters don't really fit me.

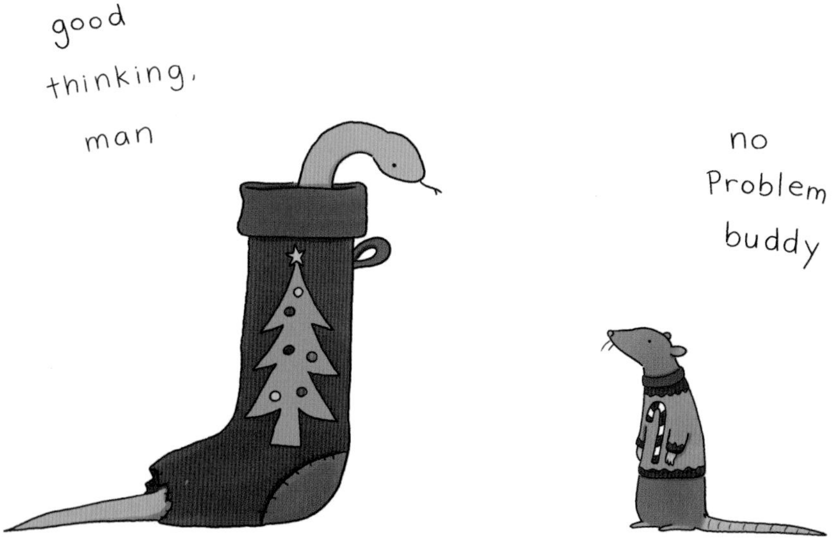
good thinking, man
no Problem buddy

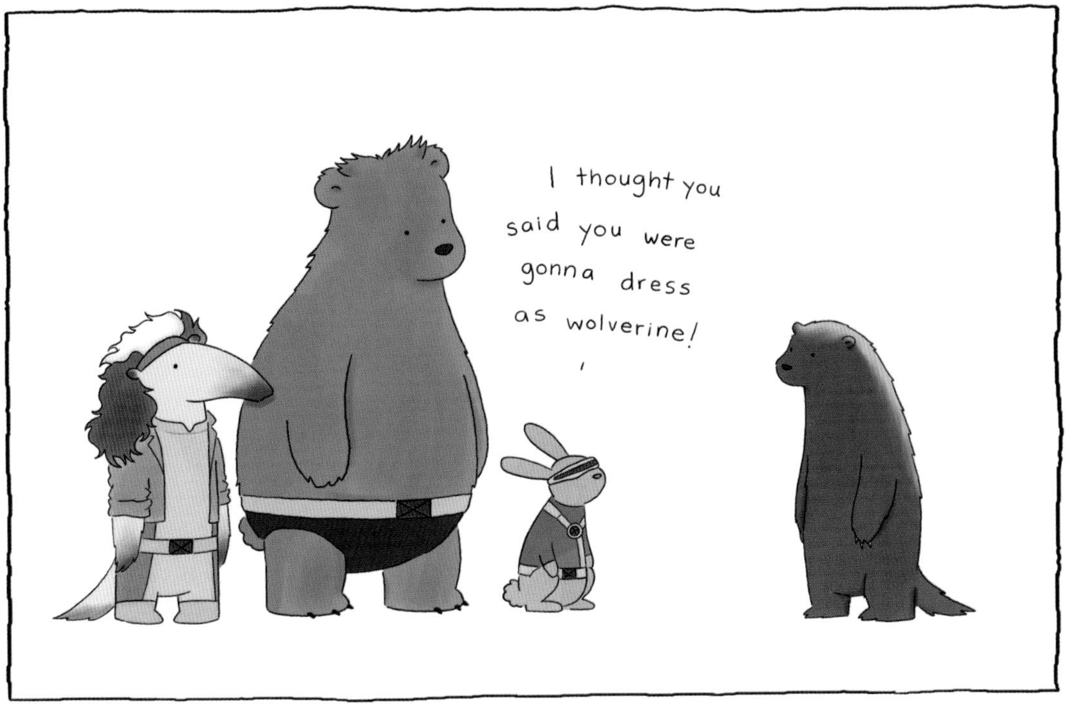
I thought you said you were gonna dress as wolverine!

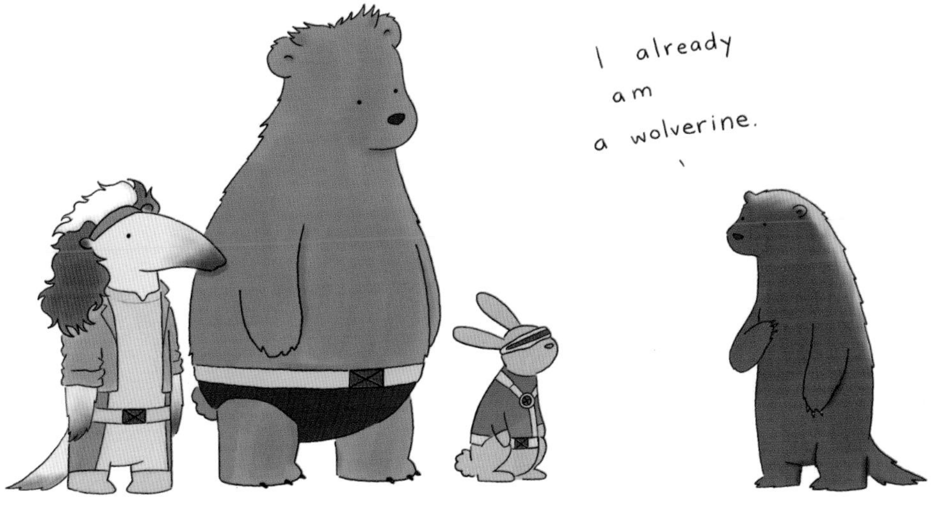
I already am a wolverine.

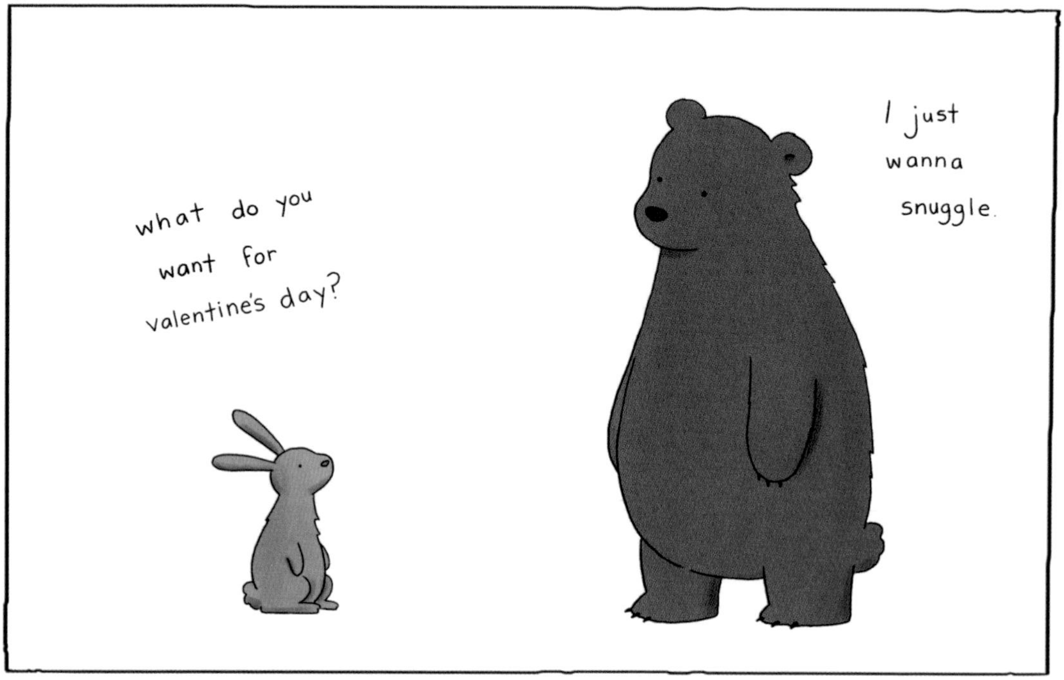
what do you want for valentine's day?
I just wanna snuggle.

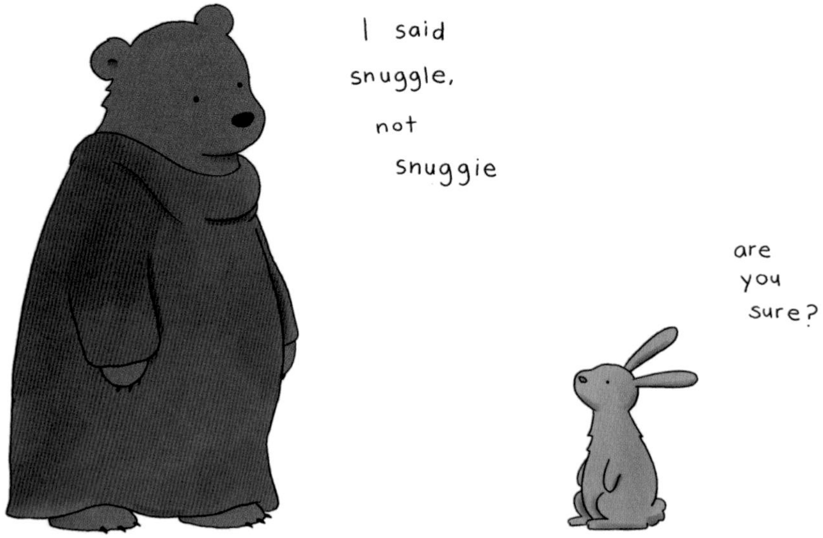
I said snuggle, not snuggie
are you sure?

here
he comes!
hide!

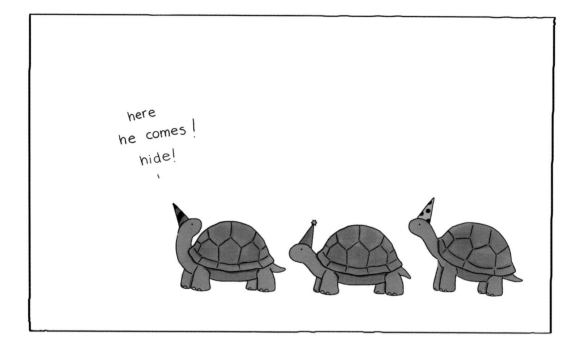

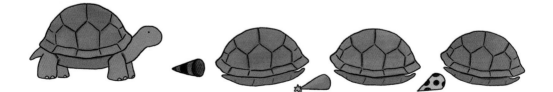

Family

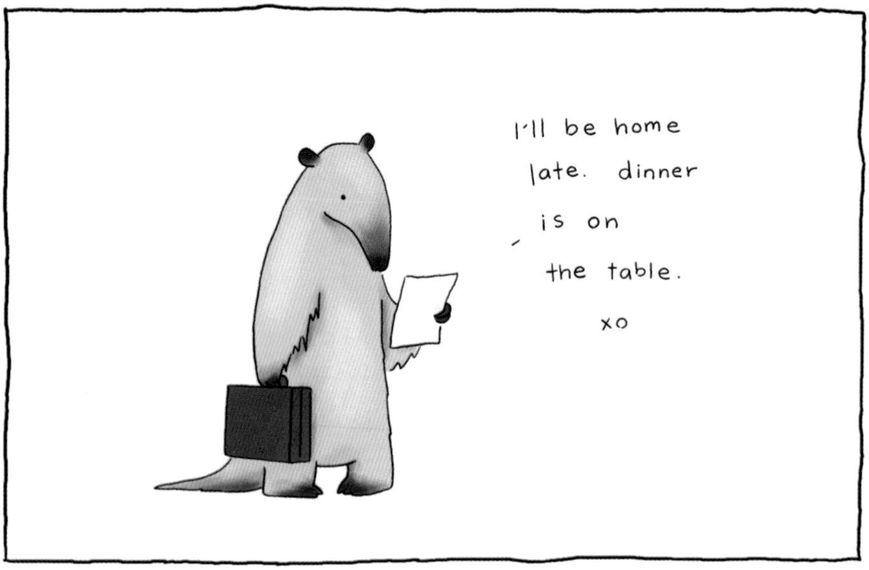
I'll be home
late. dinner
is on
the table.
xo

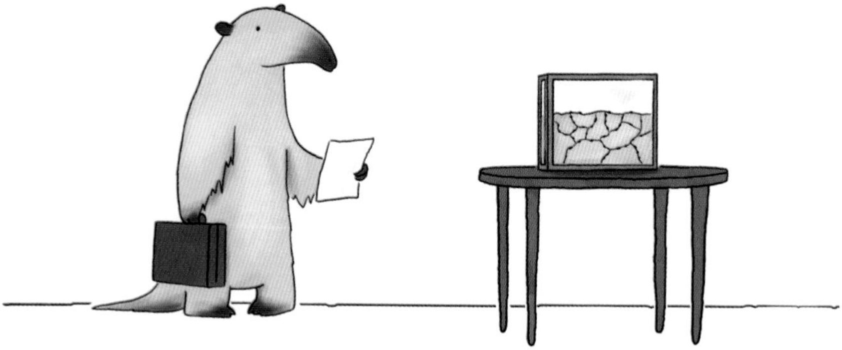

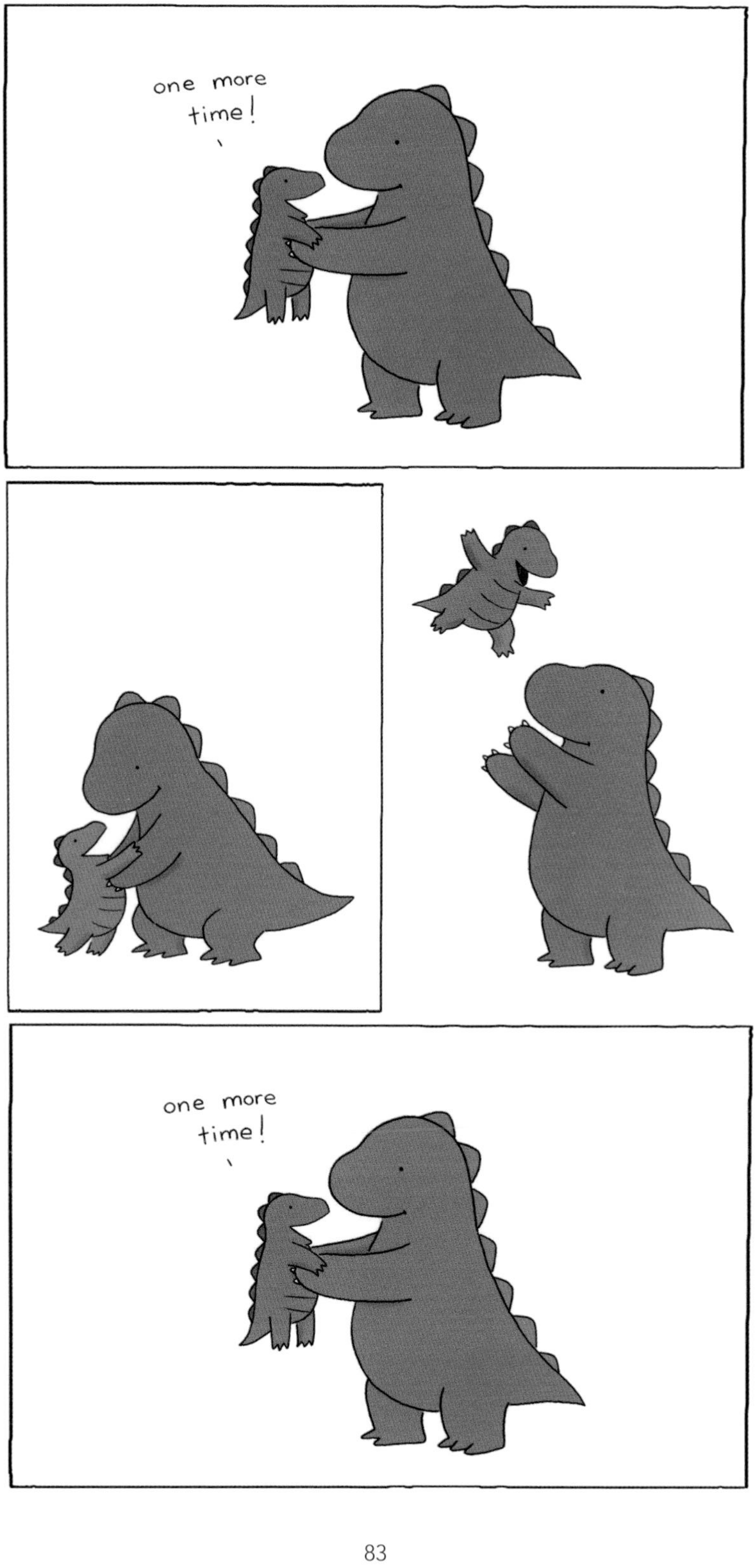
one more time!
one more time!

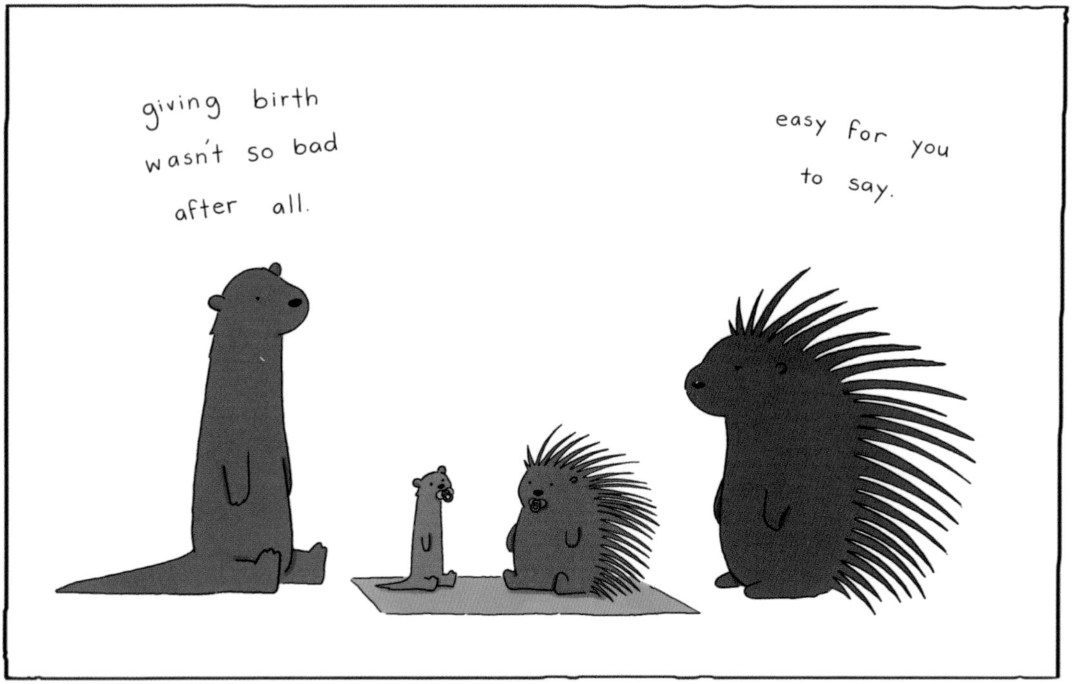
giving birth wasn't so bad after all.
easy for you to say.

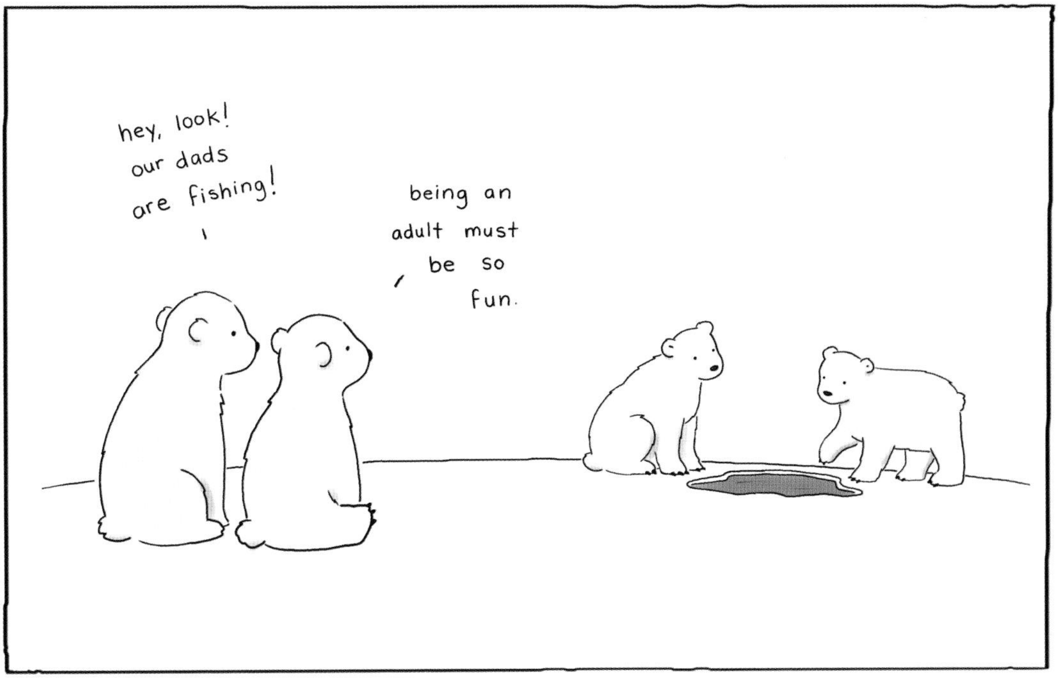
hey, look! our dads are fishing!
being an adult must be so fun.

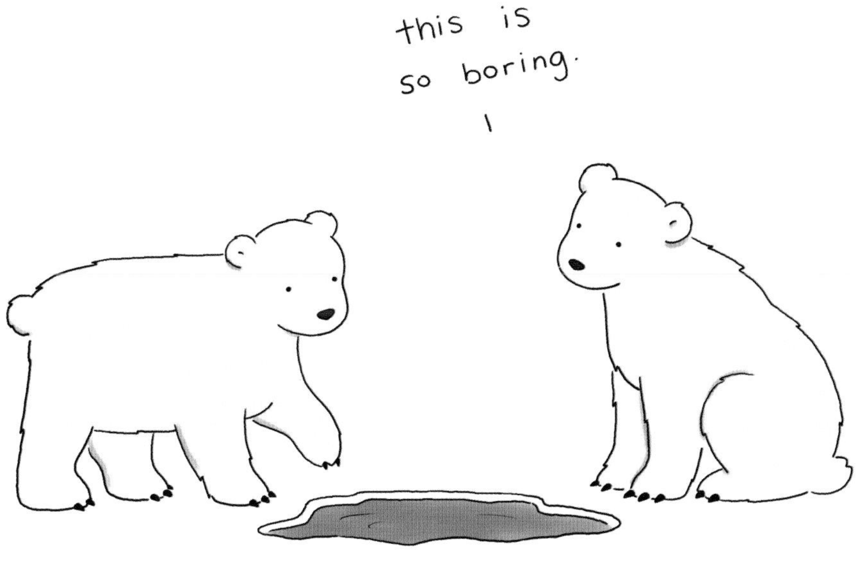
this is so boring.

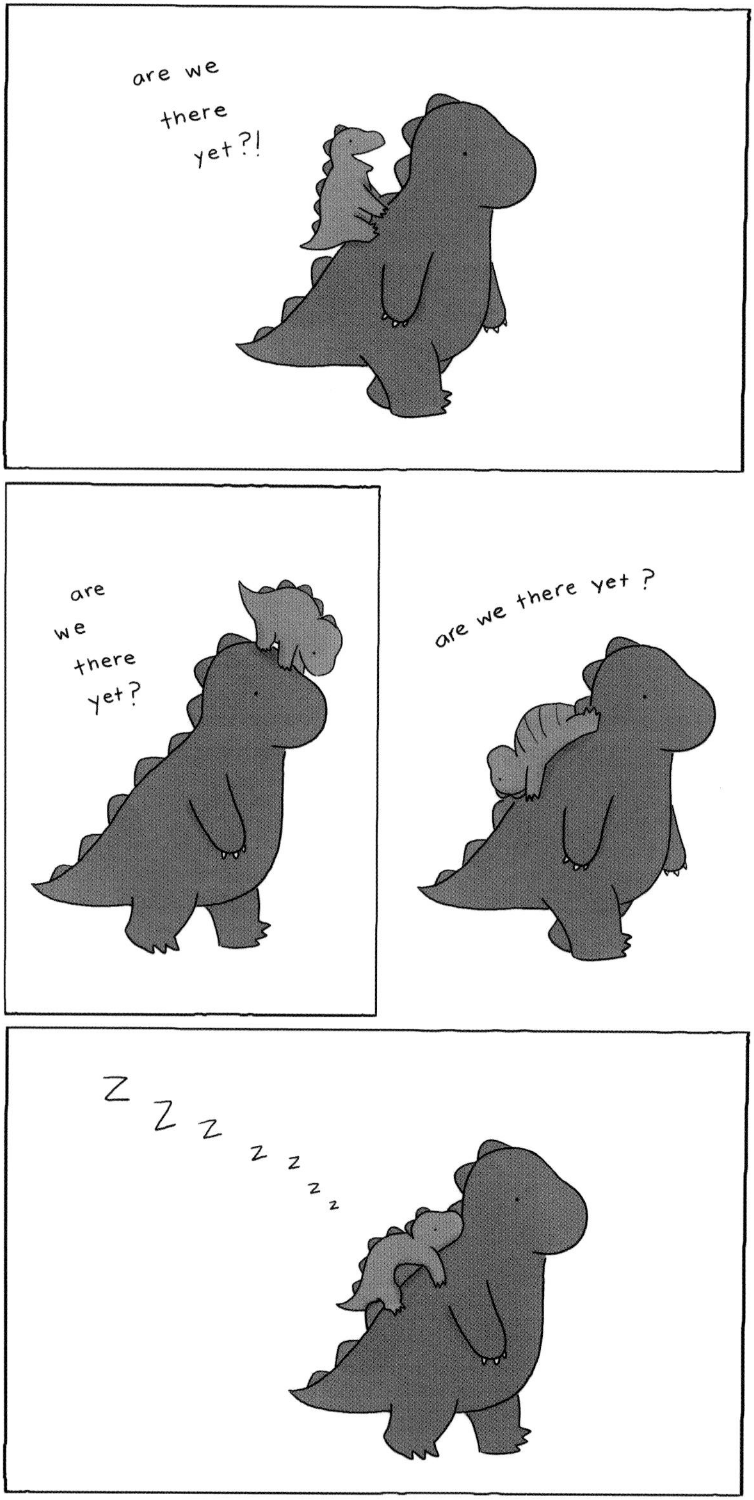
are we there yet?!
are we there yet?
are we there yet?
Z Z Z z z z z

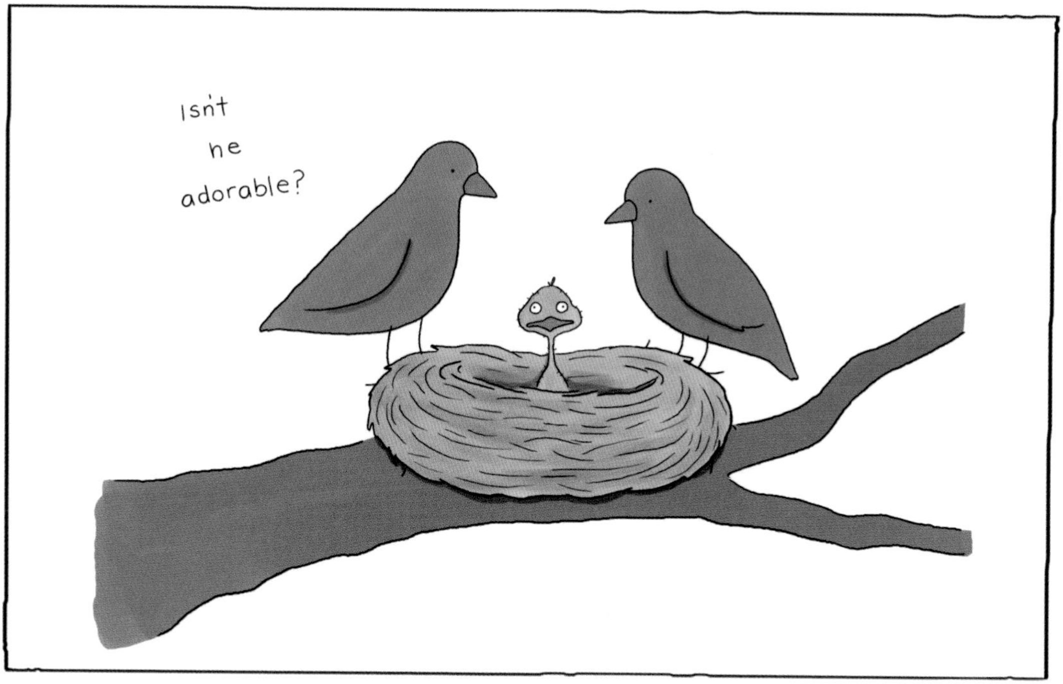
Isn't he adorable?

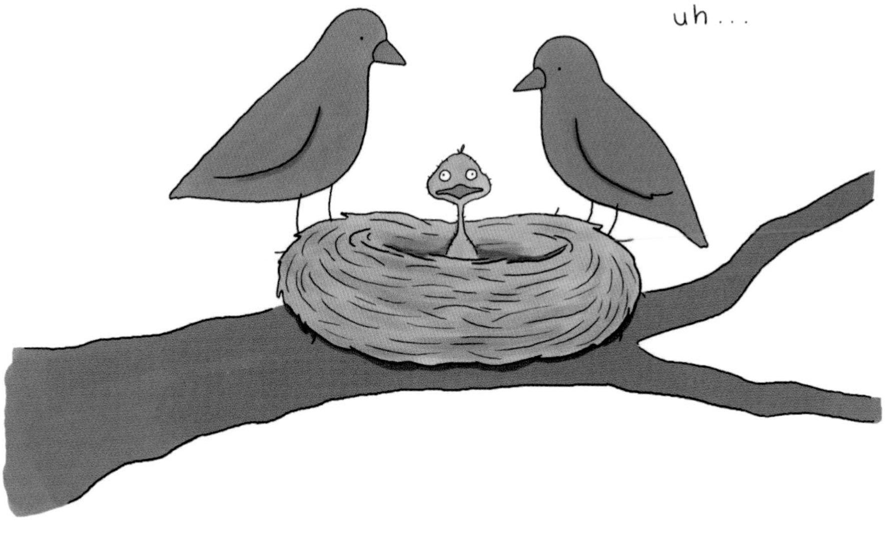
uh...

I have to tell you something.

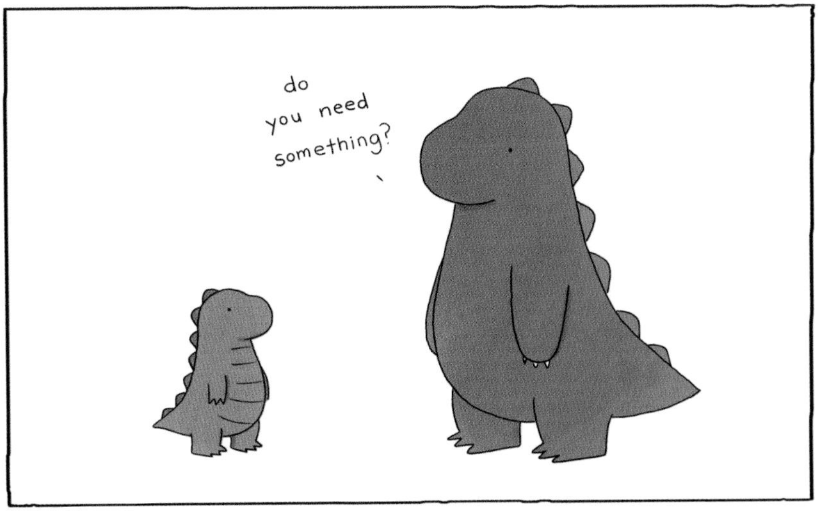
do
you need
something?

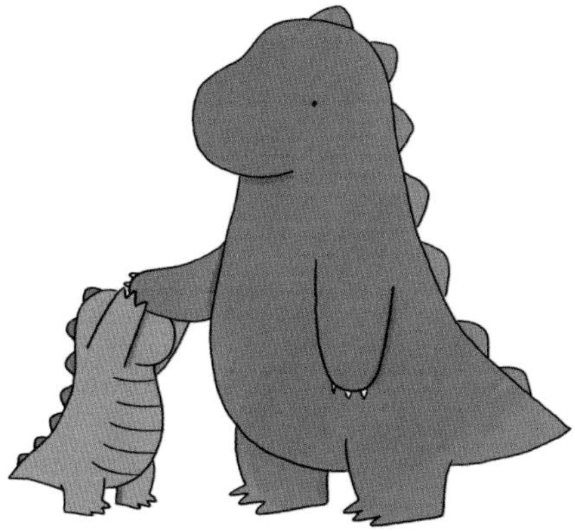

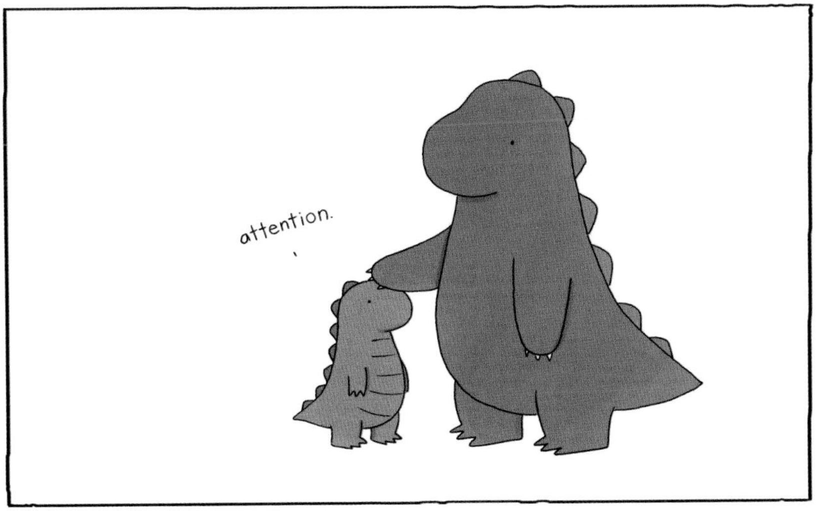
attention.

you should tell your mom
you're staying over with me and
I'll tell my mom I'm staying
over with you and then we
can stay out all night long!

I don't
think
that's
going to
work.

him? oh,
that's just
Jack. he's
a little shy.

Mom! Put me down!
You're embarrassing me
in front of my friends!

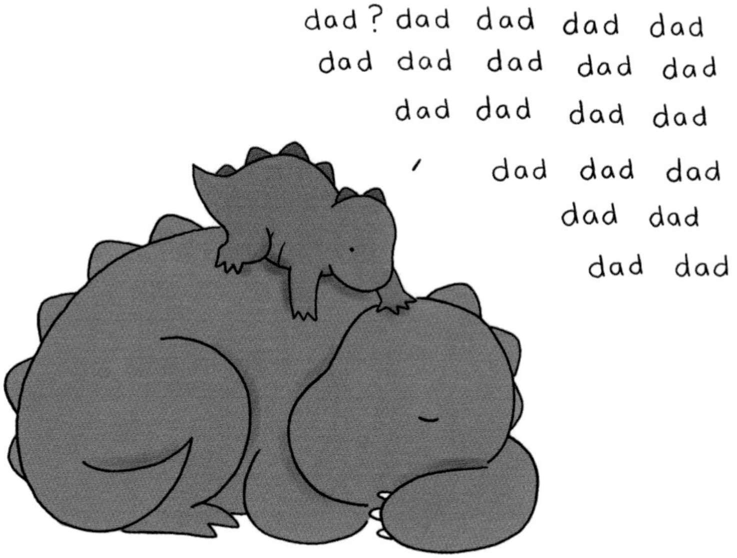
dad? dad dad dad dad
dad dad dad dad dad
dad dad dad dad
dad dad dad
dad dad
dad dad

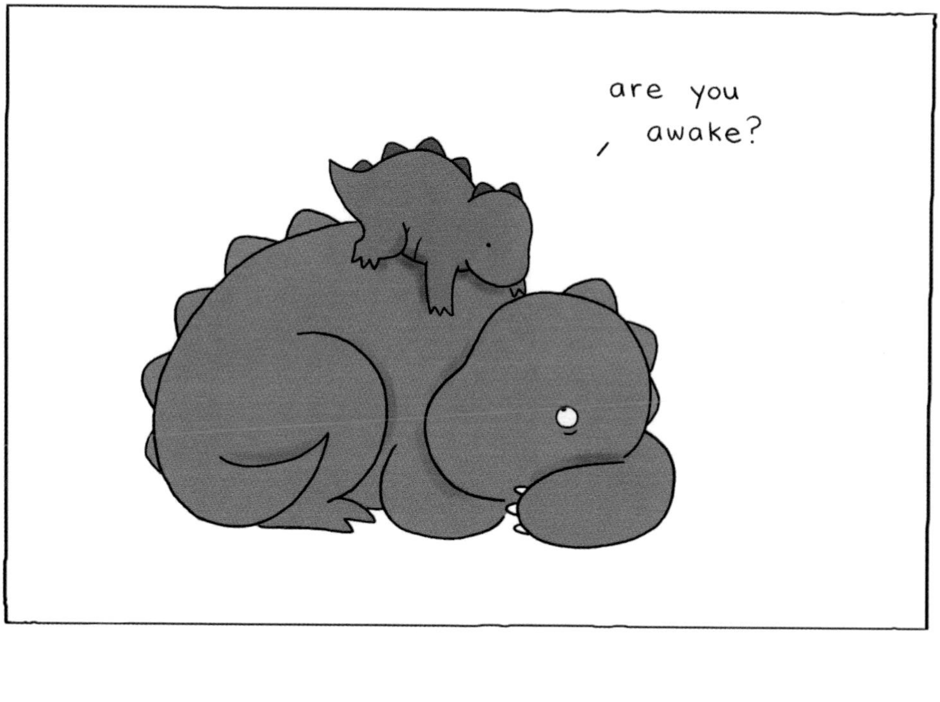
are you awake?

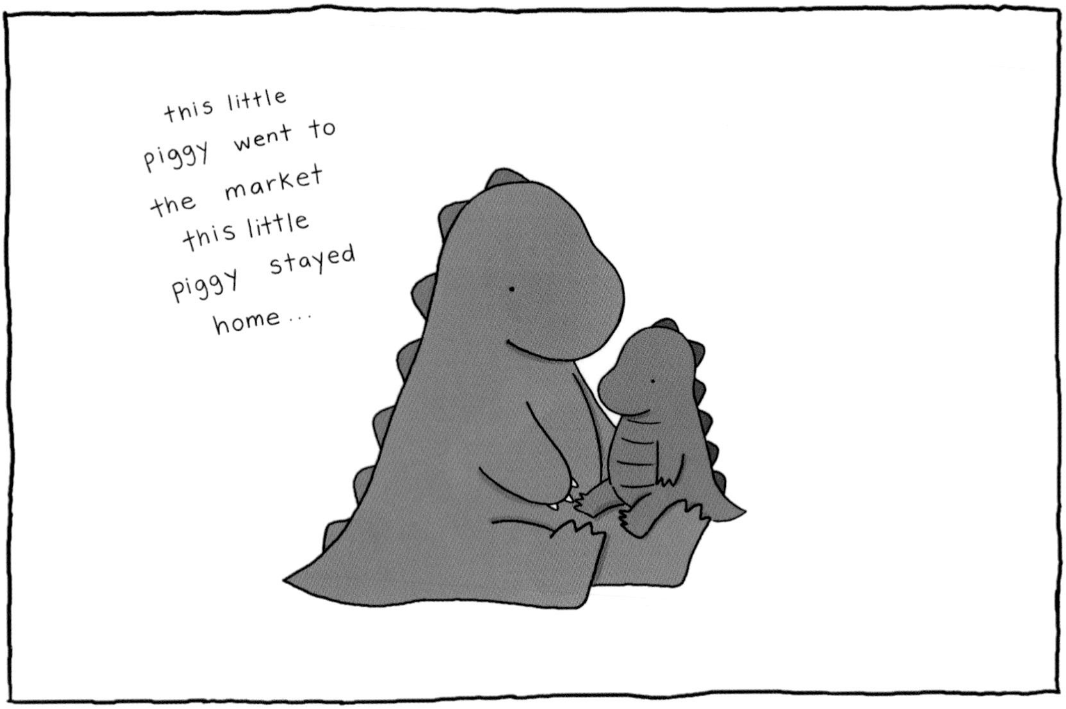
this little piggy went to the market this little piggy stayed home...

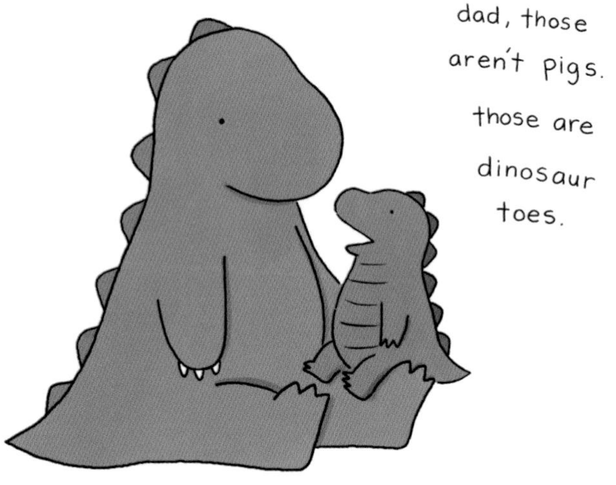
dad, those aren't pigs.
those are dinosaur toes.

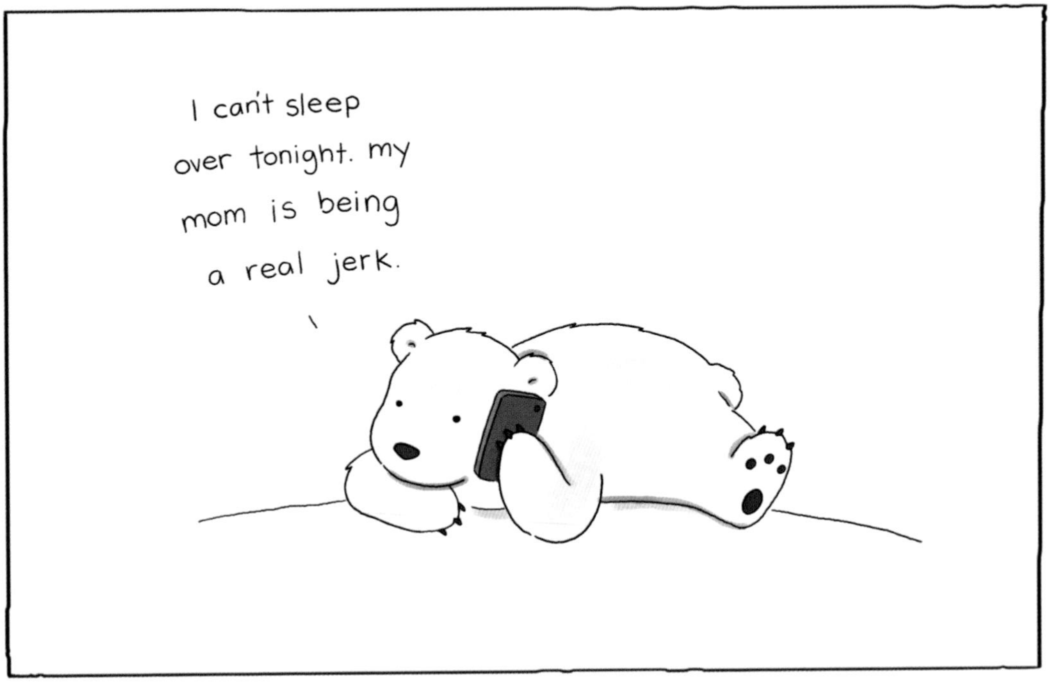
I can't sleep over tonight. my mom is being a real jerk.

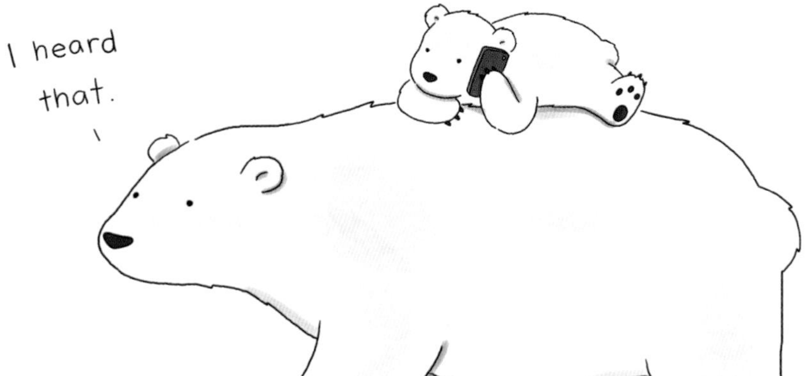
I heard that.

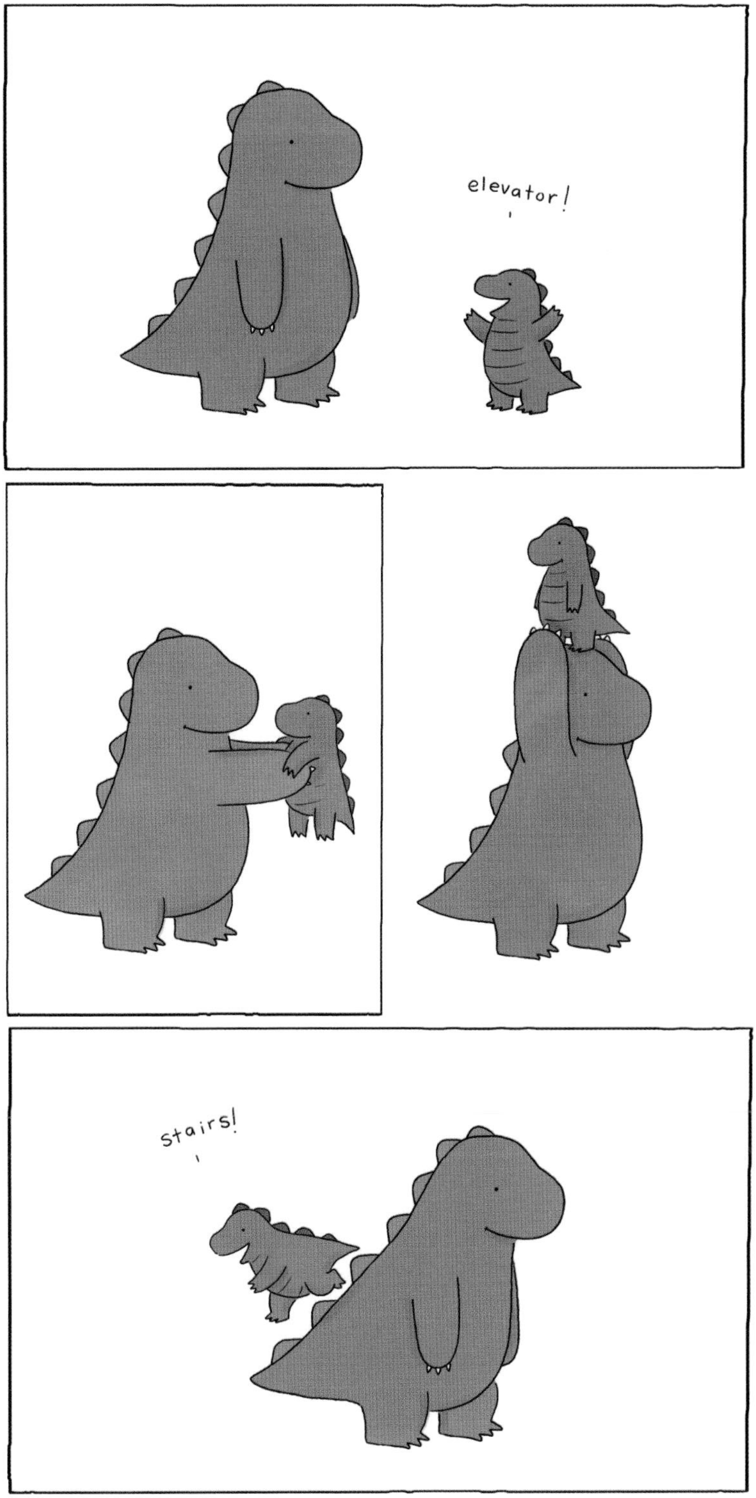
elevator!
stairs!

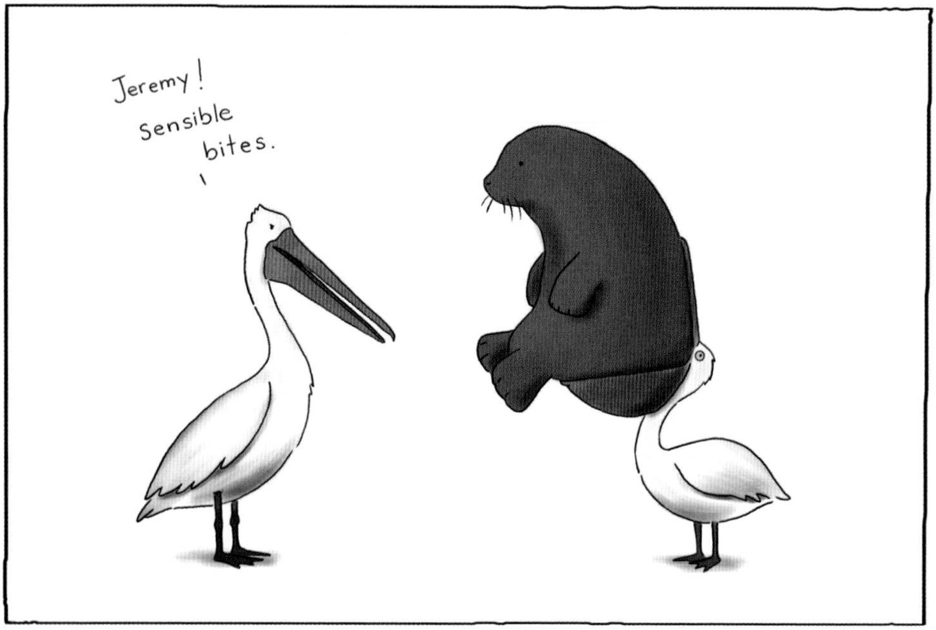
Jeremy! sensible bites.

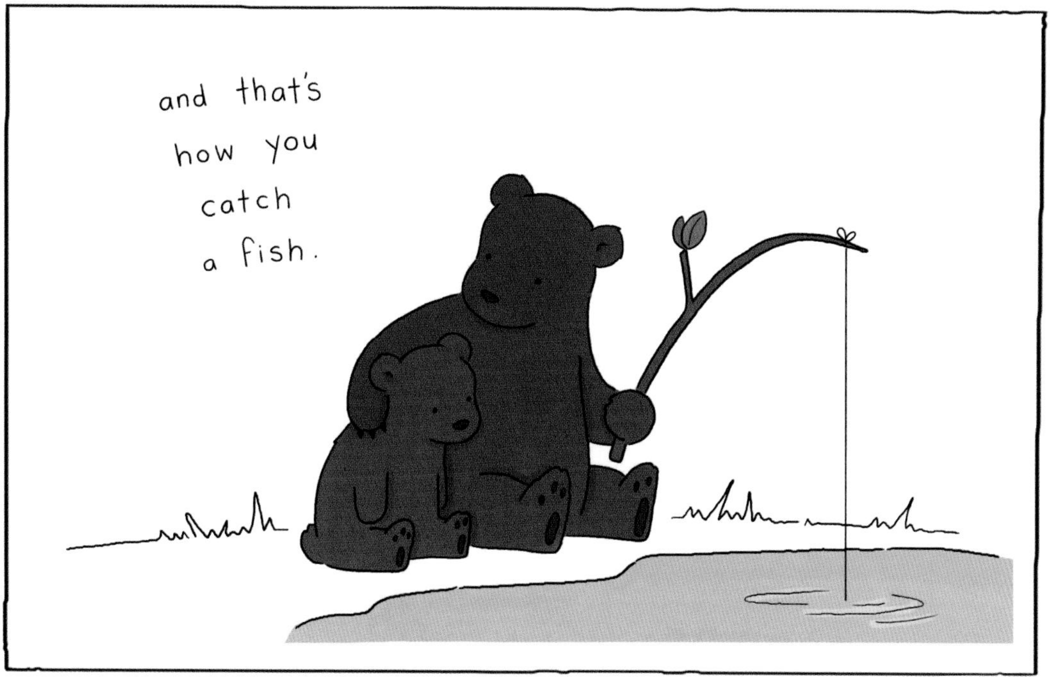
and that's
how you
catch
a fish.

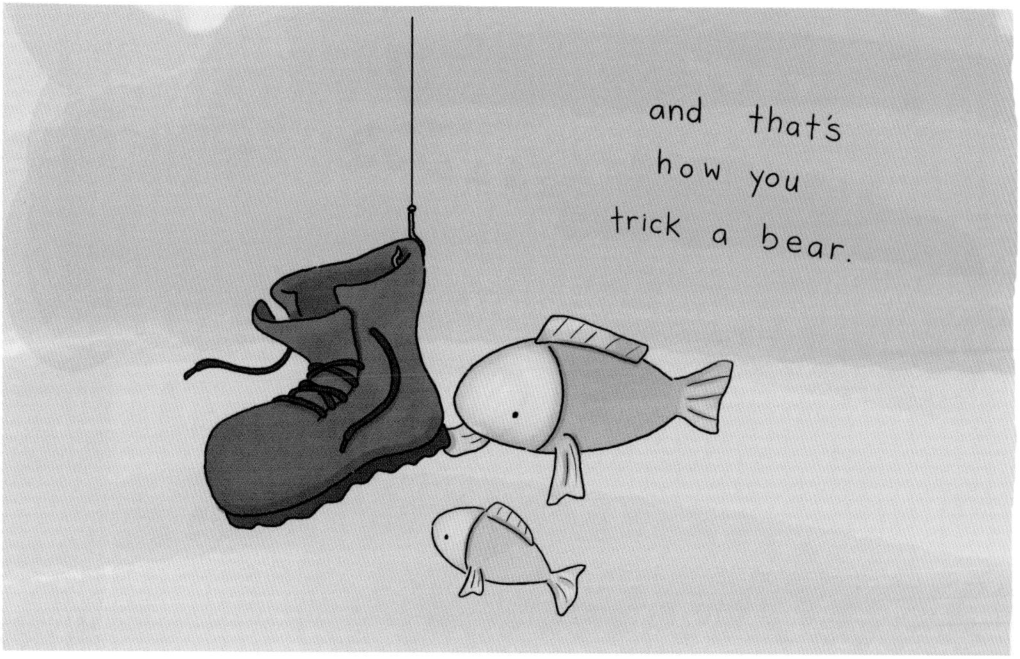
and that's
how you
trick a bear.

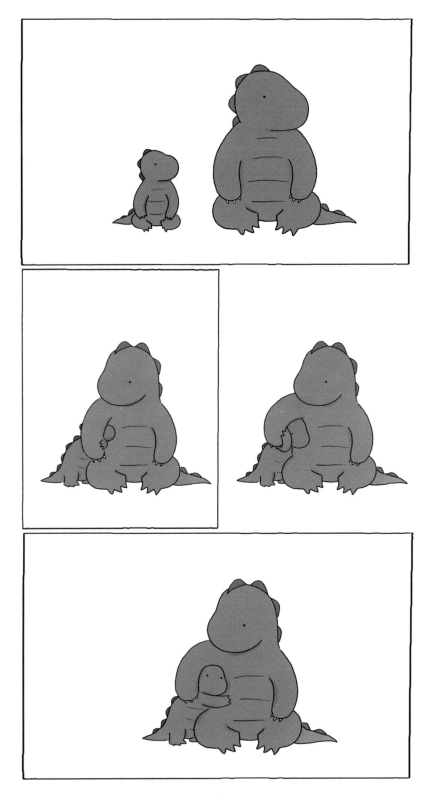

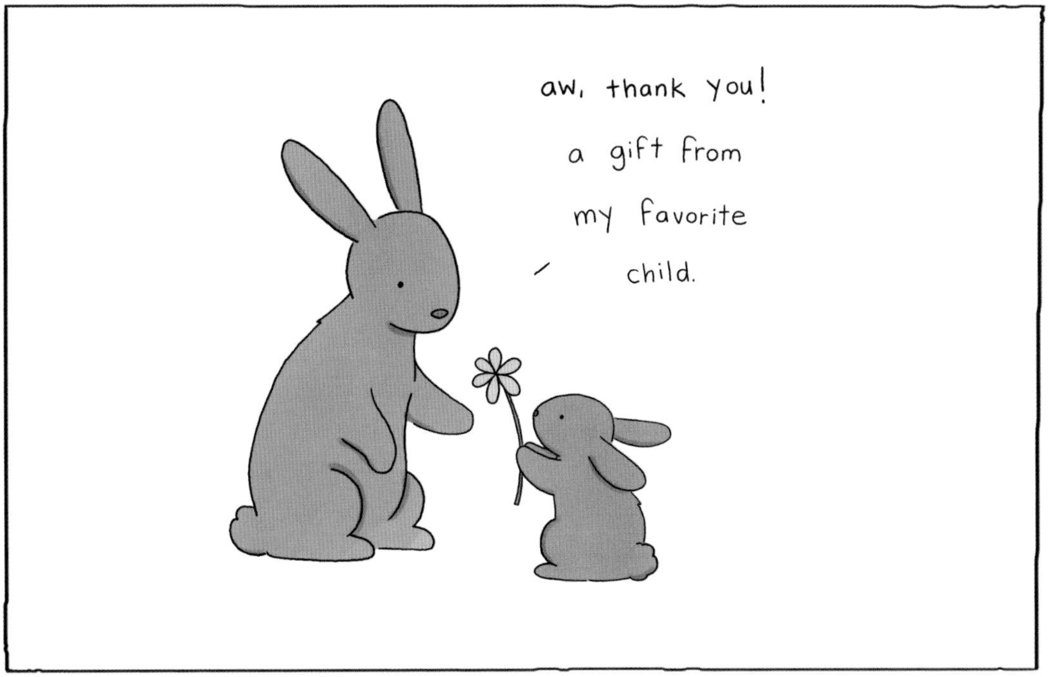
aw, thank you!
a gift from
my favorite
child.

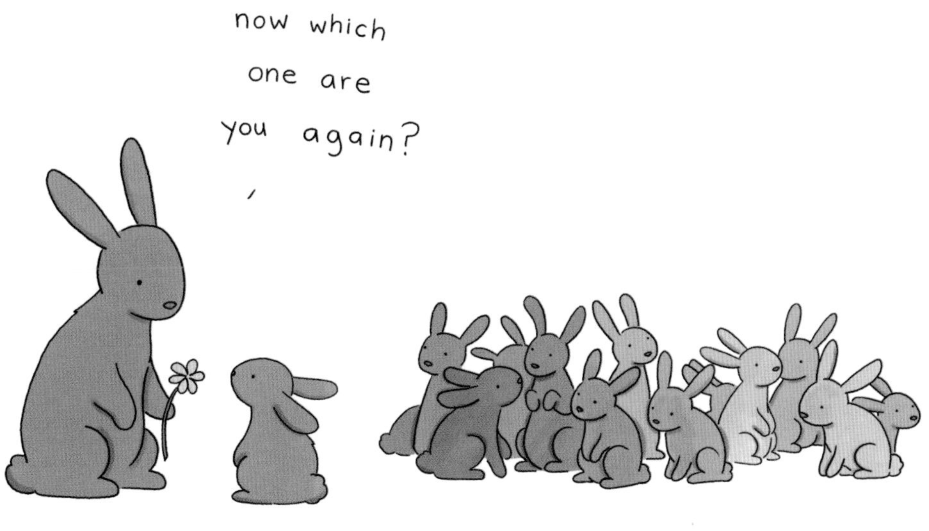
now which
one are
you again?

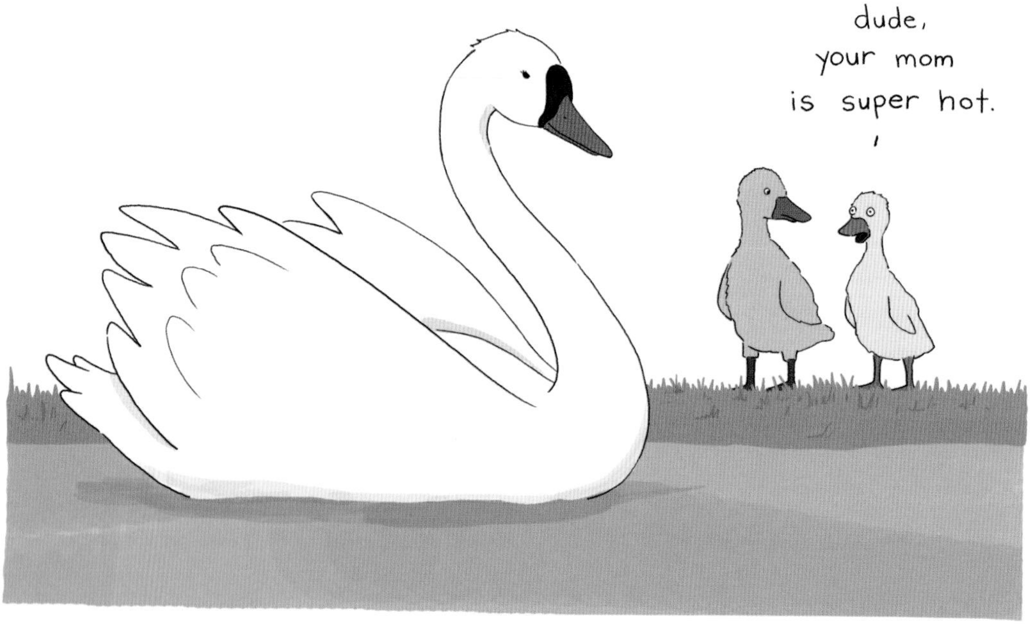
dude,
your mom
is super hot.

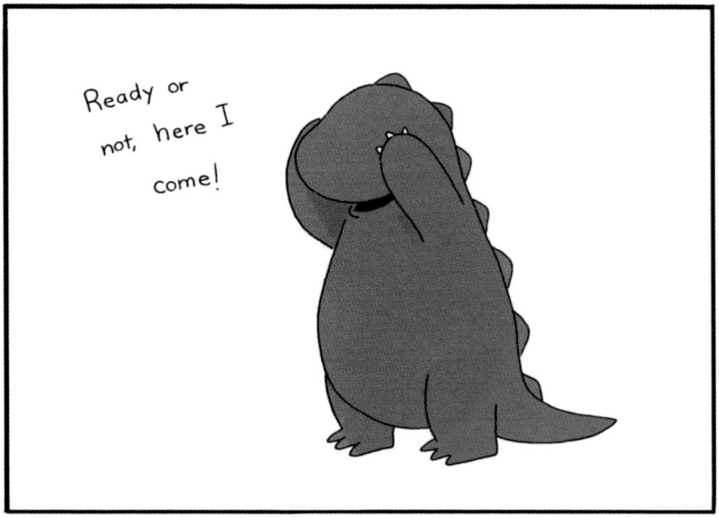
Ready or not, here I come!

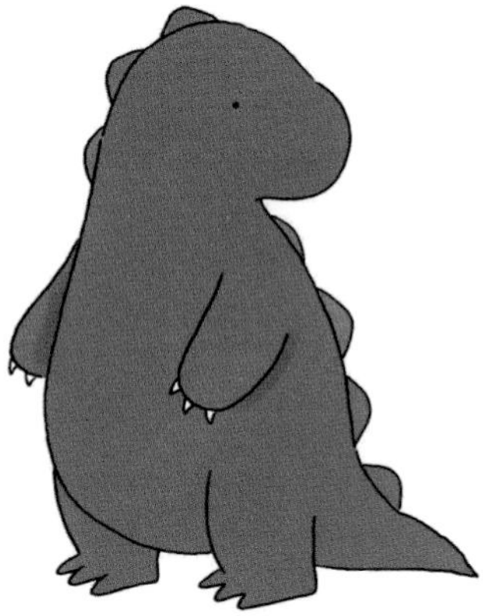

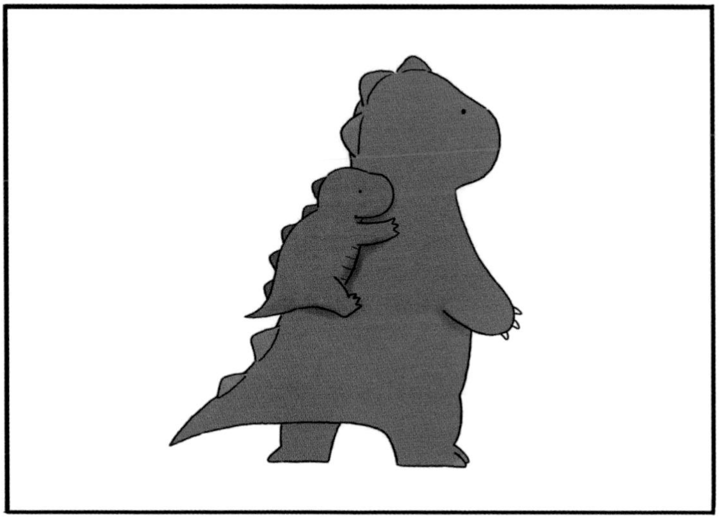

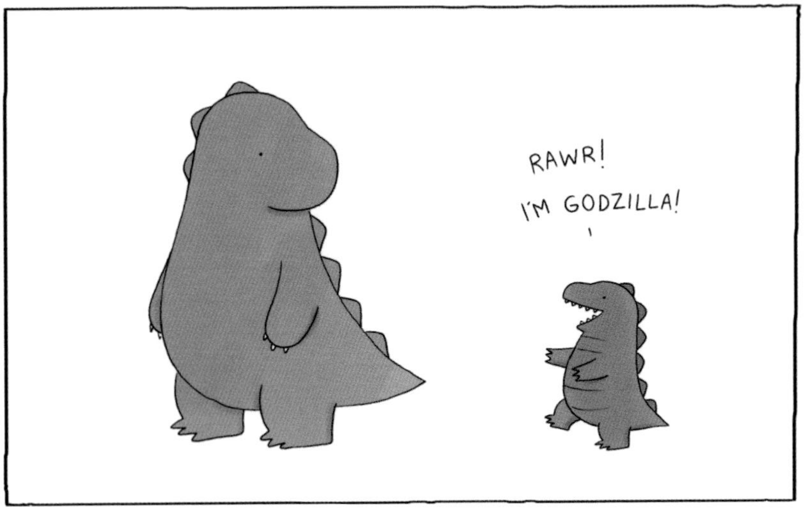
RAWR!
I'M GODZILLA!

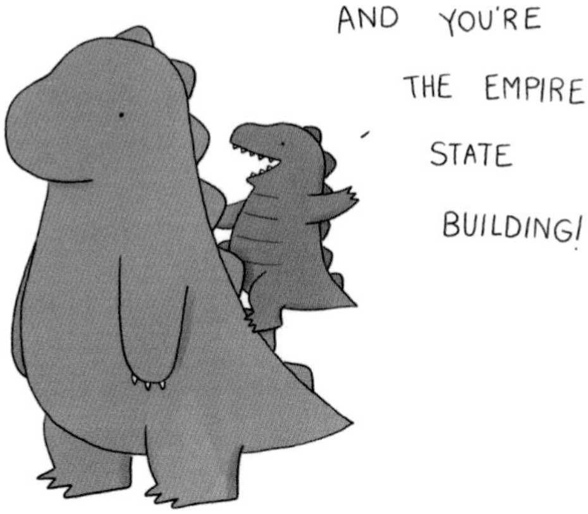
AND YOU'RE THE EMPIRE STATE BUILDING!

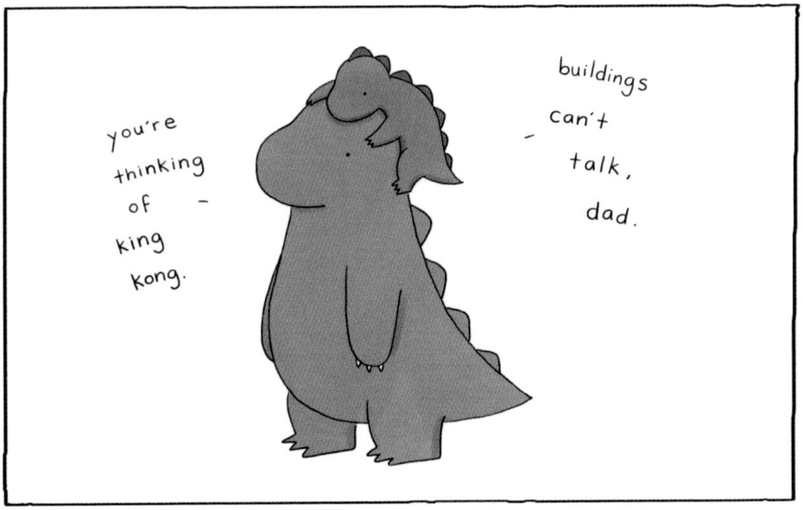
you're thinking of king kong.
buildings can't talk, dad.

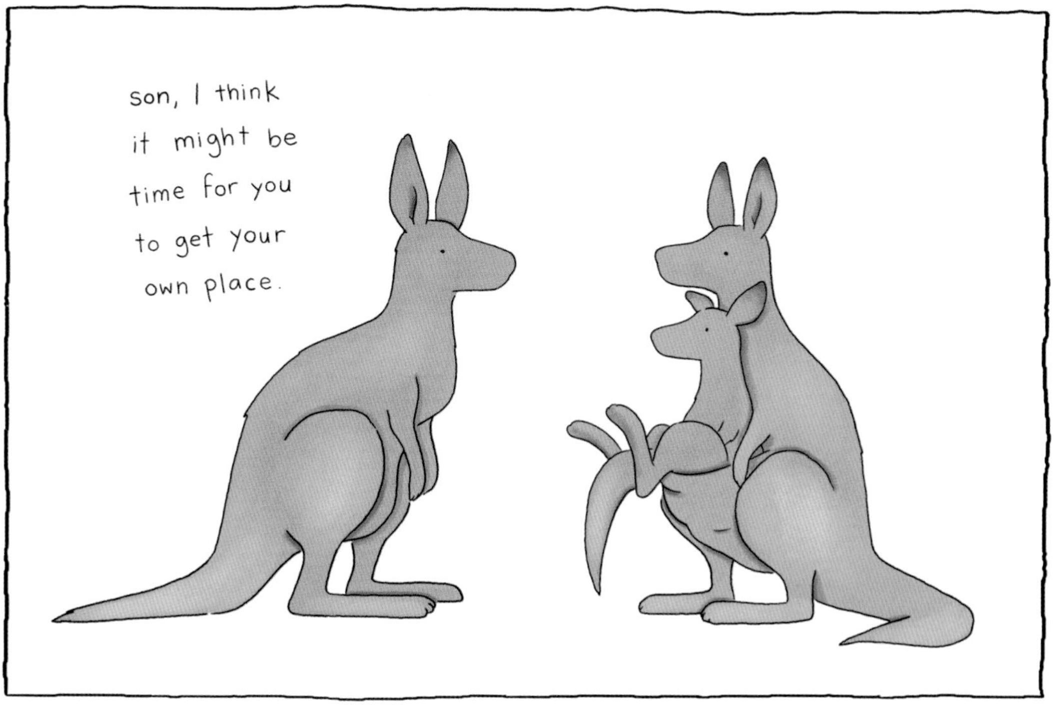
son, I think
it might be
time for you
to get your
own place.

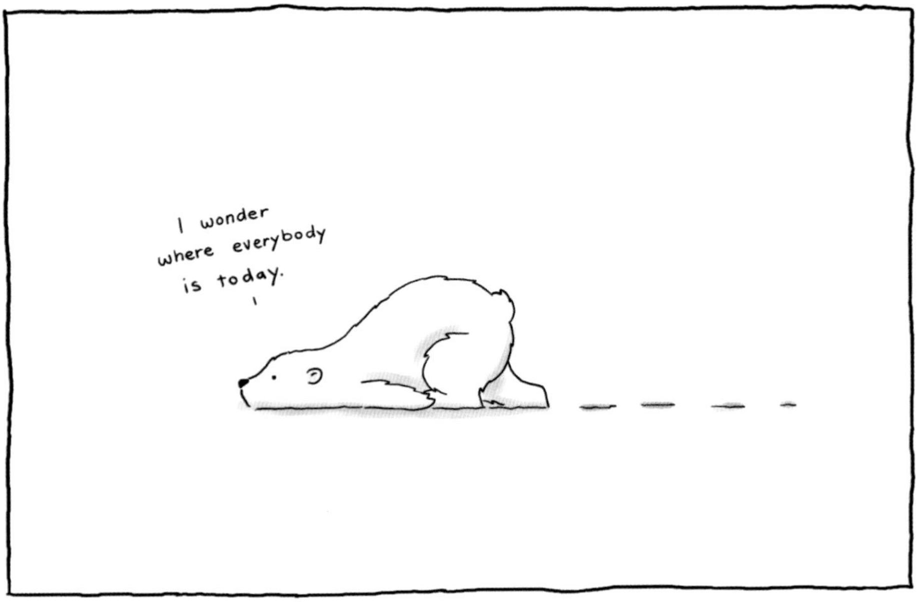
I wonder where everybody is today.

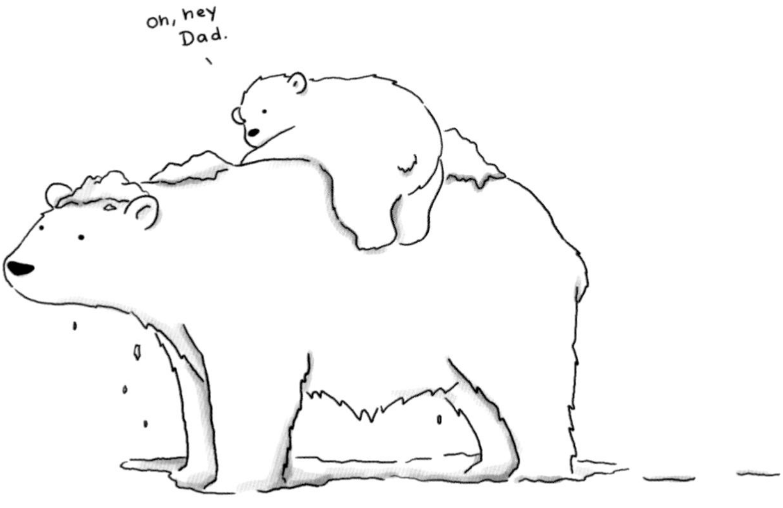
Oh, hey Dad.

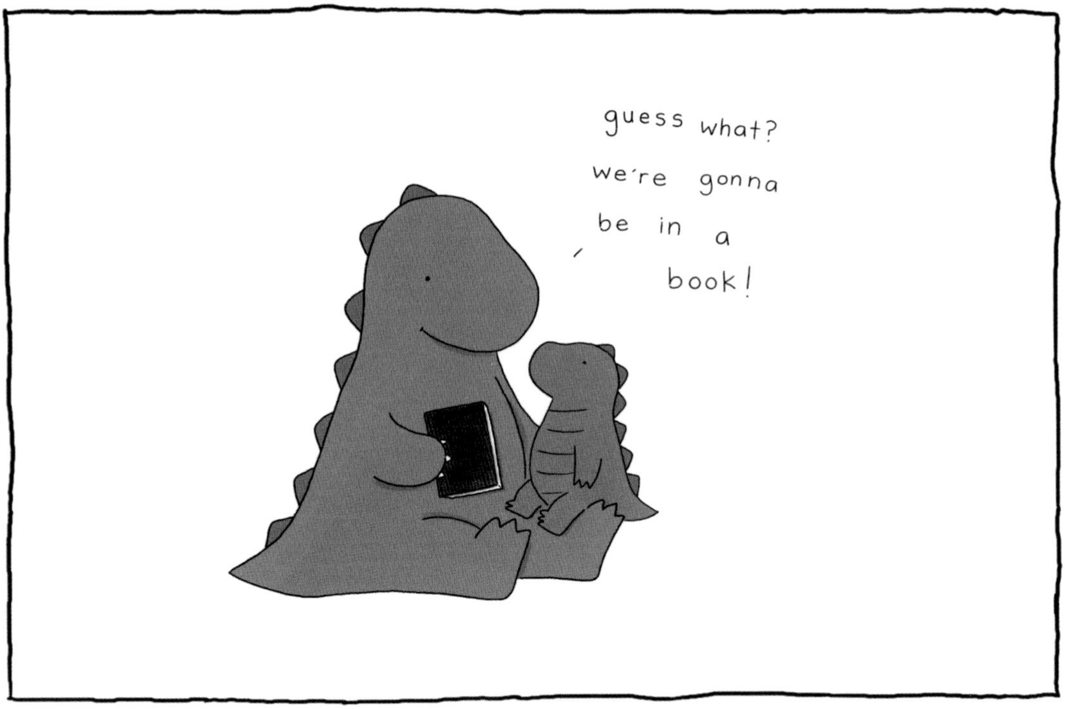
guess what? we're gonna be in a book!

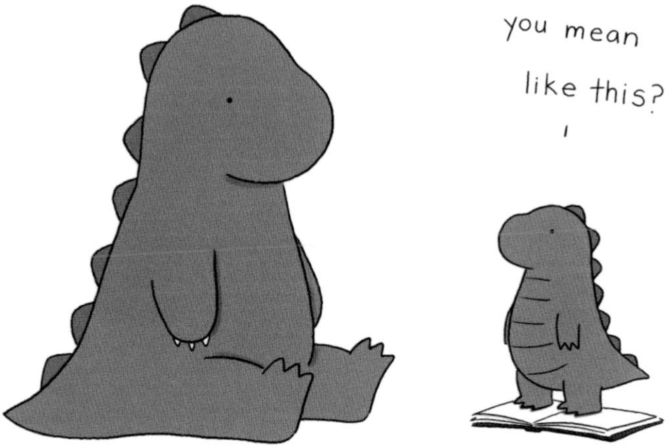
you mean like this?

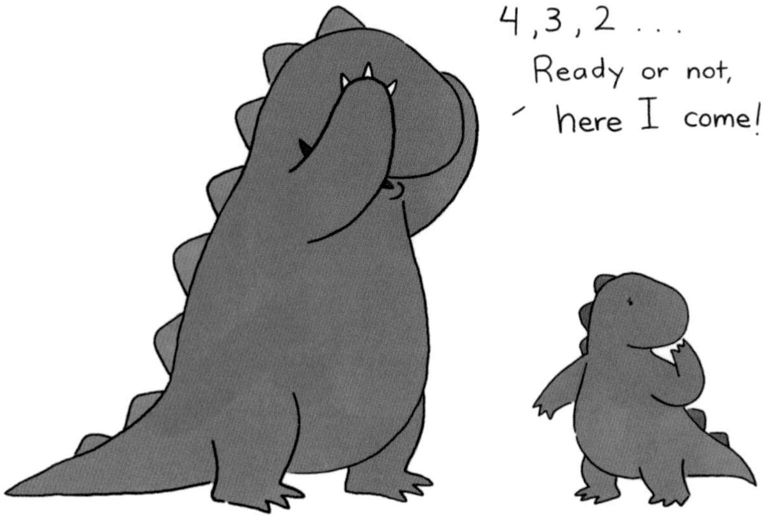
4, 3, 2 . . .
Ready or not,
here I come!

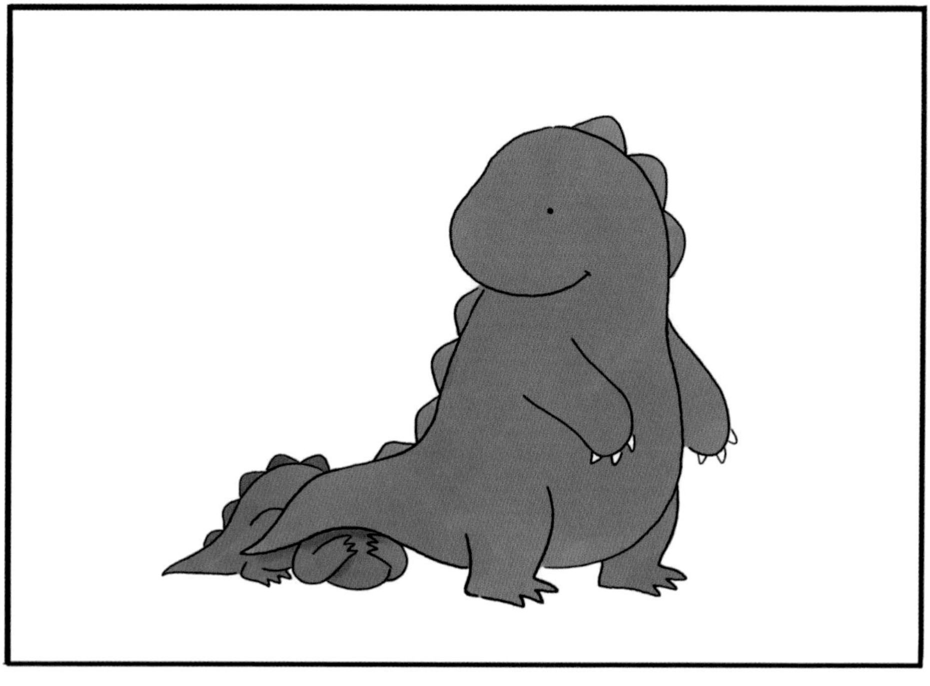

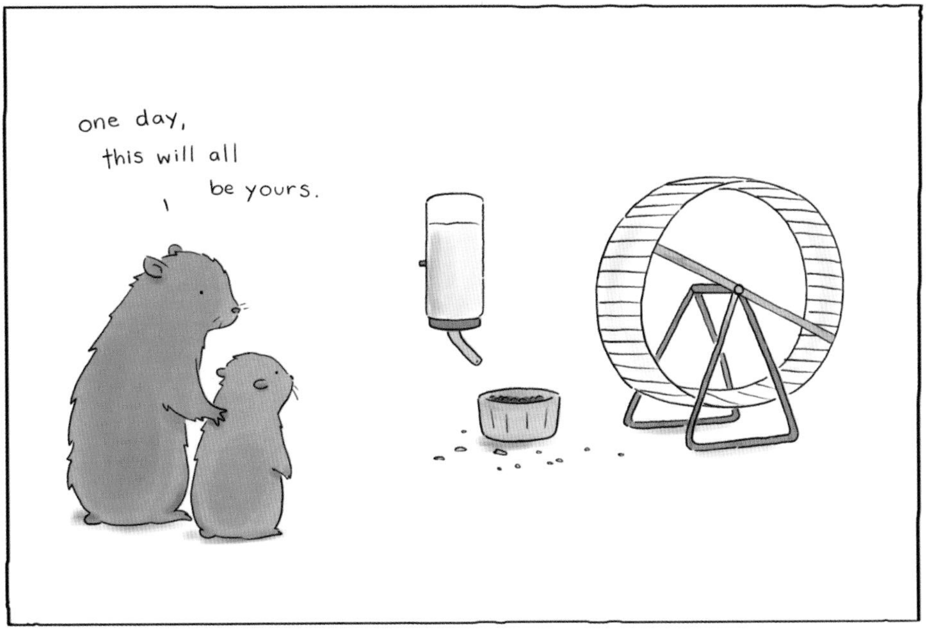
one day,
this will all
be yours.

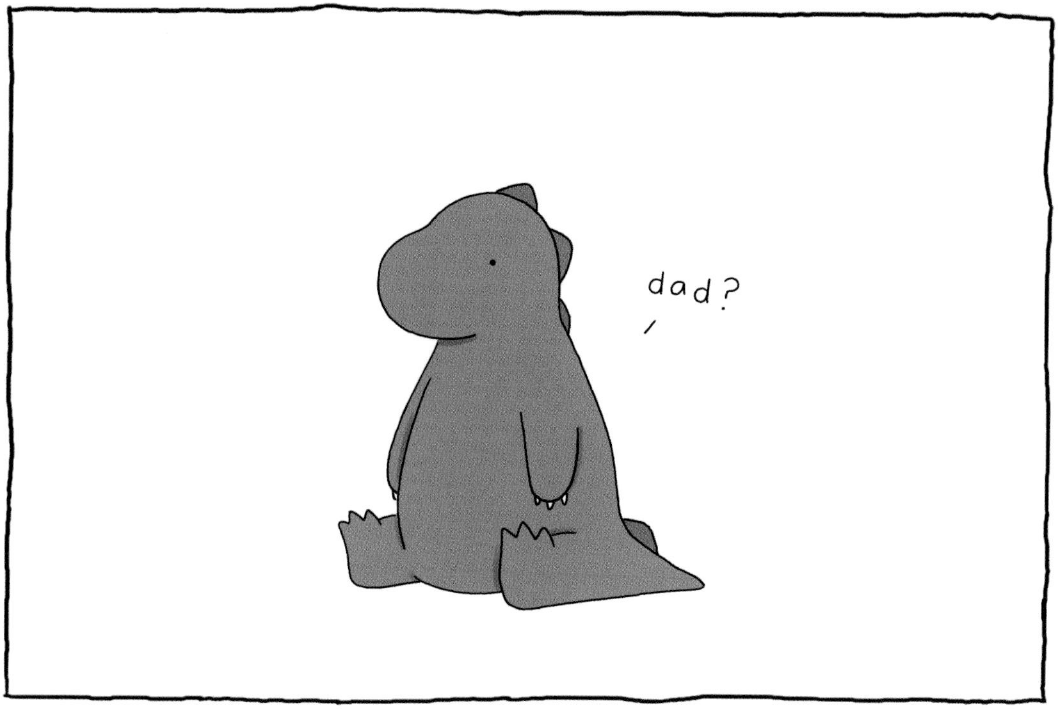
dad?

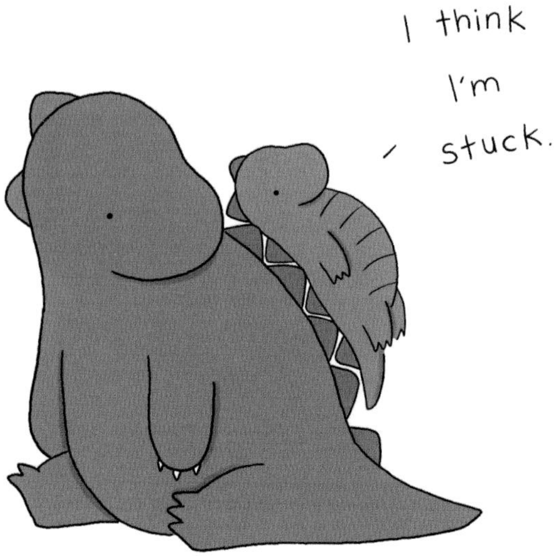
I think I'm stuck.

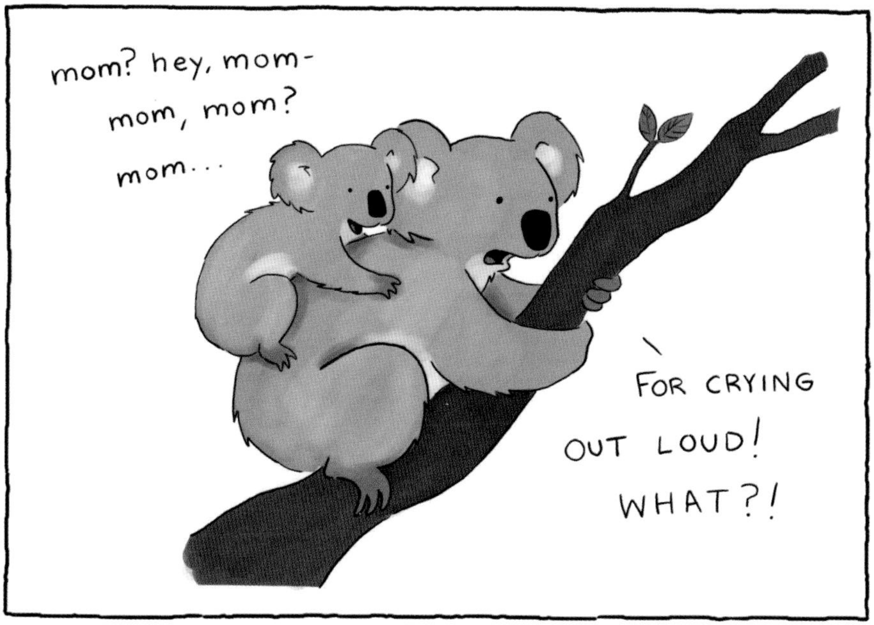
mom? hey, mom-
mom, mom?
mom...
FOR CRYING OUT LOUD! WHAT?!

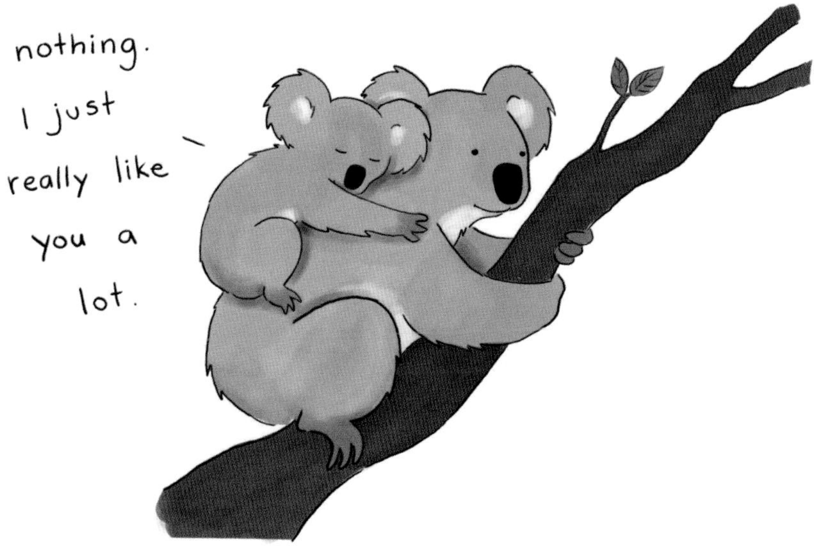
nothing. I just really like you a lot.

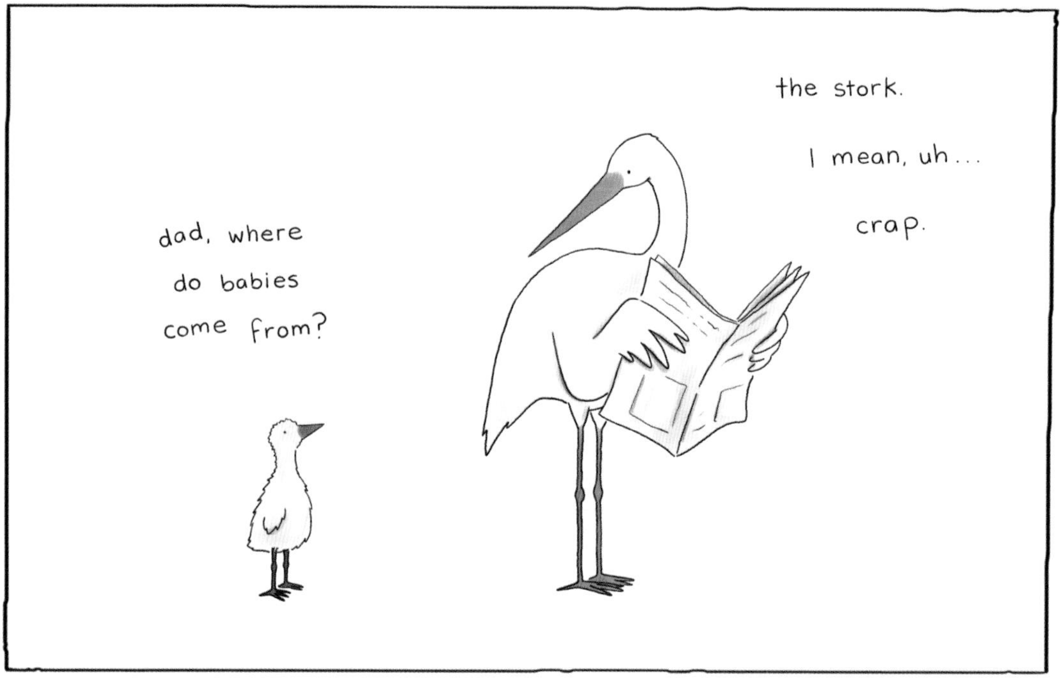
dad, where do babies come from?
the stork.
I mean, uh...
crap.

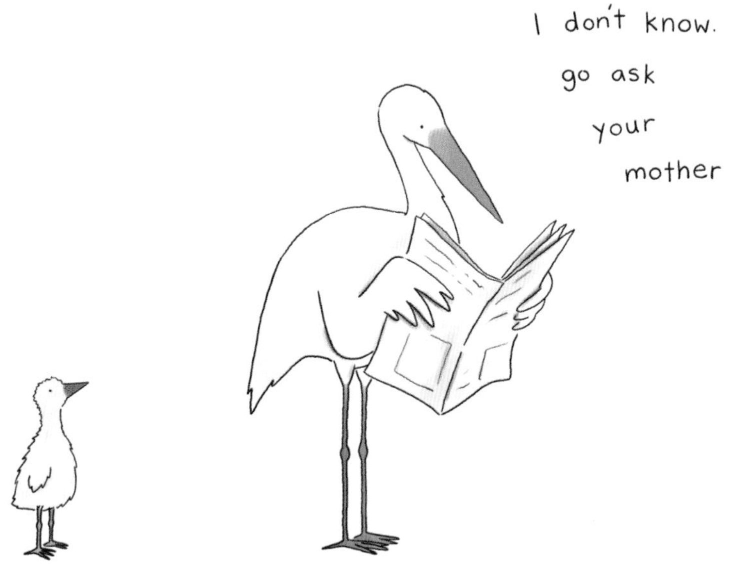
I don't know. go ask your mother

daily life

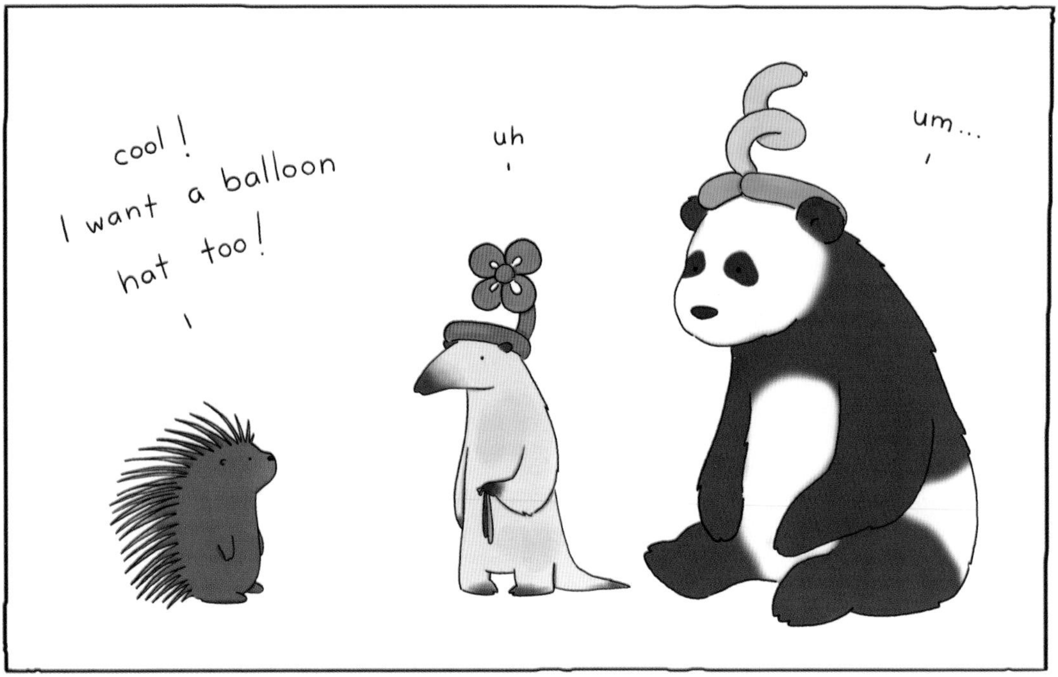
cool! I want a balloon hat too!
uh
um...

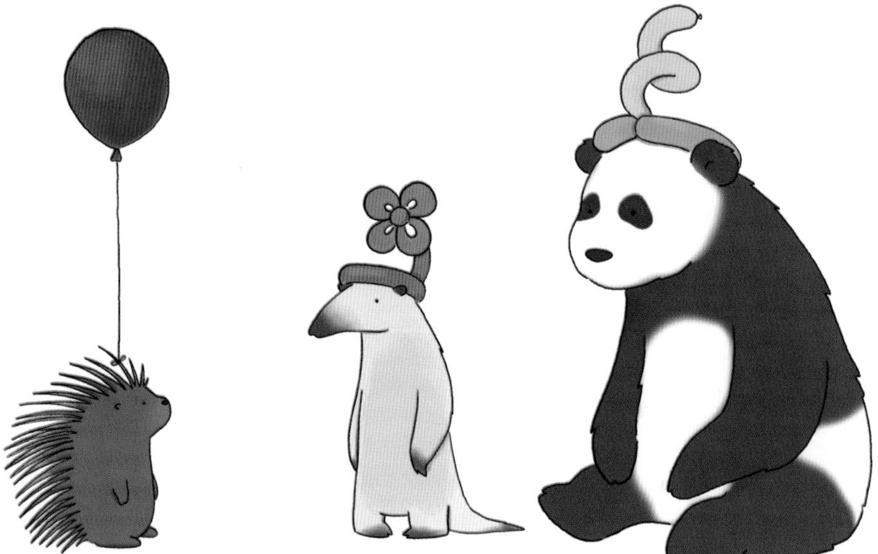

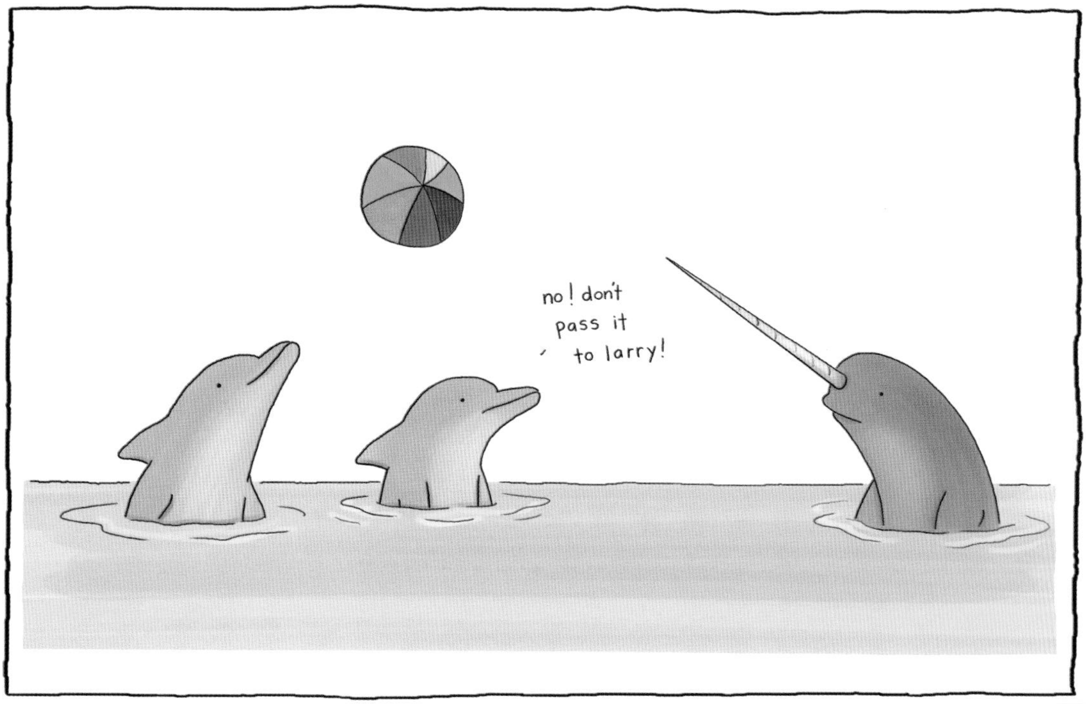
no! don't
pass it
to larry!

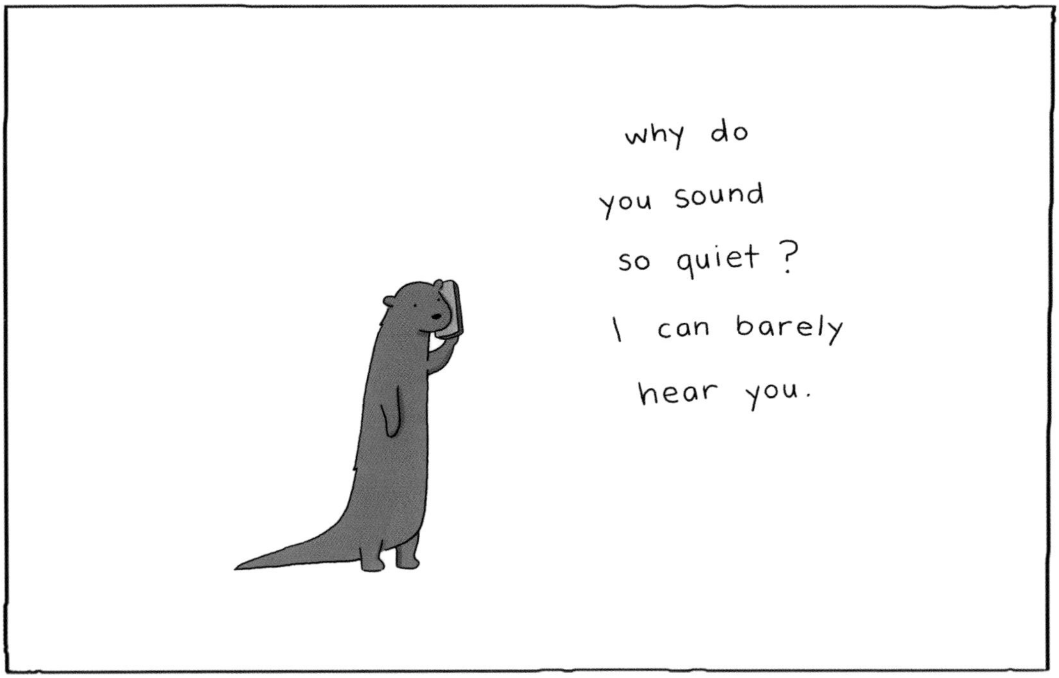
why do you sound so quiet ? I can barely hear you.

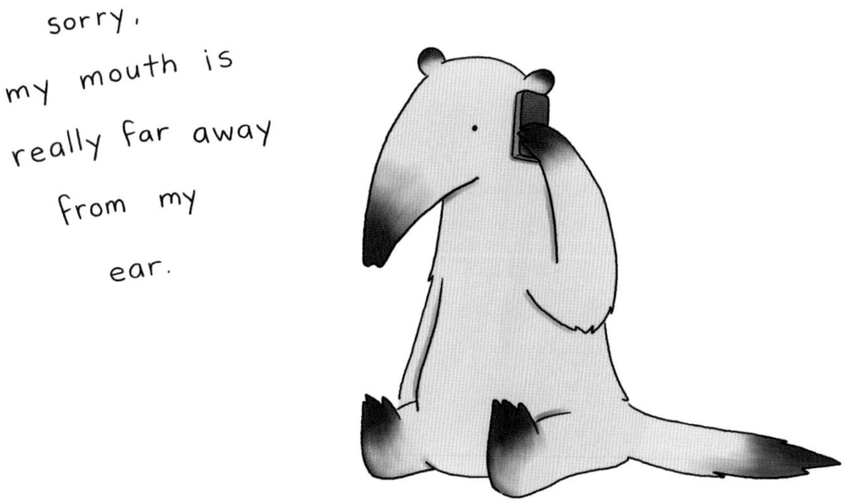
sorry, my mouth is really far away from my ear.

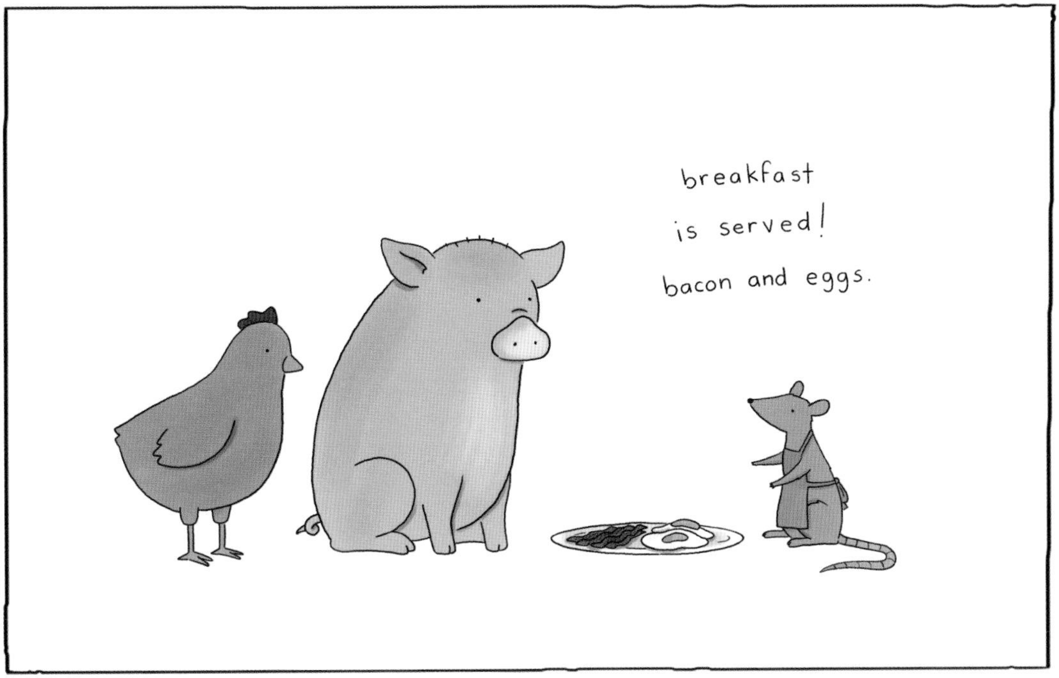
breakfast
is served!
bacon and eggs.

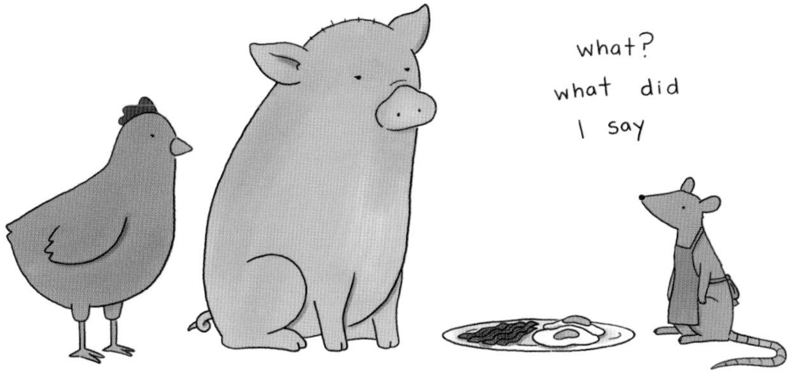
what?
what did
I say

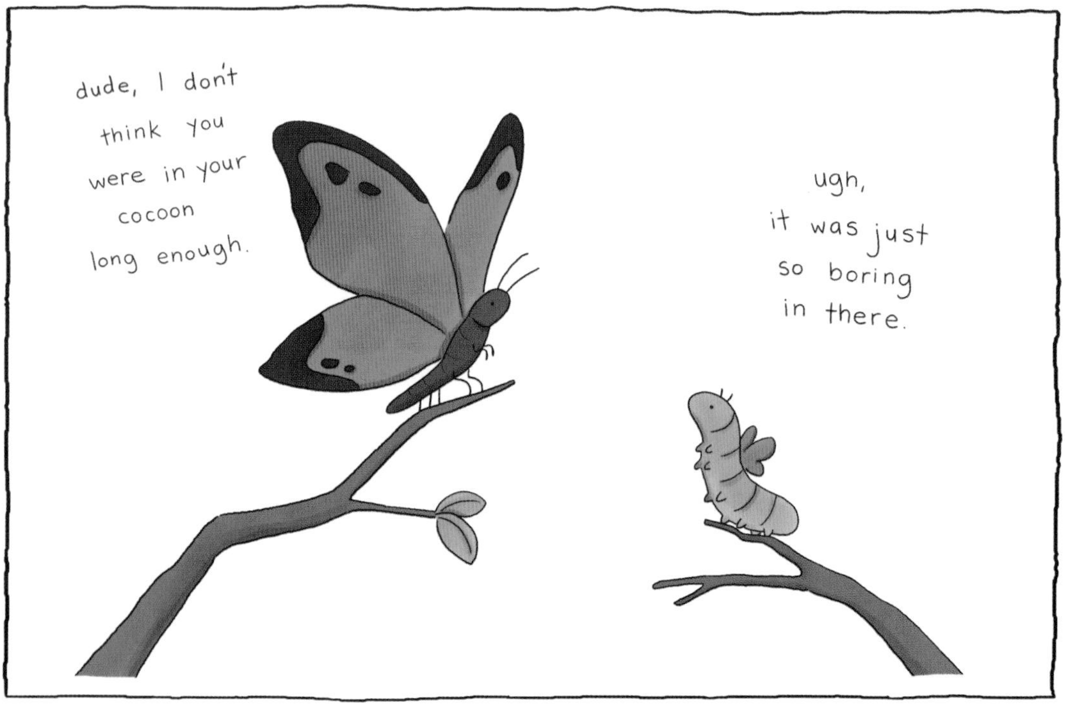
dude, I don't think you were in your cocoon long enough.
ugh, it was just so boring in there.

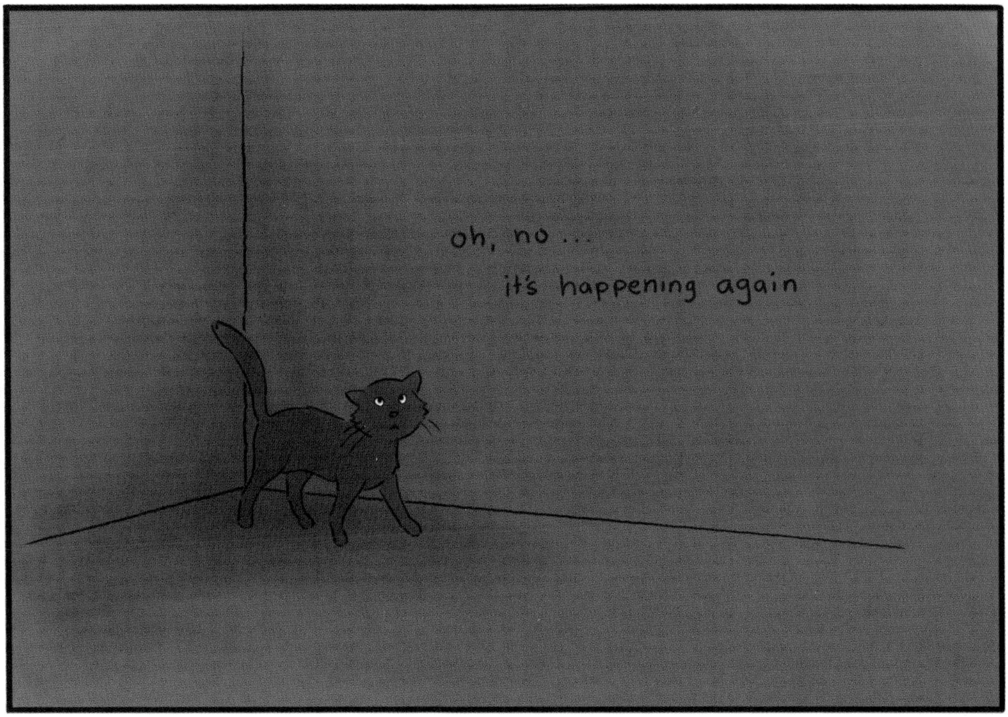
oh, no ...
it's happening again

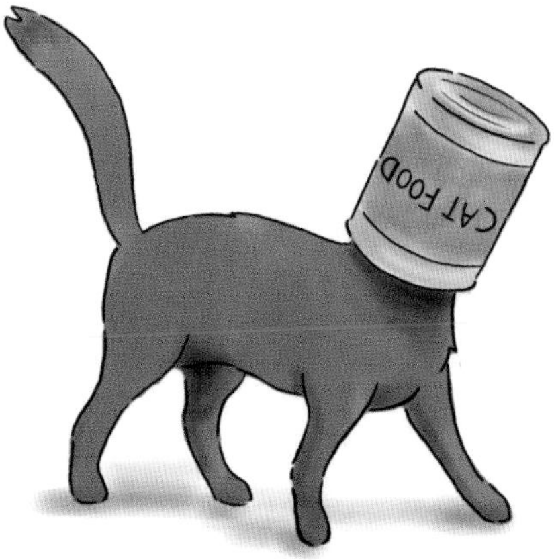
CAT FOOD

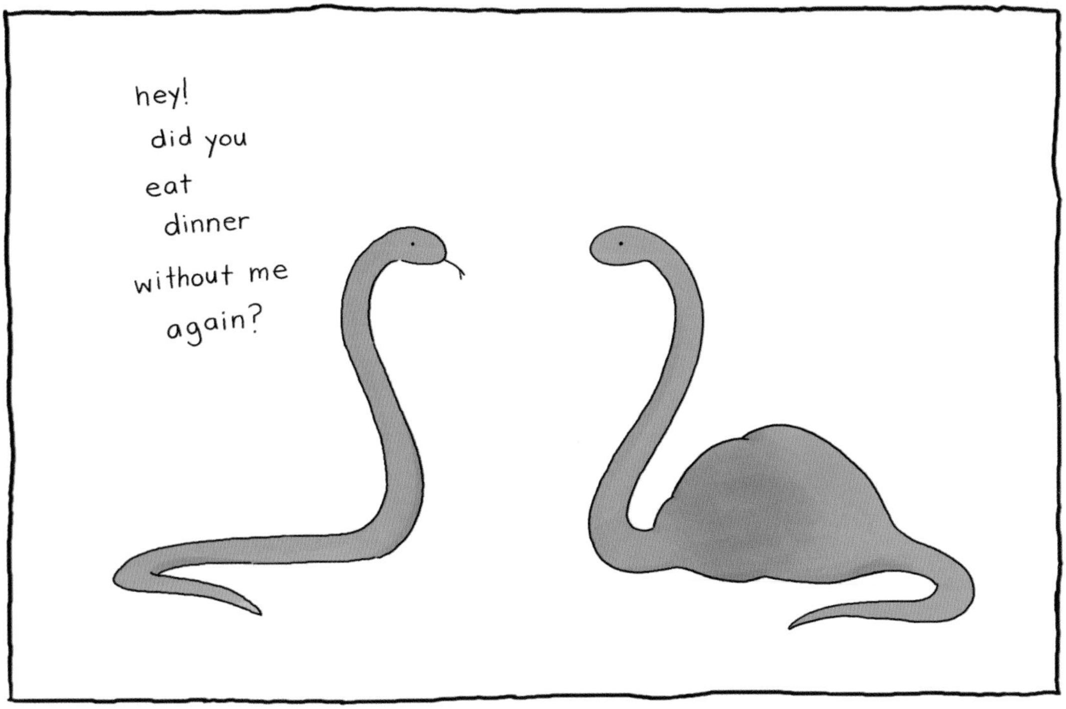
hey! did you eat dinner without me again?

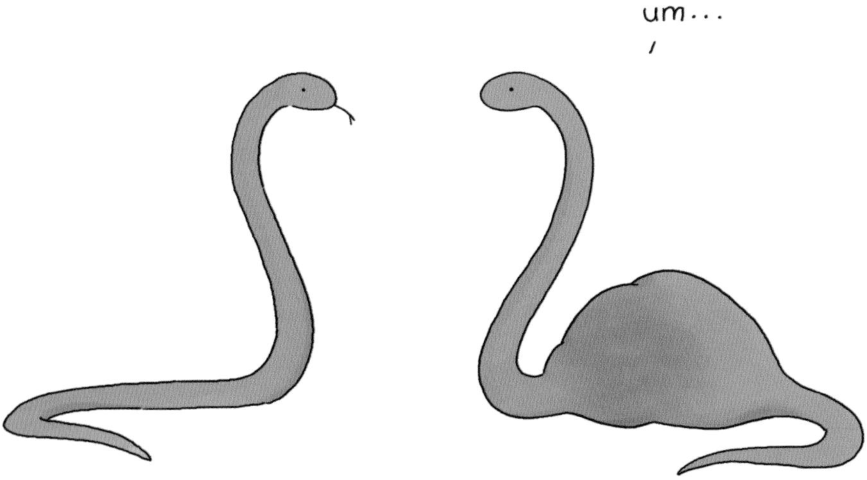
um...

Woolly bully.

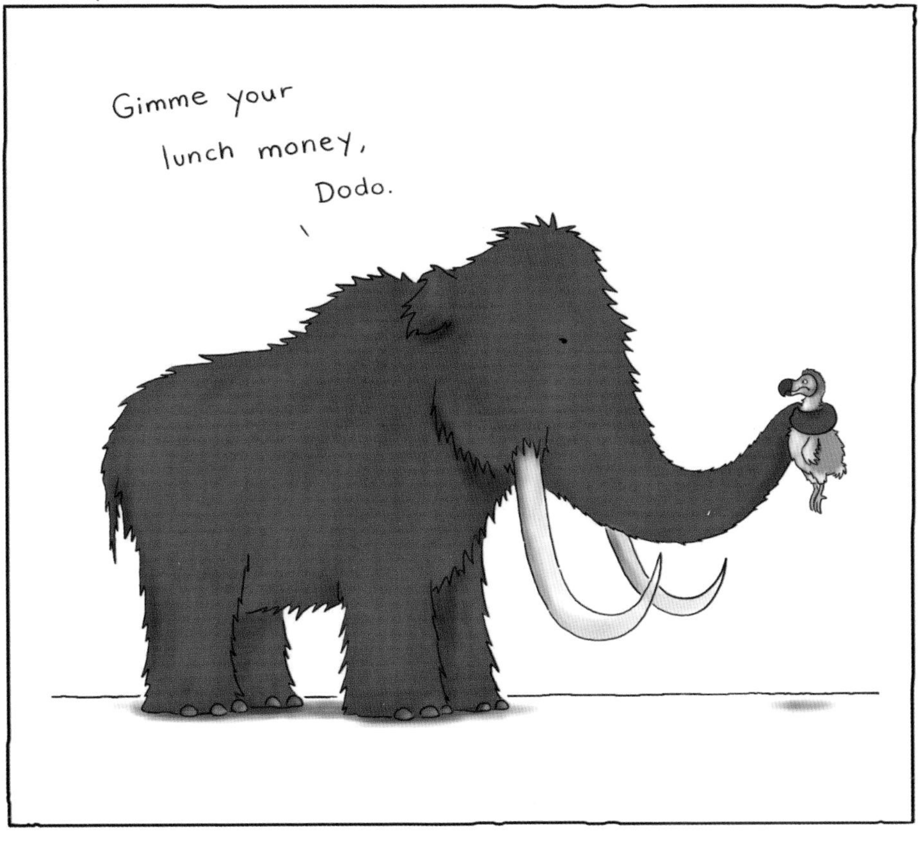
Gimme your lunch money, Dodo.

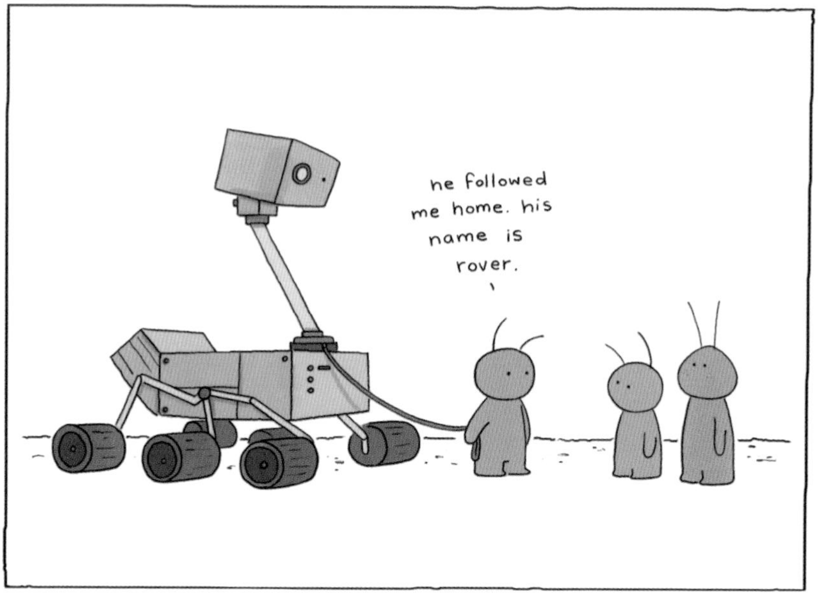
he followed me home. his name is rover.

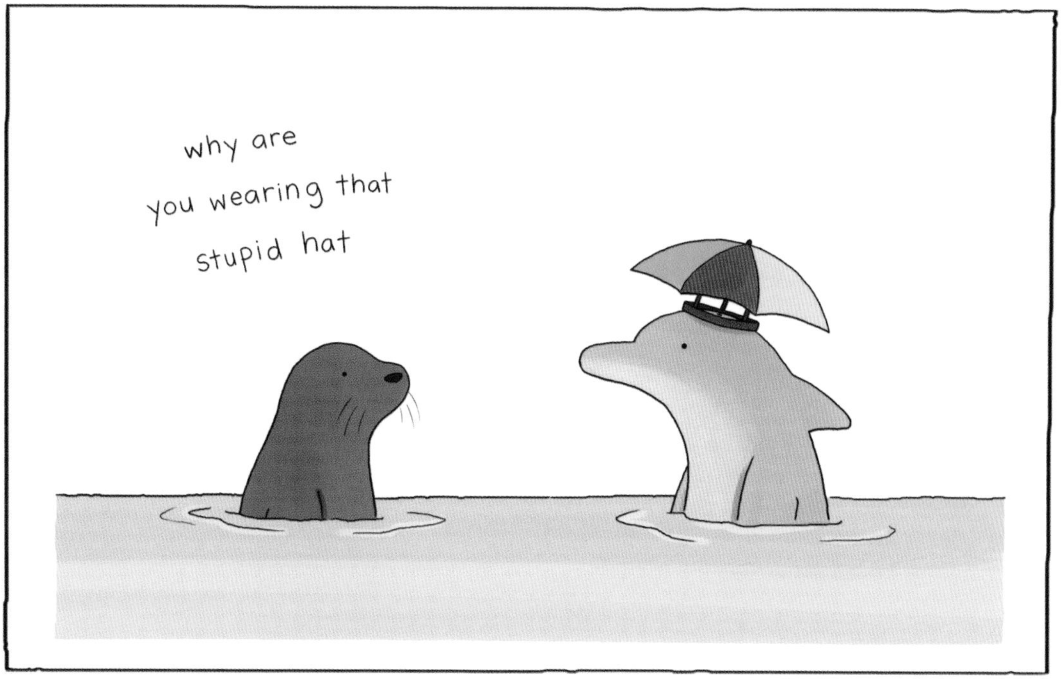
why are you wearing that stupid hat

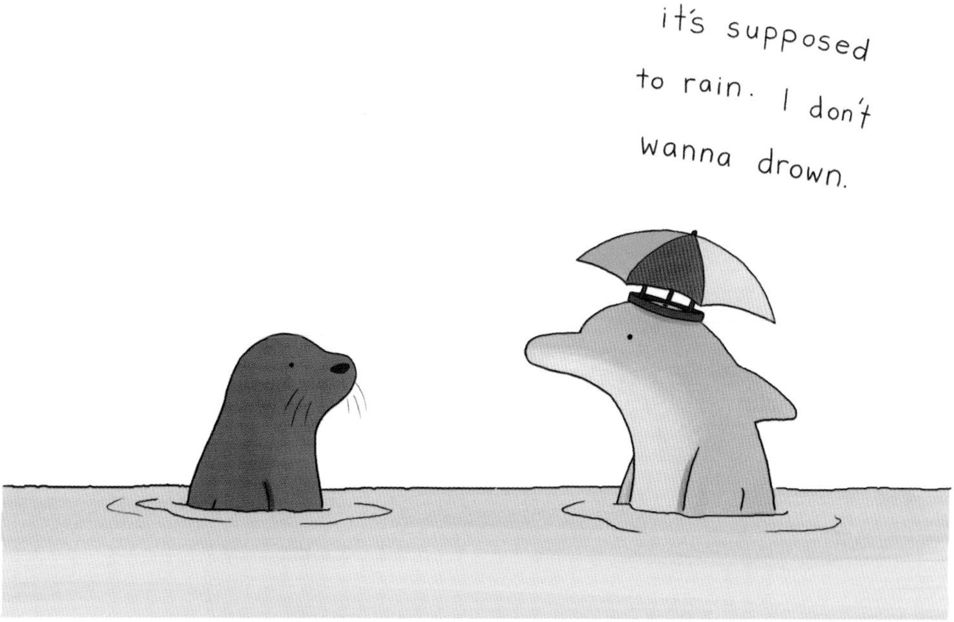
it's supposed to rain. I don't wanna drown.

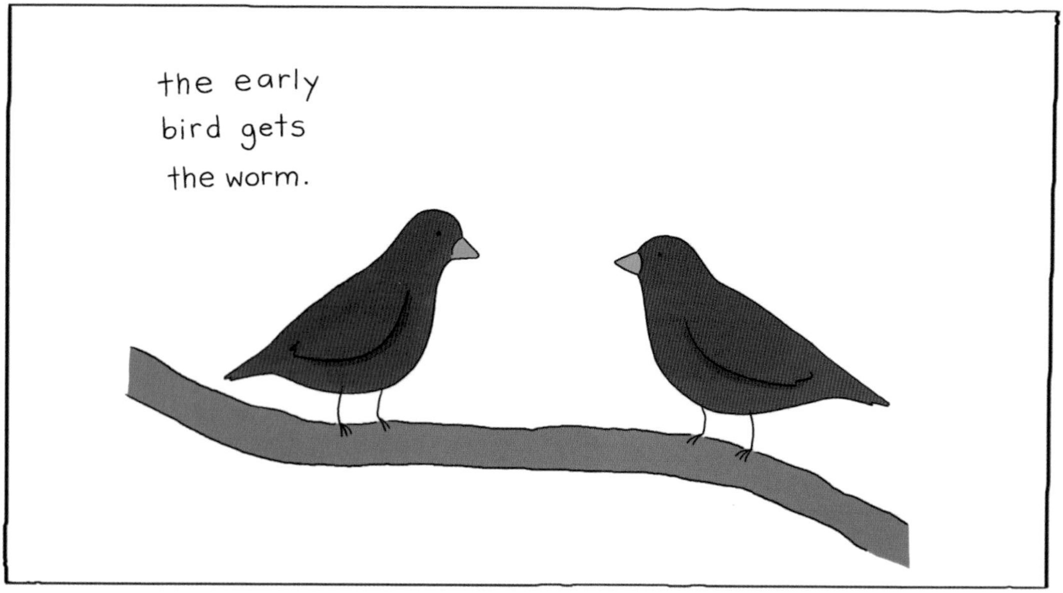
the early bird gets the worm.

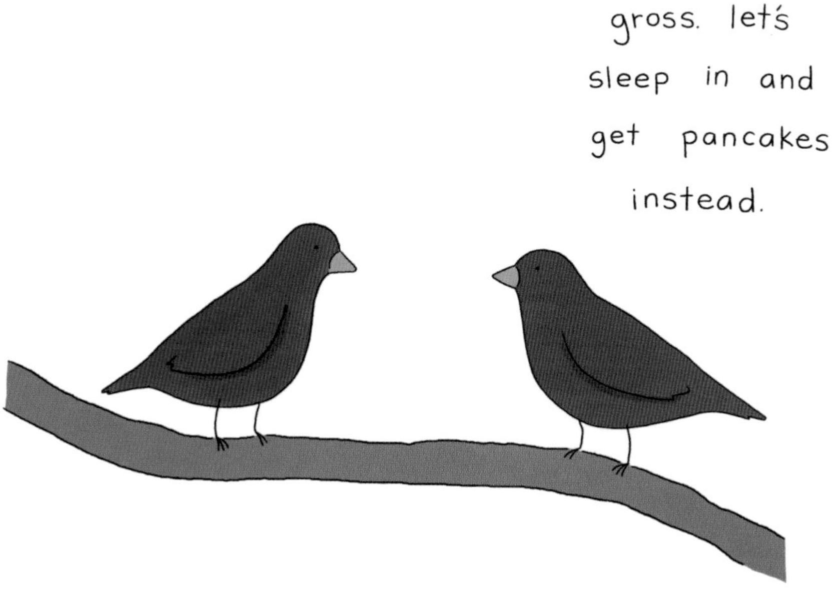
gross. let's sleep in and get pancakes instead.

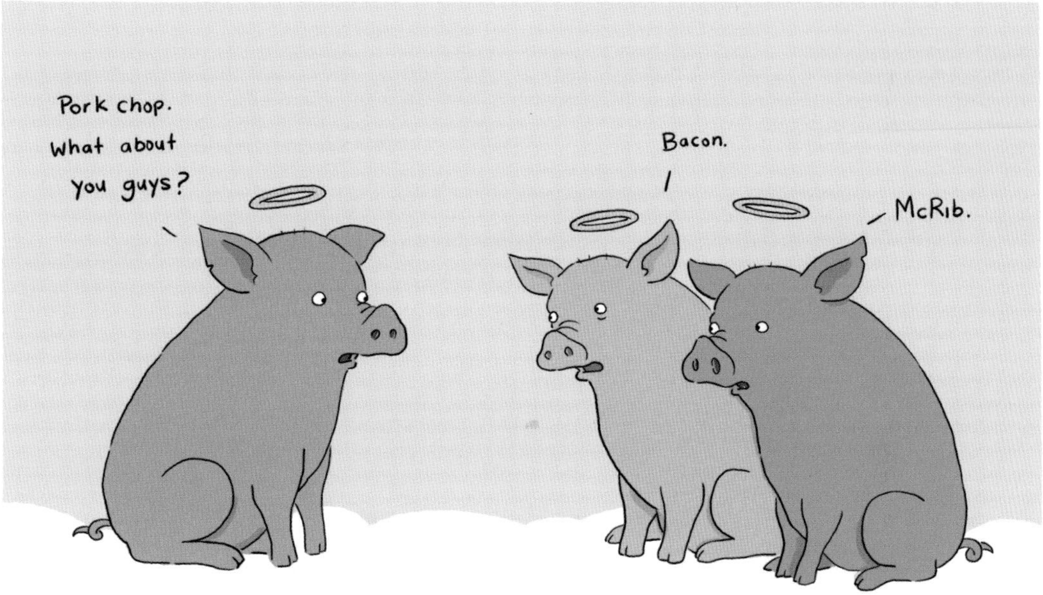
Pork chop.
What about
you guys?
Bacon.
McRib.

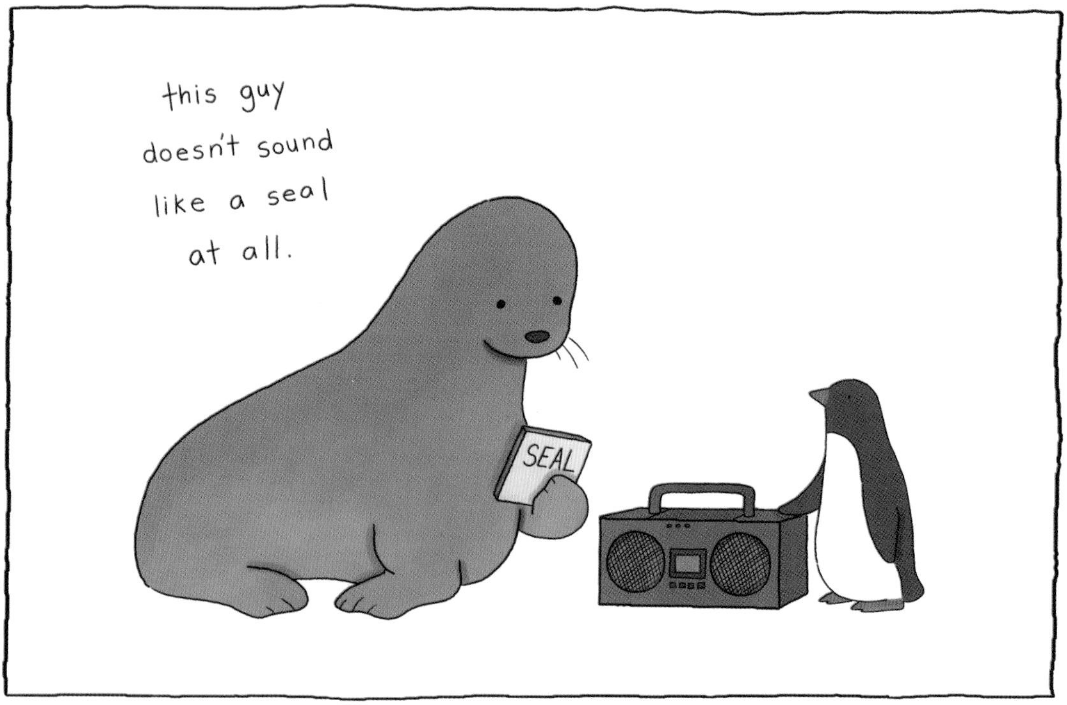
this guy doesn't sound like a seal at all.
SEAL

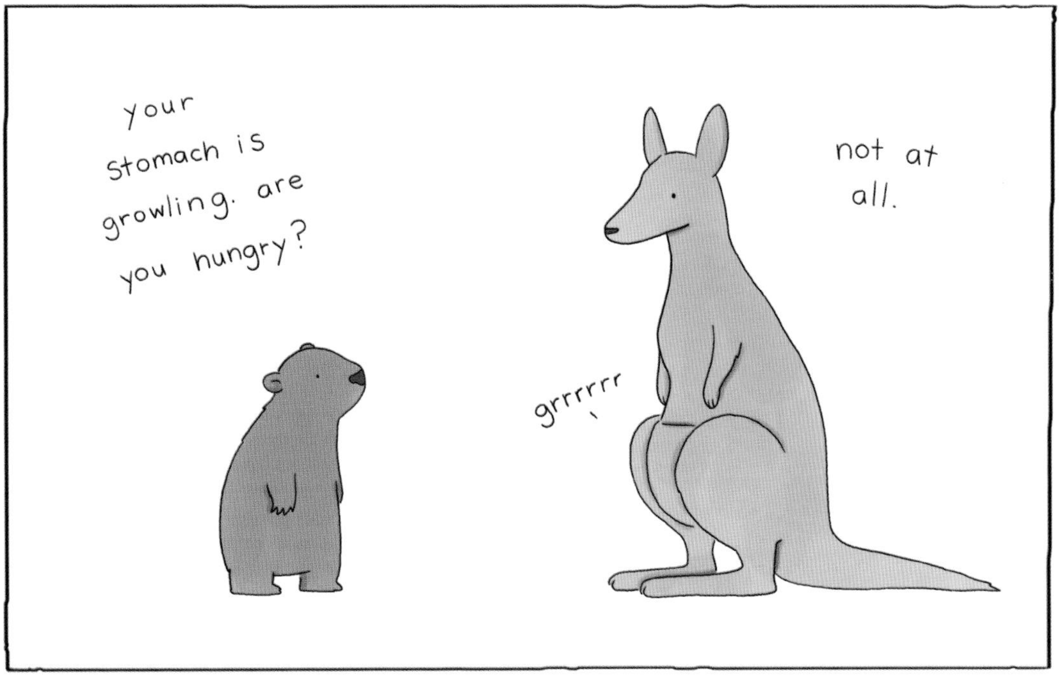
your stomach is growling. are you hungry?
not at all.
grrrrrr

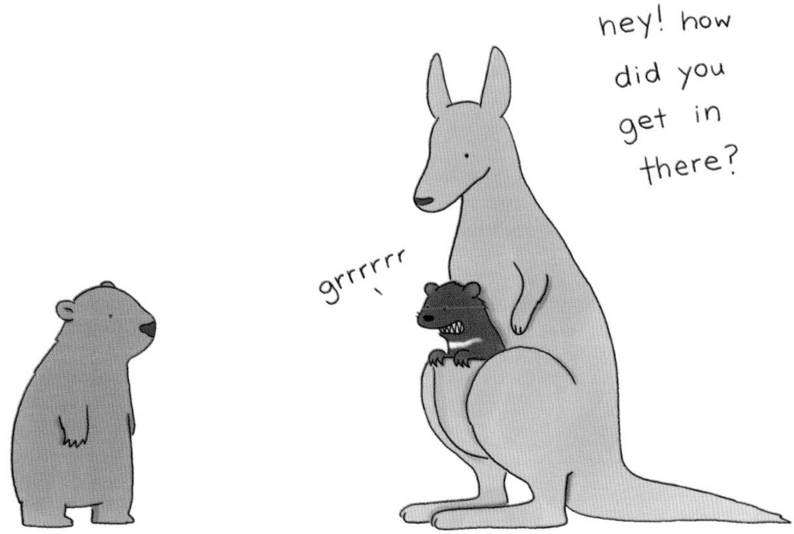
hey! how did you get in there?
grrrrrr

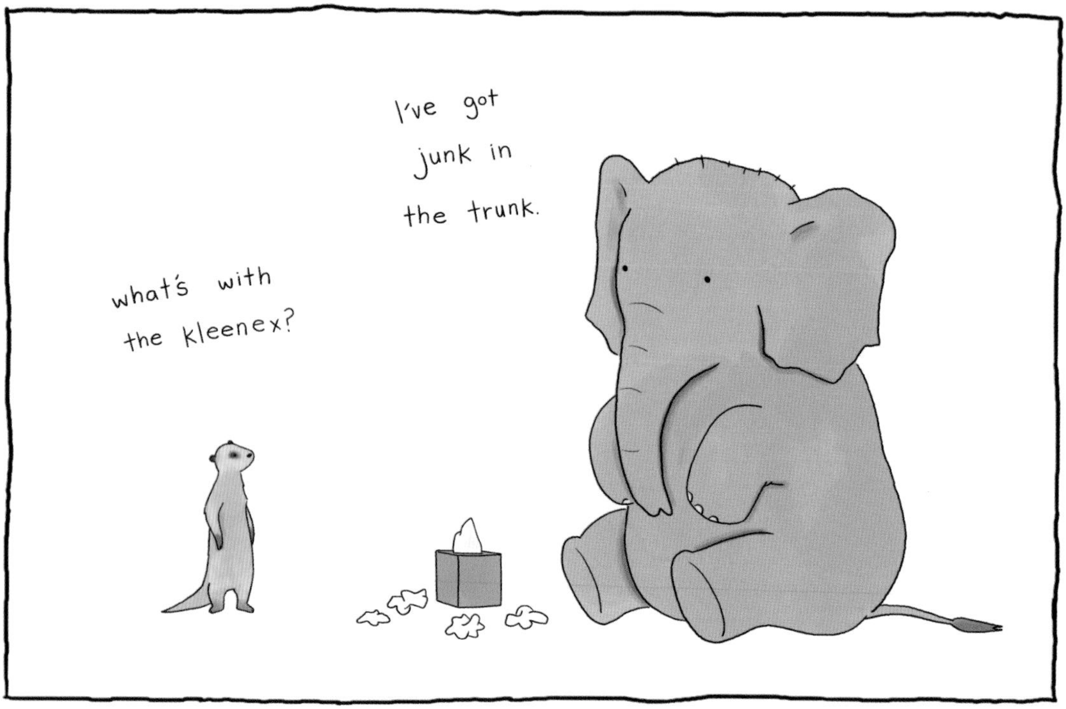

what's with the kleenex?
I've got junk in the trunk.

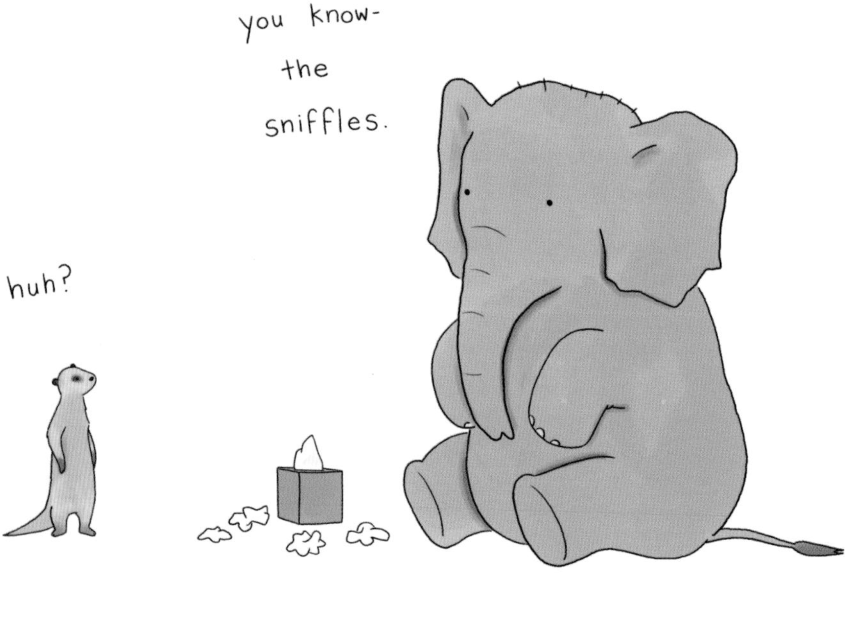

huh?
you know- the sniffles.

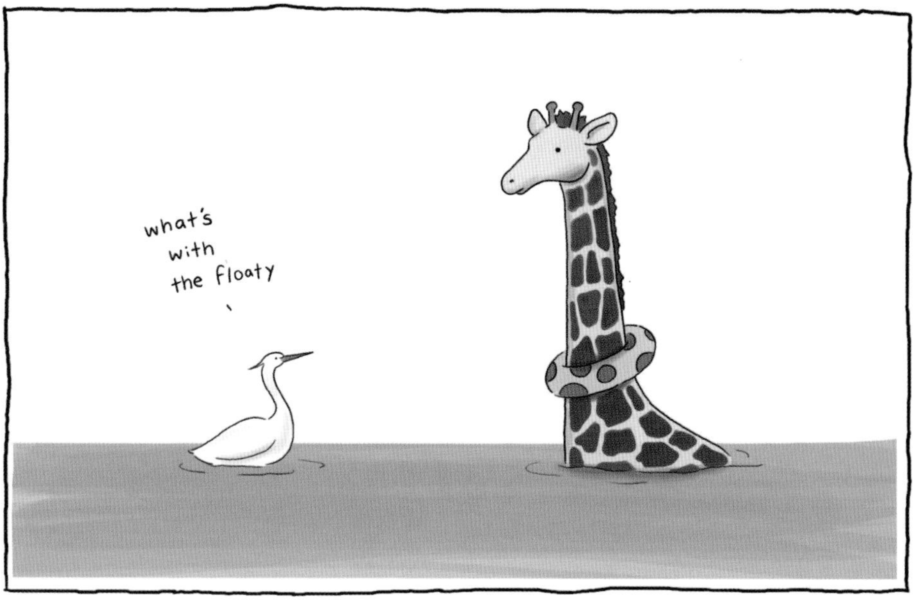
what's with the floaty

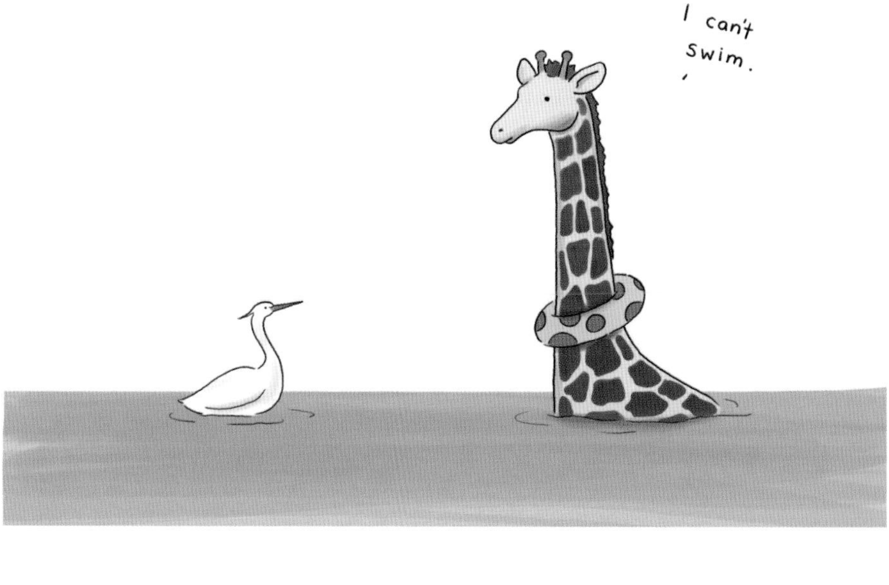
I can't swim.

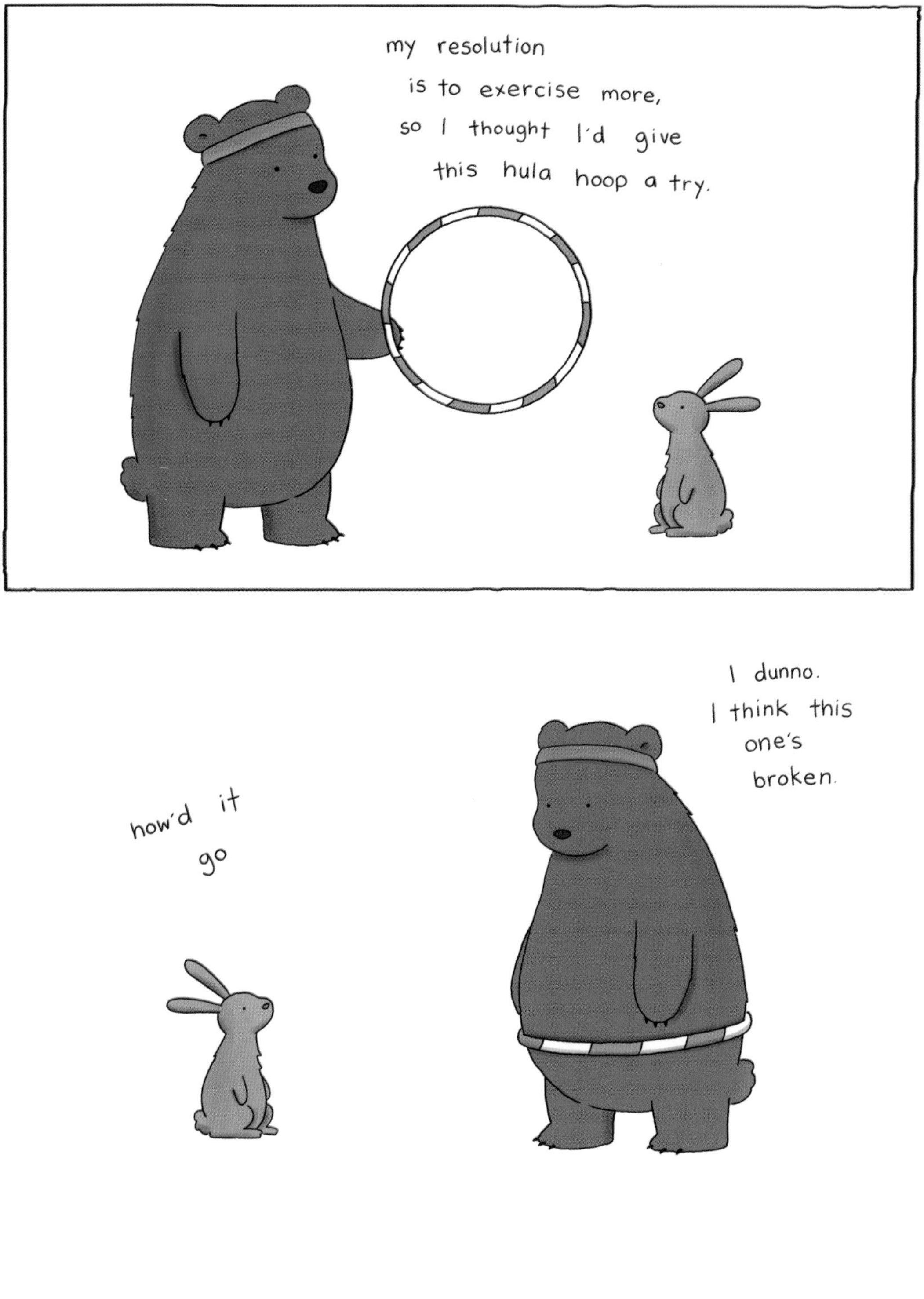
my resolution is to exercise more, so I thought I'd give this hula hoop a try.
how'd it go
I dunno. I think this one's broken.

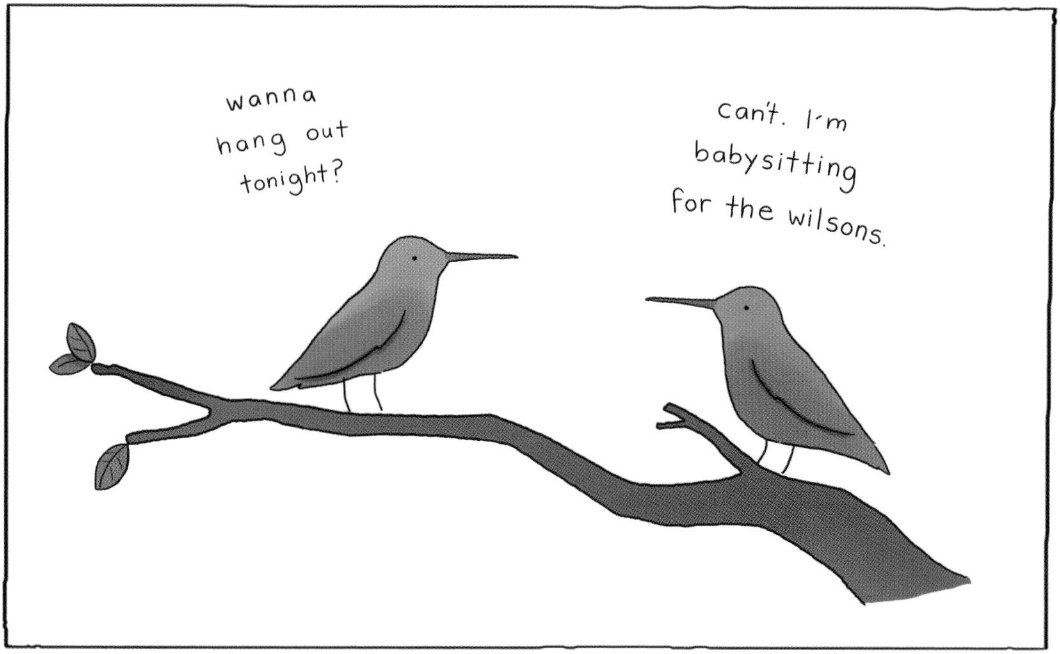
wanna hang out tonight?
can't. I'm babysitting for the wilsons.

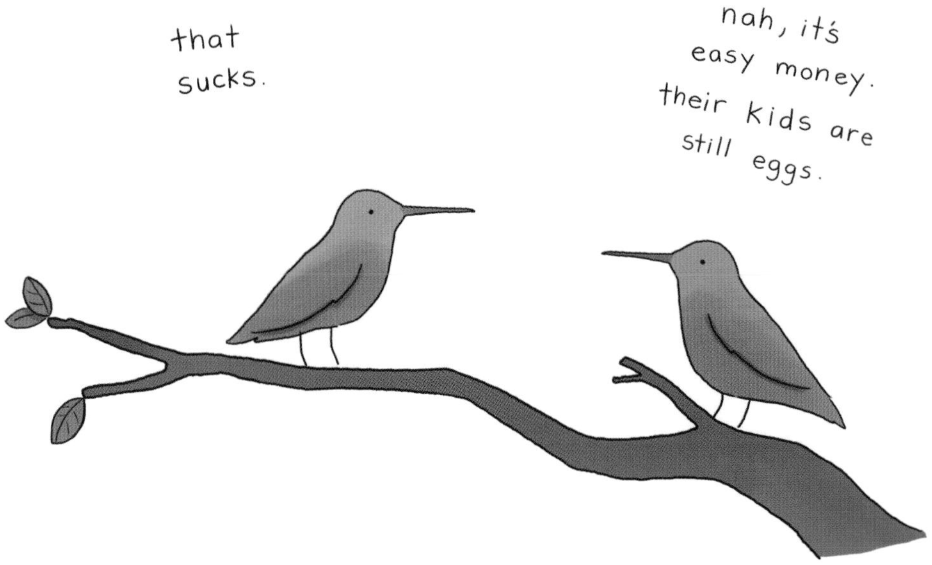
that sucks.
nah, it's easy money. their kids are still eggs.

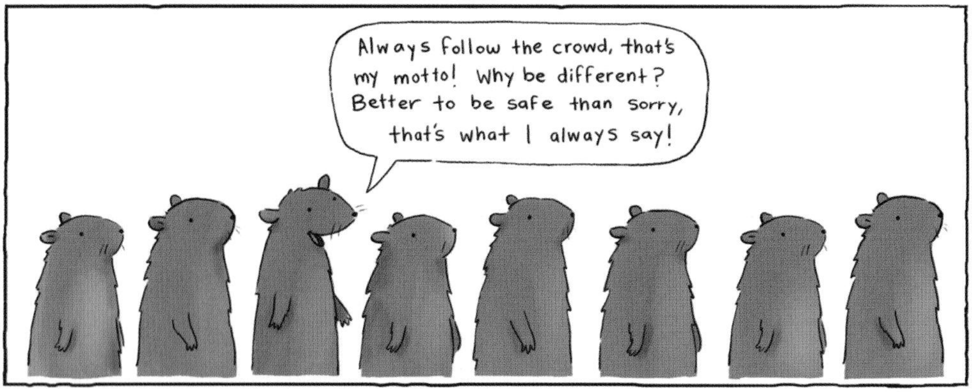
Always follow the crowd, that's my motto! Why be different? Better to be safe than sorry, that's what I always say!

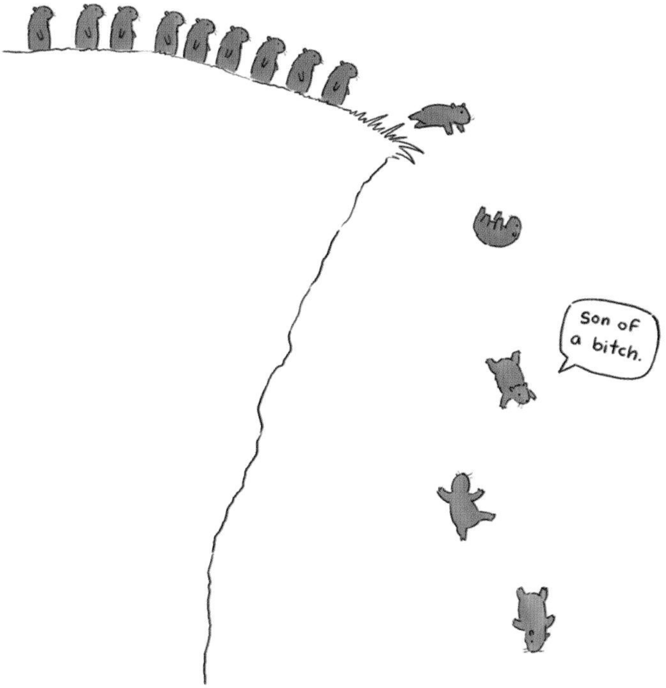
Son of a bitch.

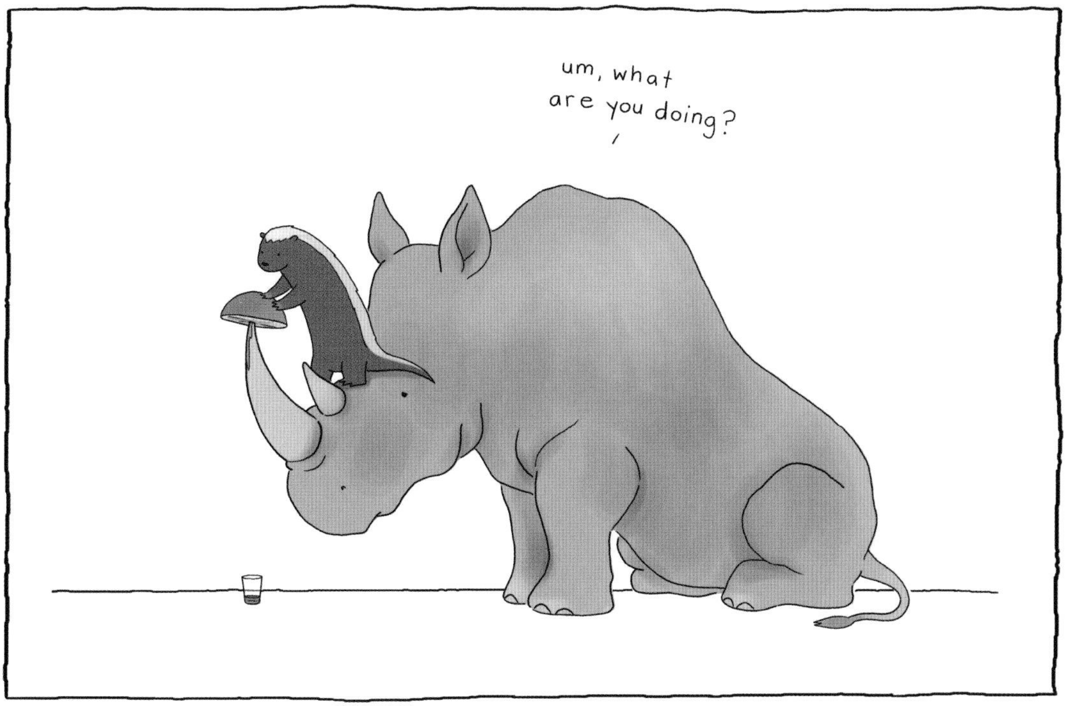
um, what are you doing?

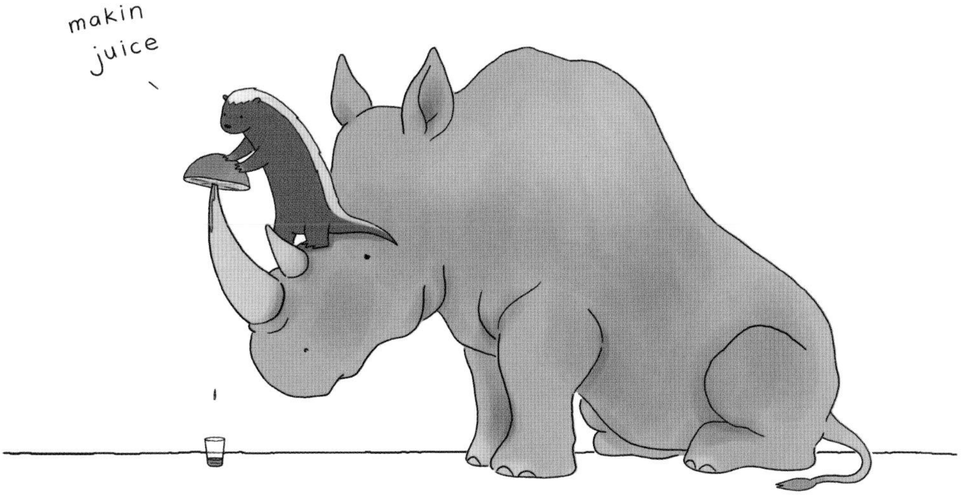
makin juice

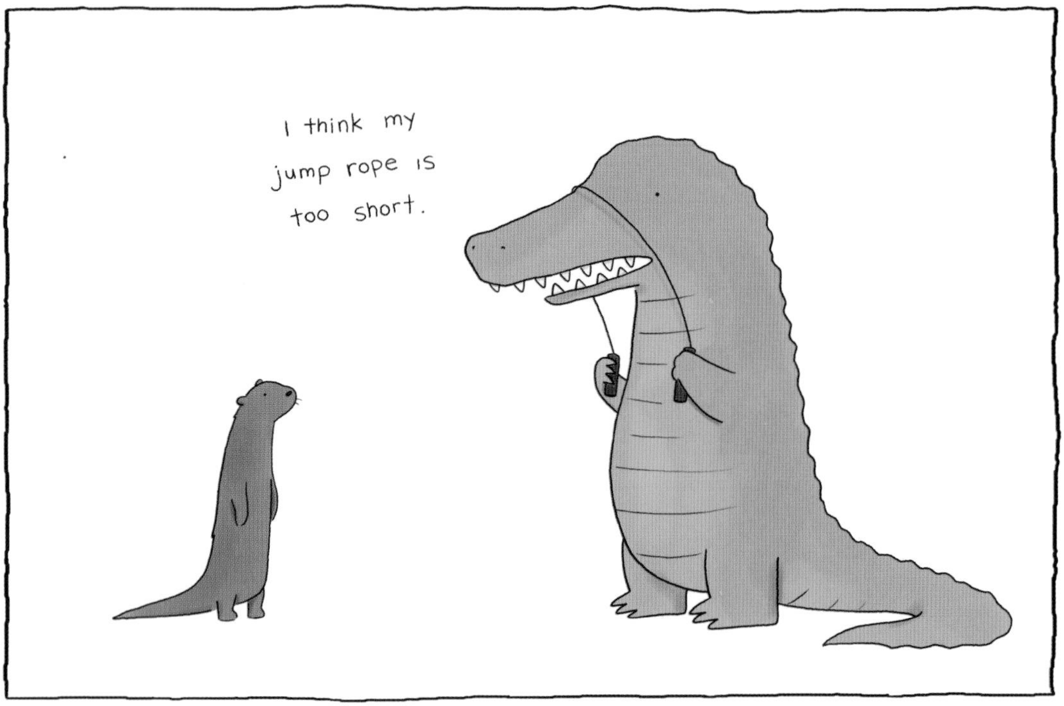
I think my jump rope is too short.

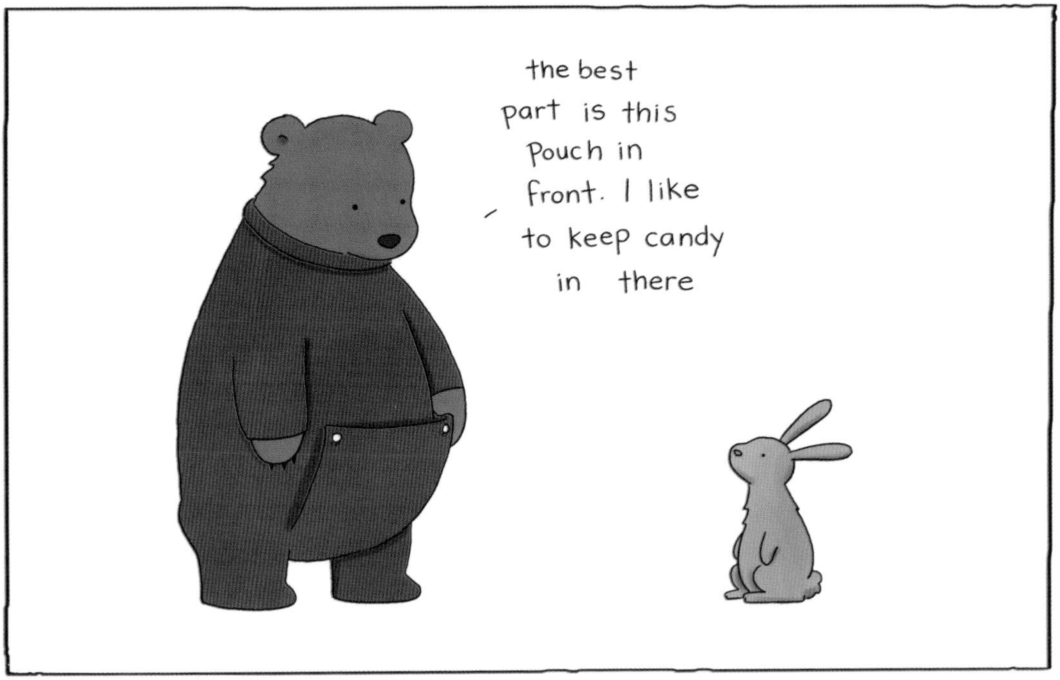
the best part is this pouch in front. I like to keep candy in there

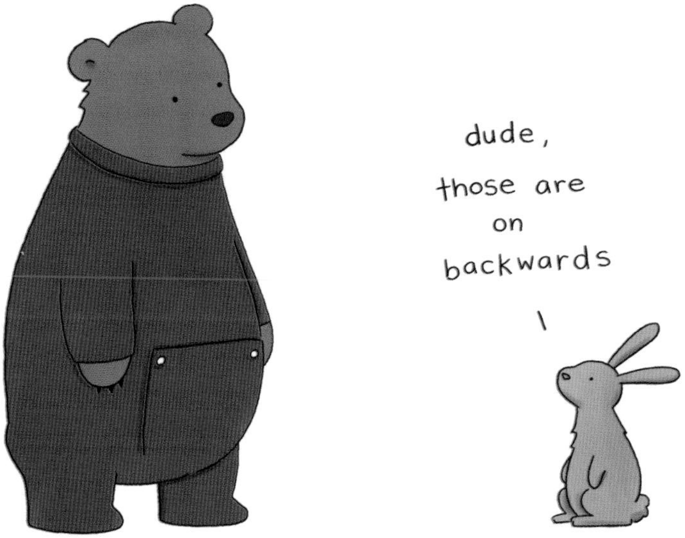
dude, those are on backwards

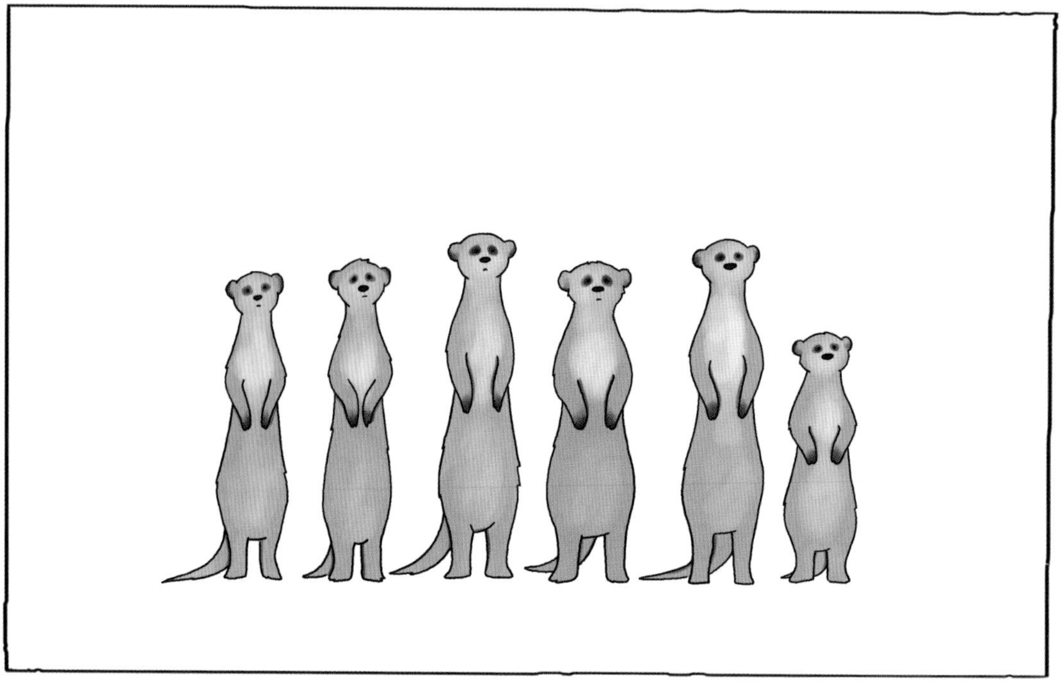

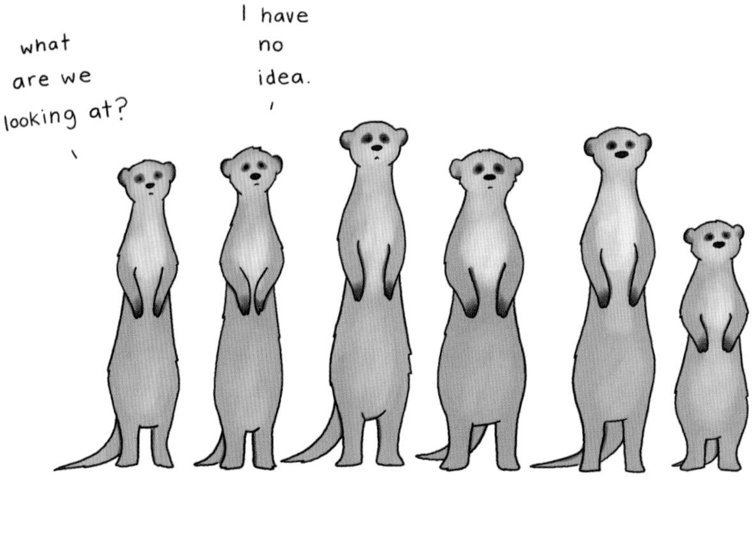
what are we looking at?
I have no idea.

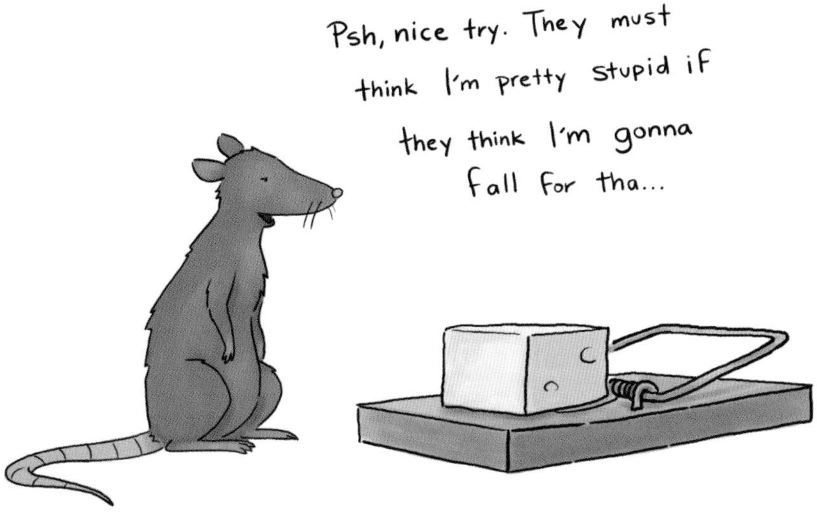
Psh, nice try. They must think I'm pretty stupid if they think I'm gonna fall for tha...

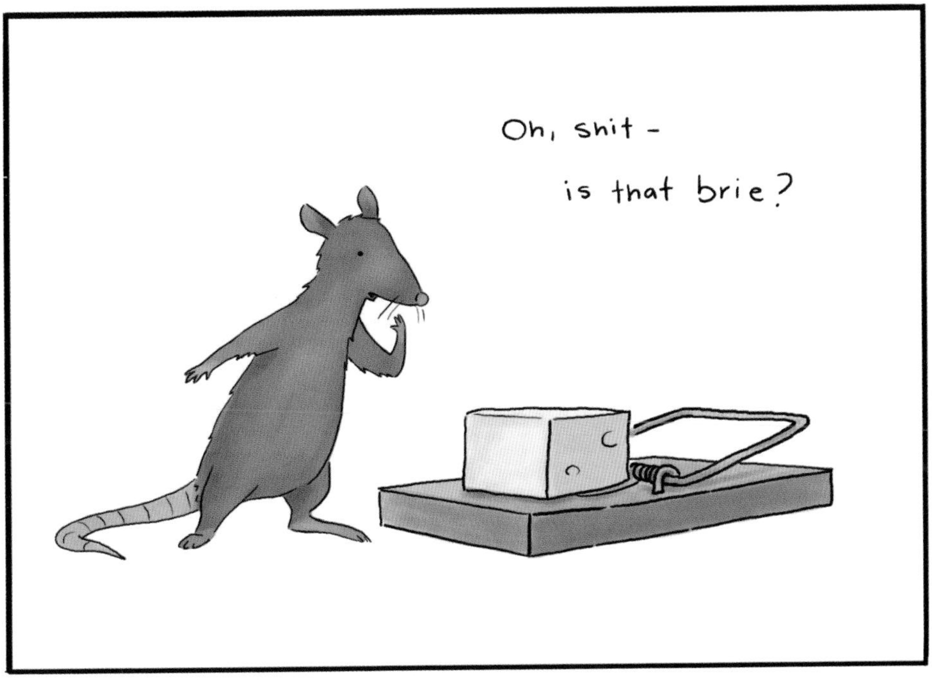
Oh, shit -
- is that brie?

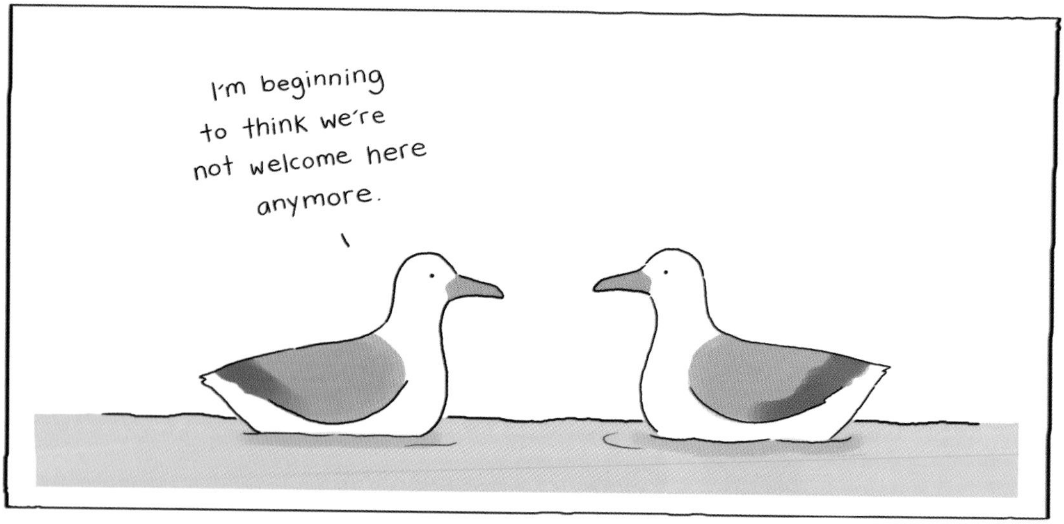
I'm beginning to think we're not welcome here anymore.

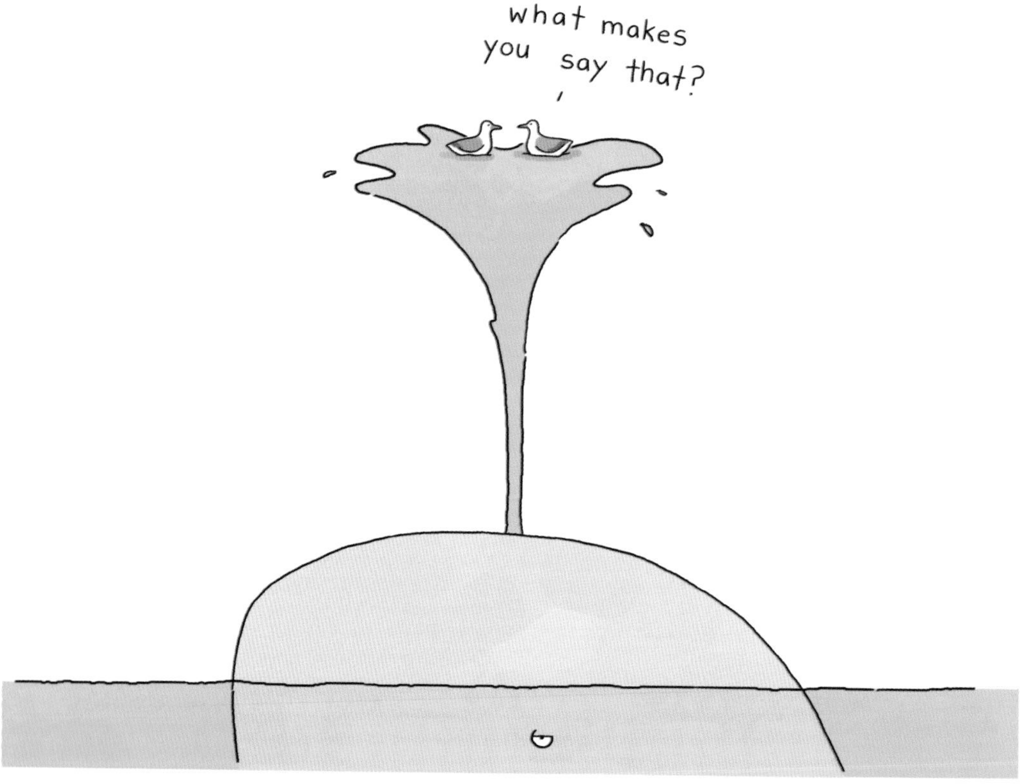
what makes you say that?

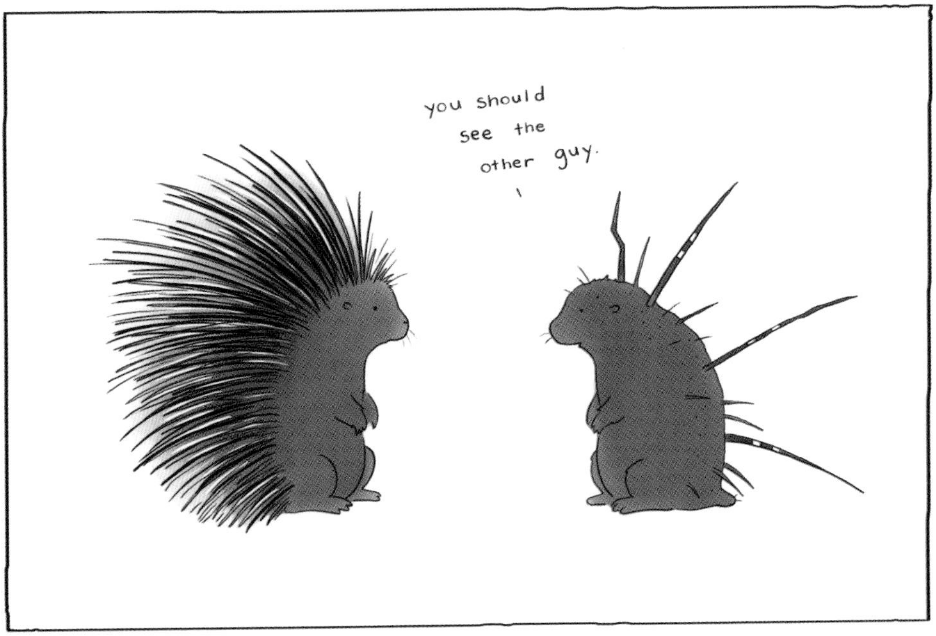
you should
see the
other guy.

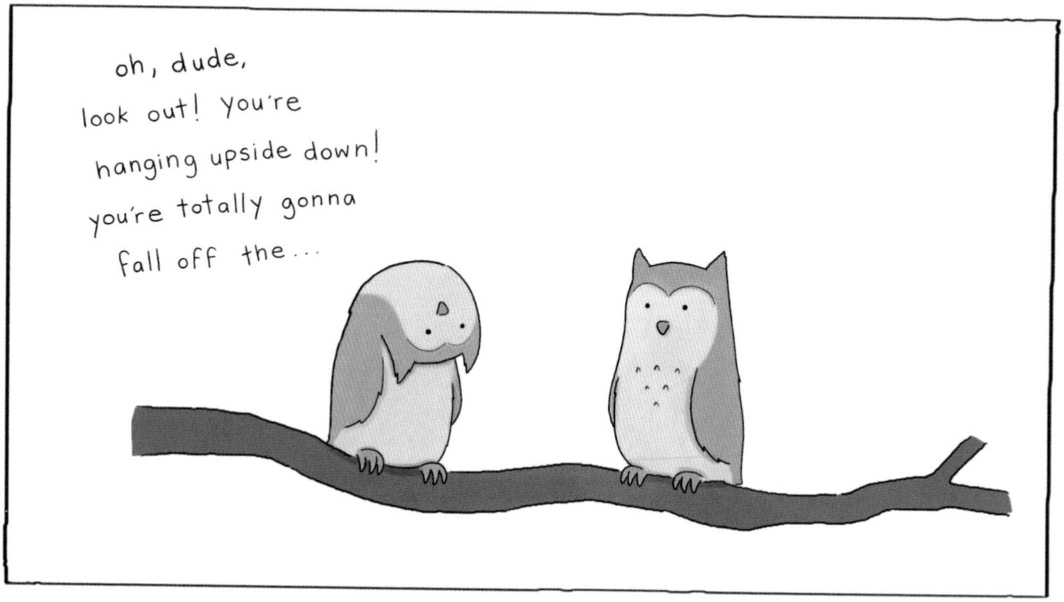
oh, dude, look out! you're hanging upside down! you're totally gonna fall off the...

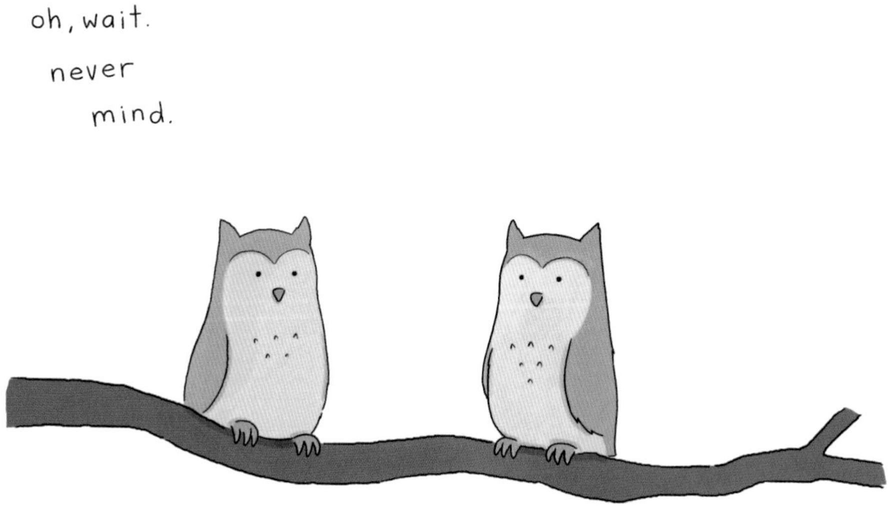
oh, wait. never mind.

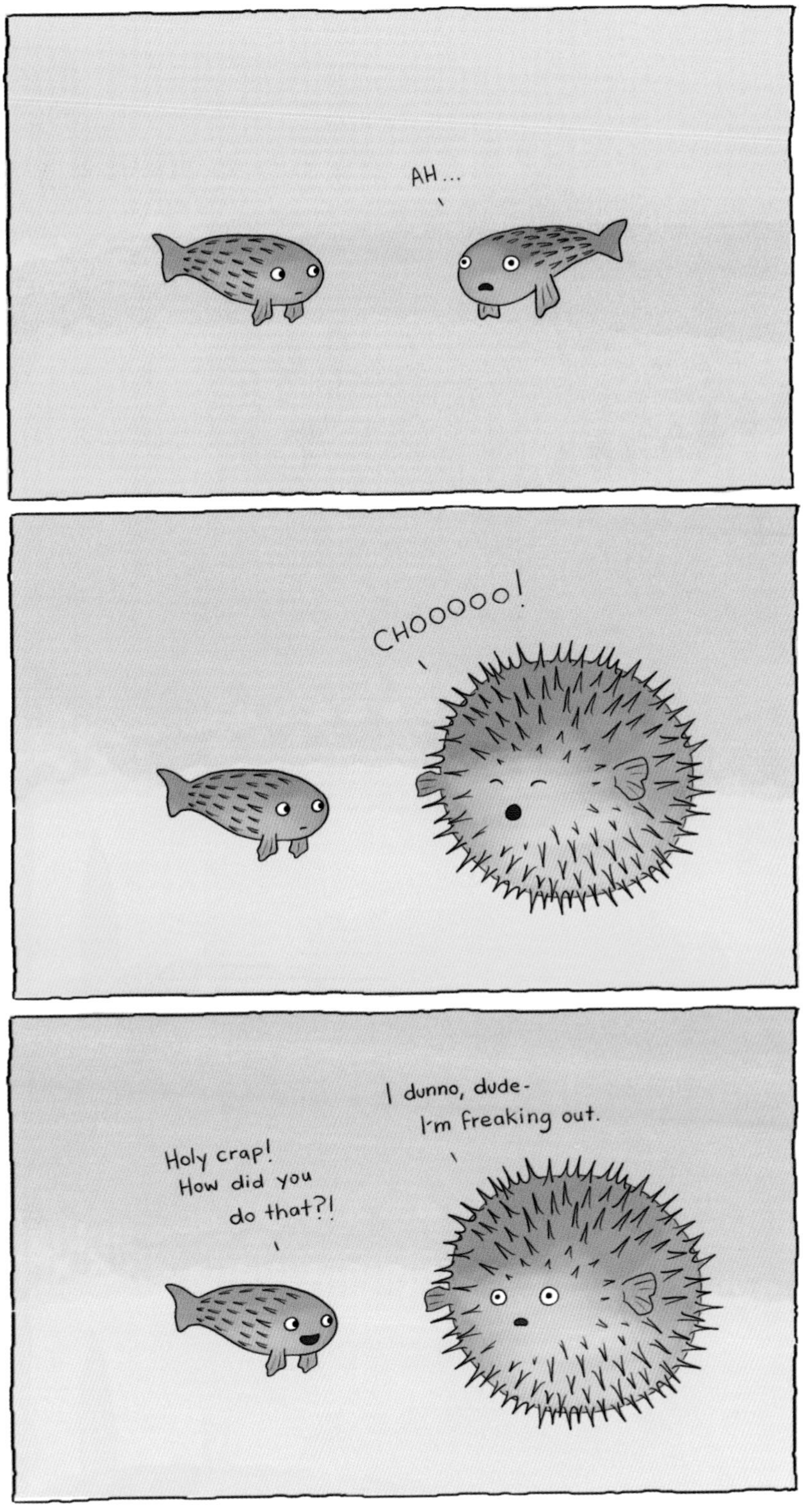
AH...
CHOOOOO!
Holy crap! How did you do that?!
I dunno, dude- I'm freaking out.

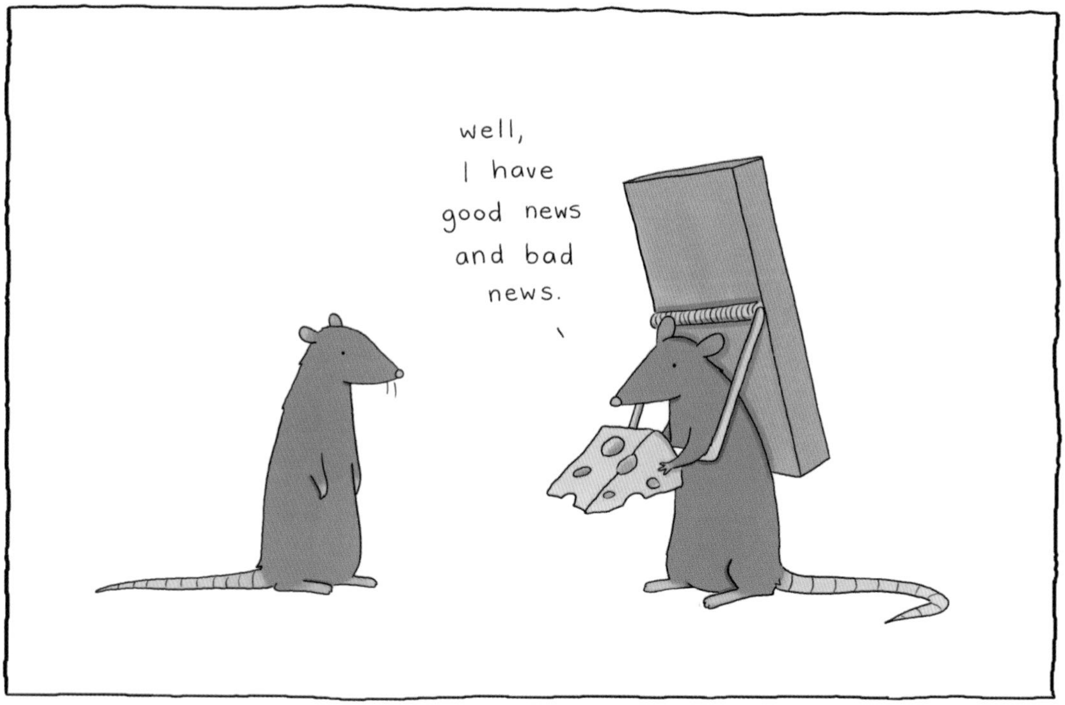
well,
I have
good news
and bad
news.

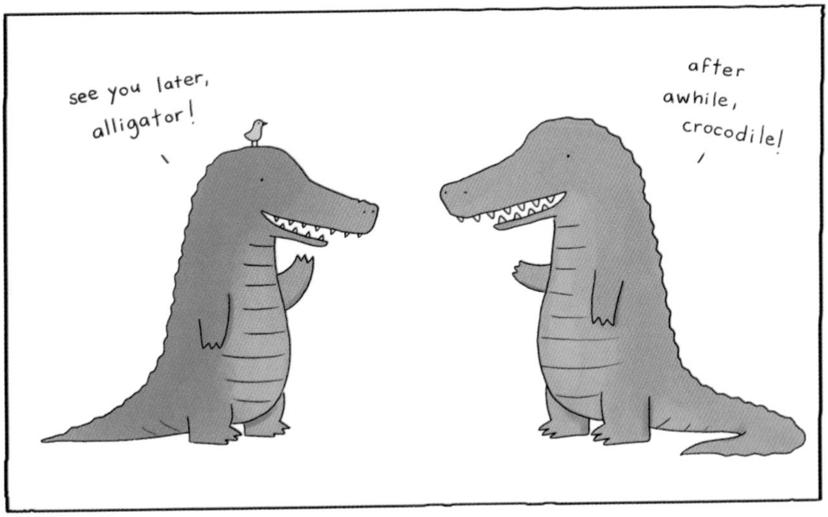
see you later, alligator!
after awhile, crocodile!
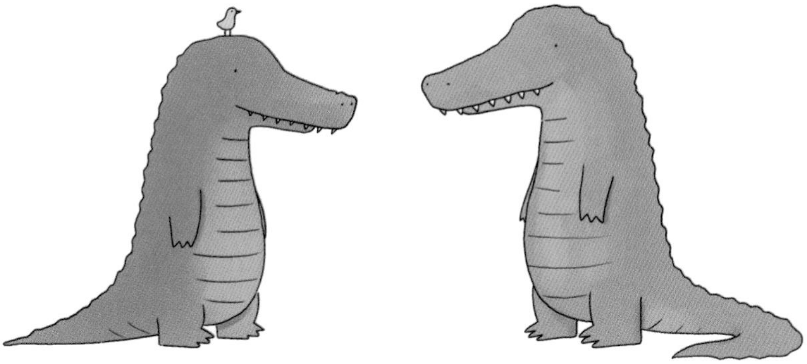
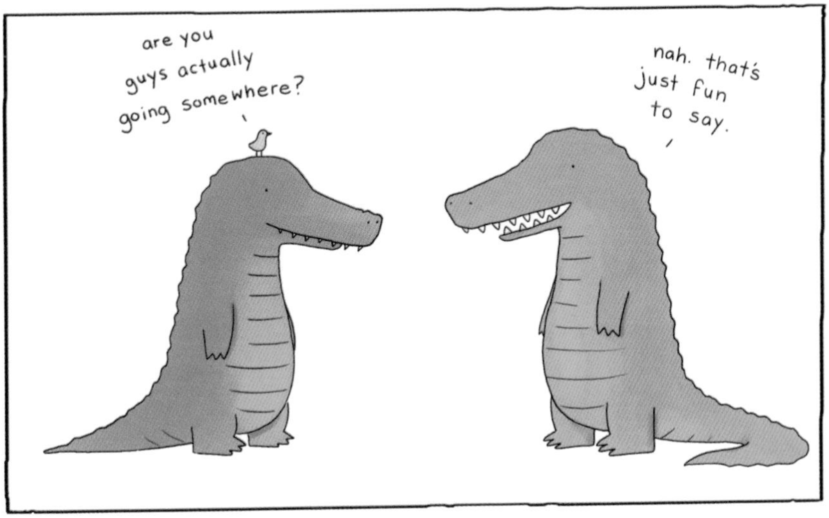
are you guys actually going somewhere?
nah. that's just fun to say.

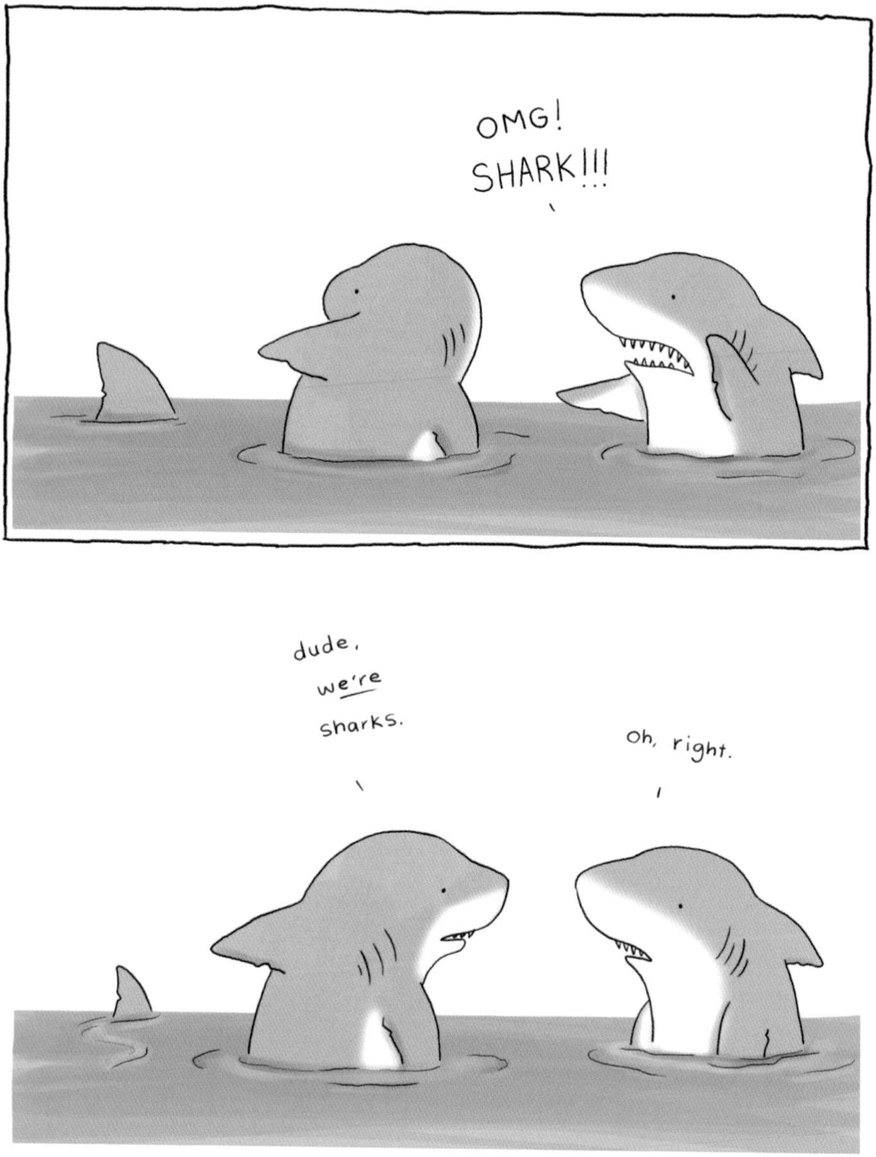
OMG!
SHARK!!!
dude,
we're
sharks.
Oh, right.

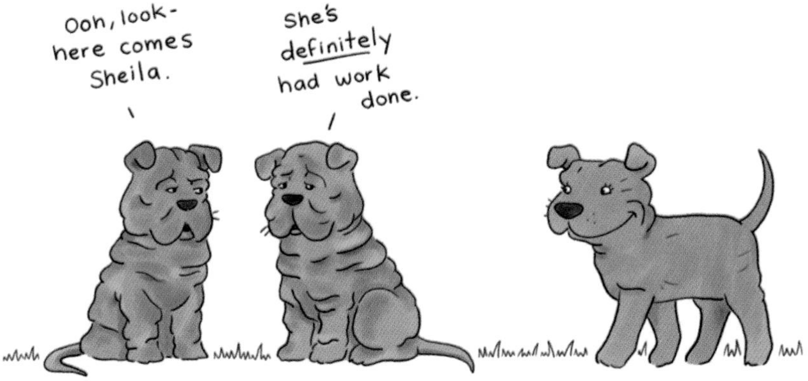
Ooh, look-
here comes
Sheila.
She's
definitely
had work
done.

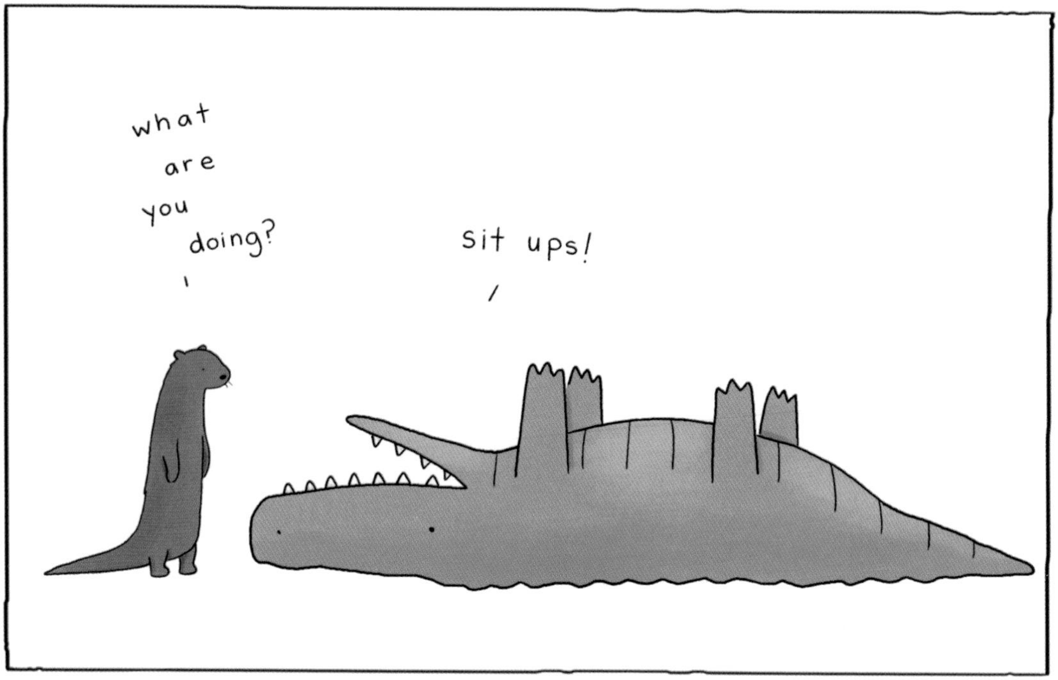
what are you doing?
sit ups!

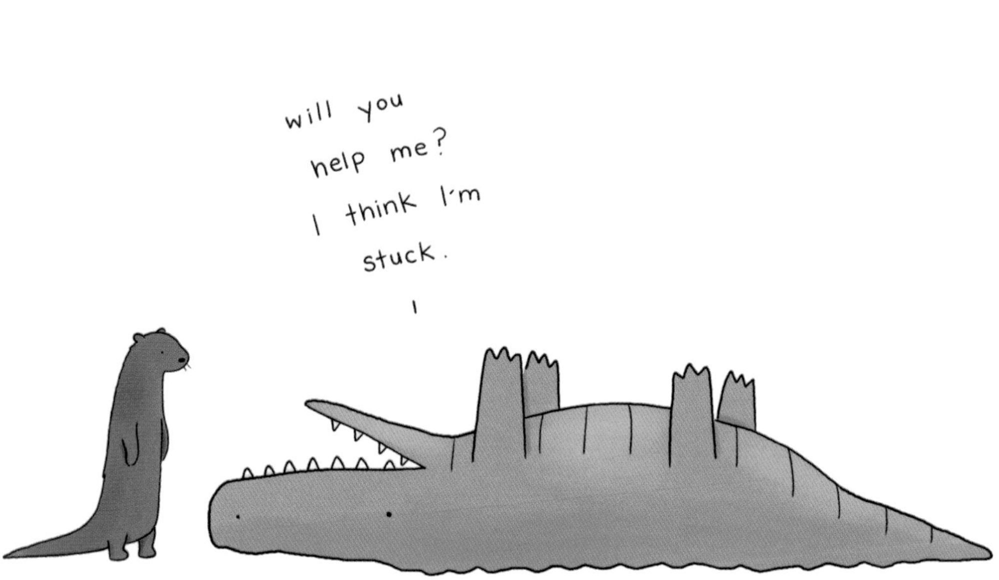
will you help me? I think I'm stuck.

you wanna
meet for lunch?
cool, I'll
be there in
like 7½
hours.

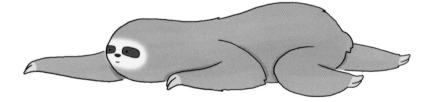

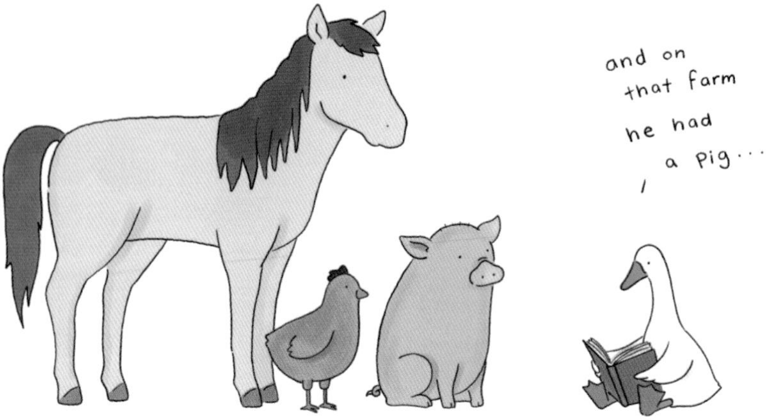
and on that farm he had a pig...

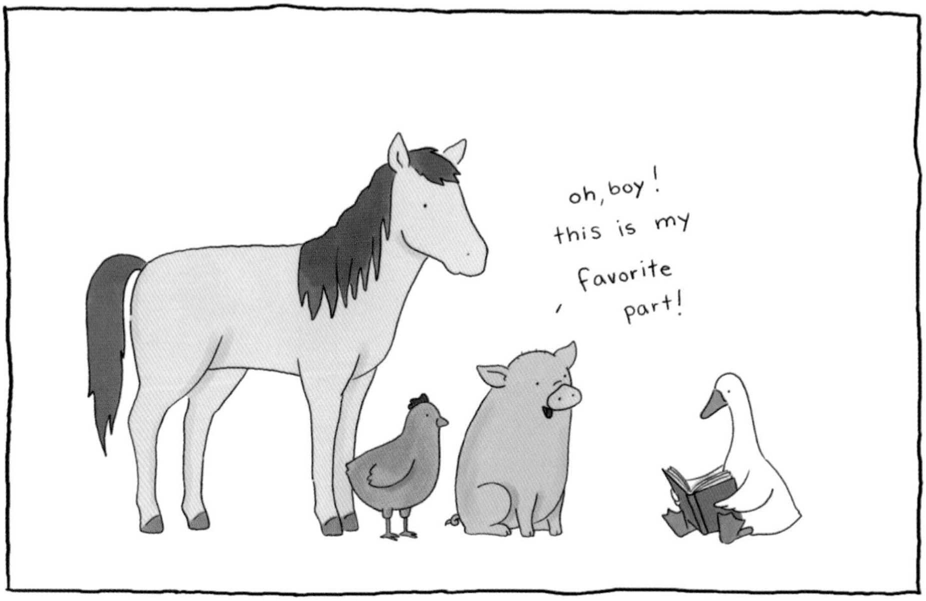
oh, boy! this is my favorite part!

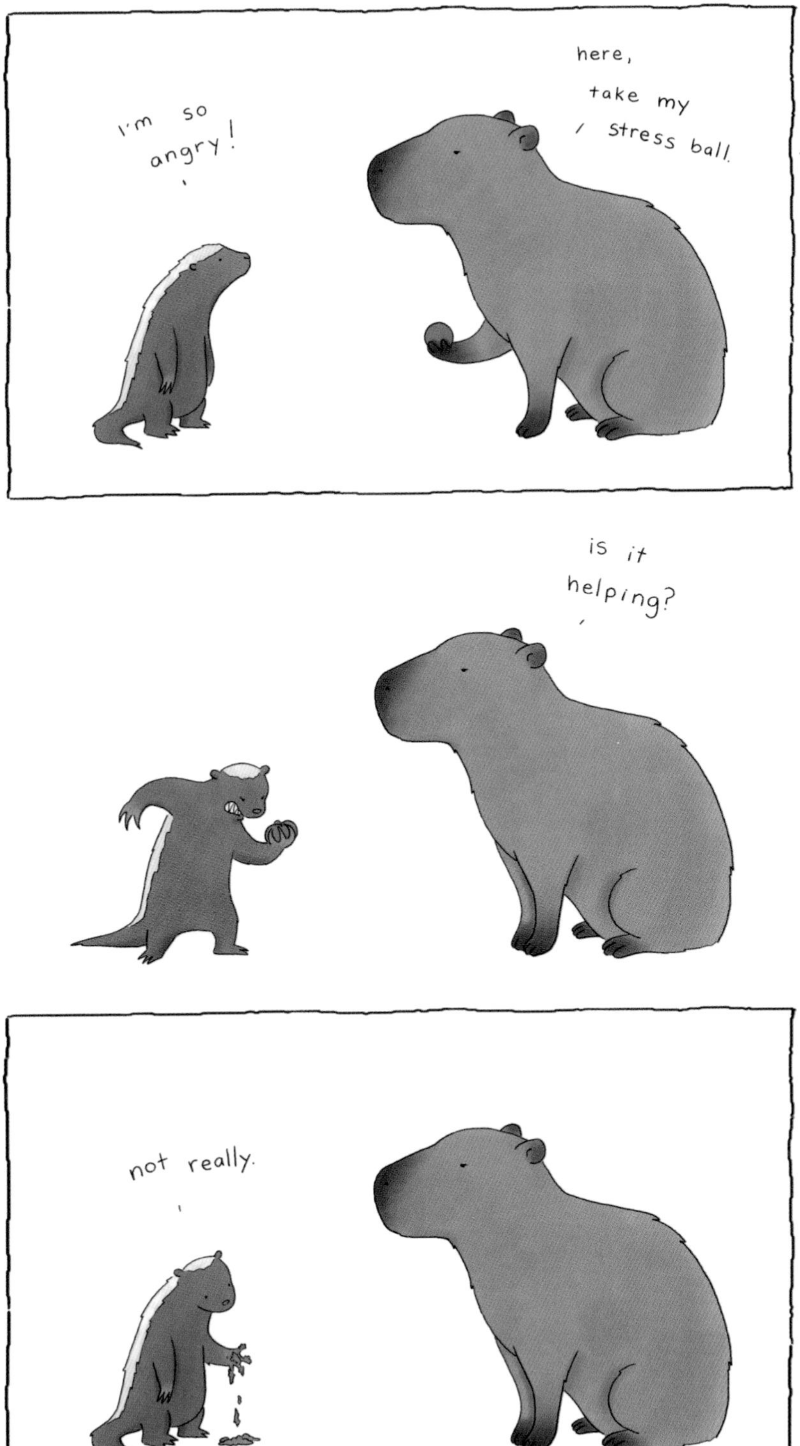
I'm so angry!
here, take my stress ball.
is it helping?
not really.

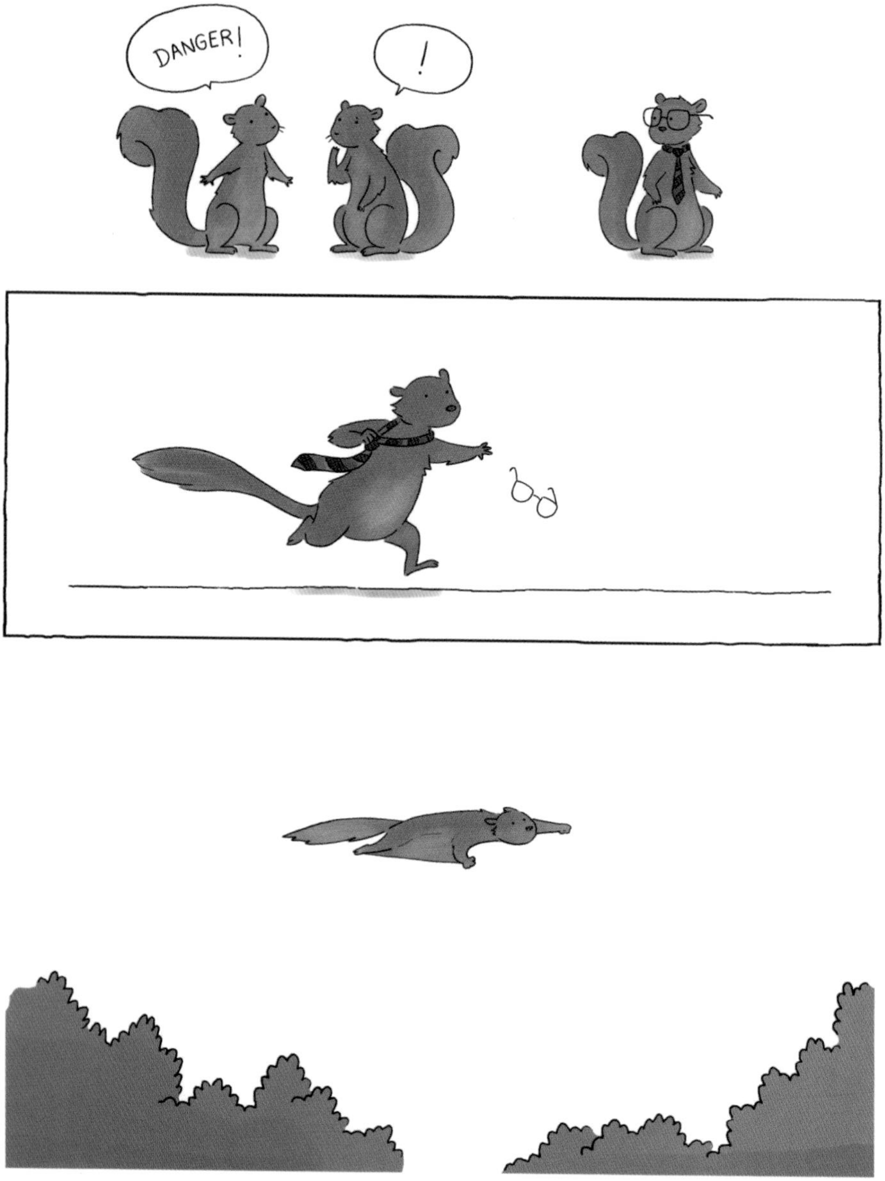
DANGER!
!

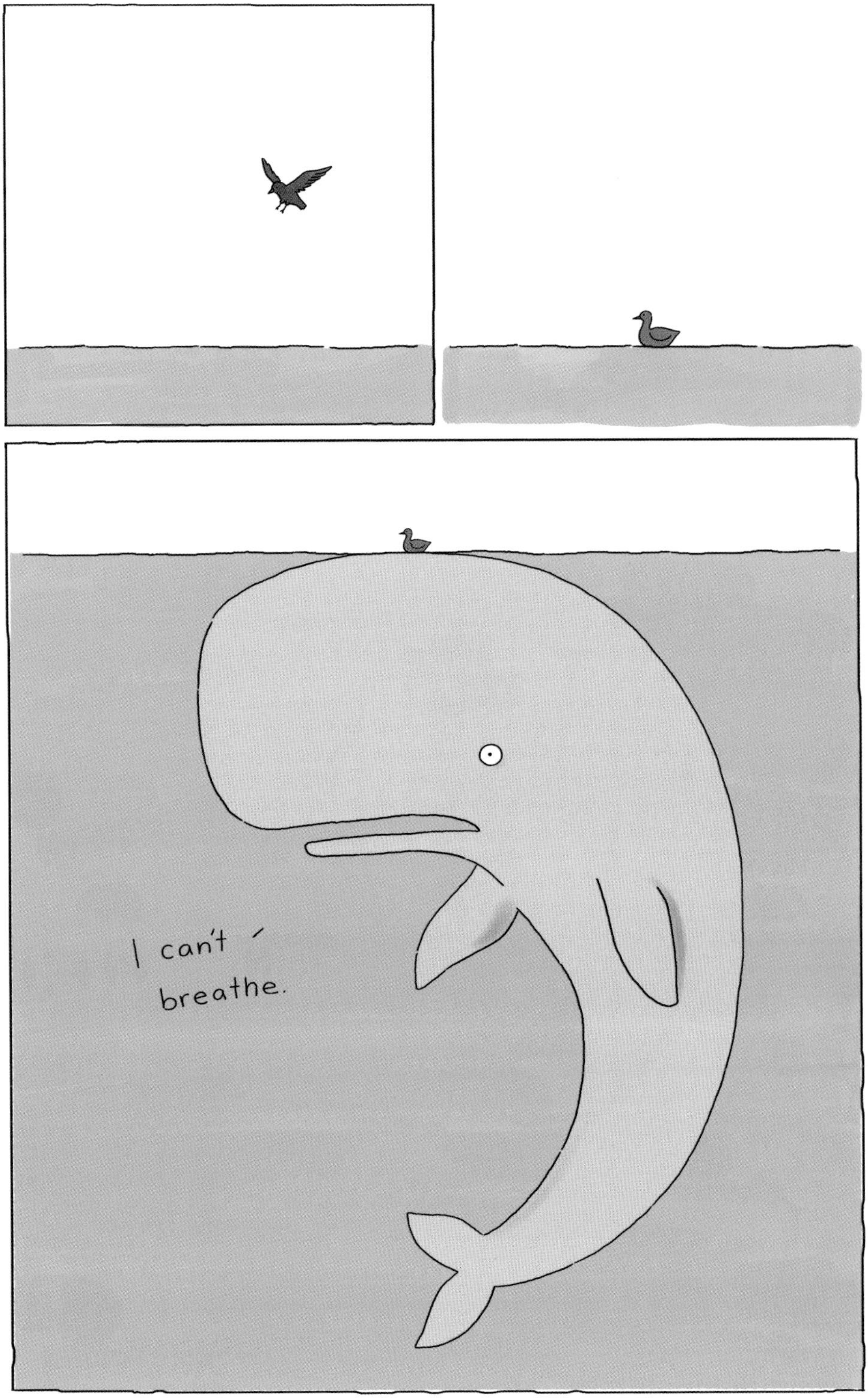
I can't breathe.

First one home wins.
Deal.

Dammit.

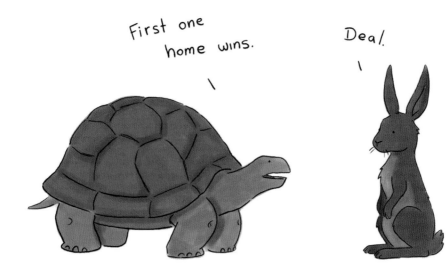

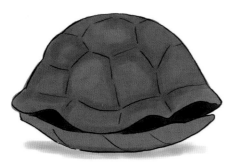

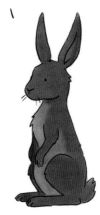

Excuse me, could you not stand on my lawn?

You're making it look tacky.

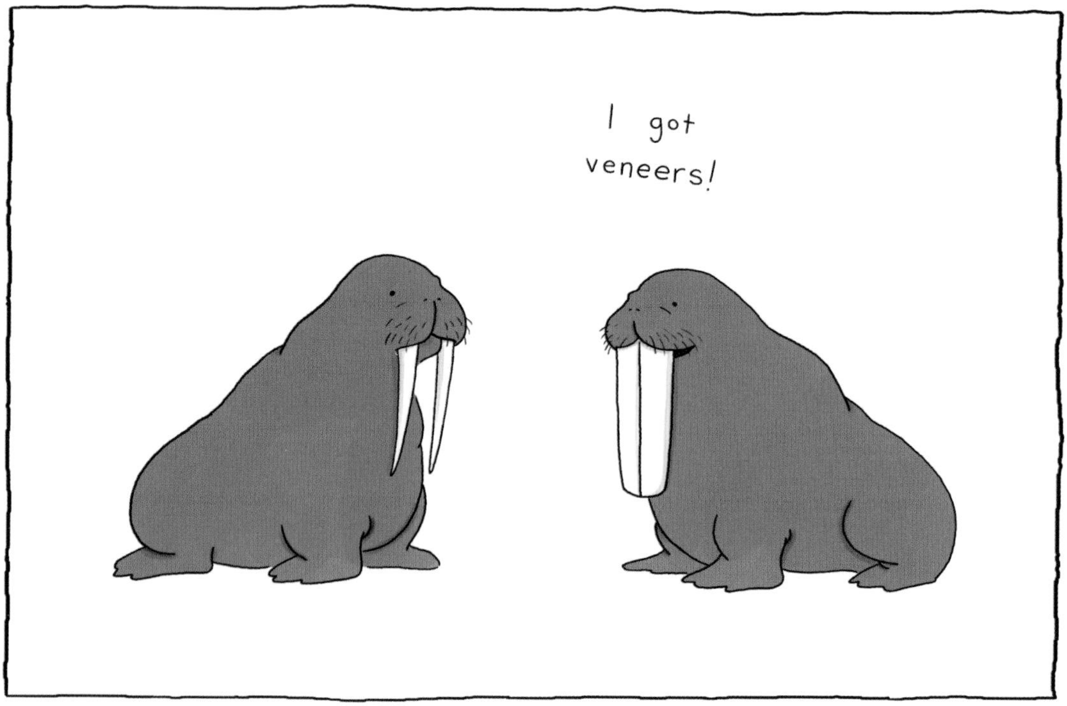
I got
veneers!

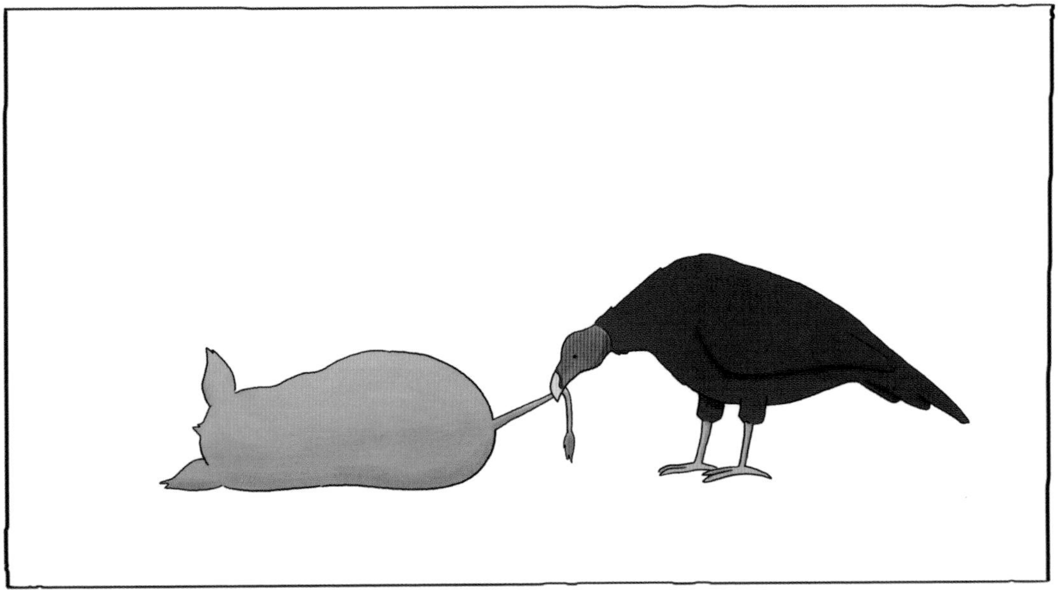

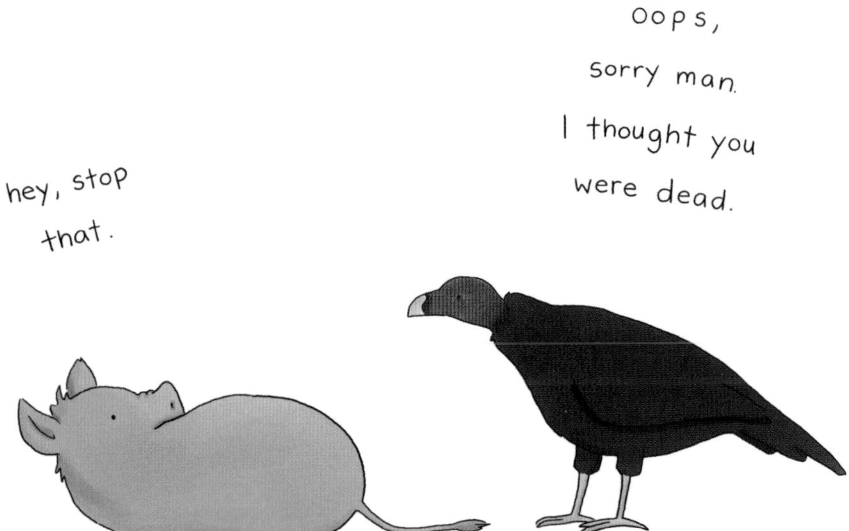
hey, stop that.
oops, sorry man. I thought you were dead.

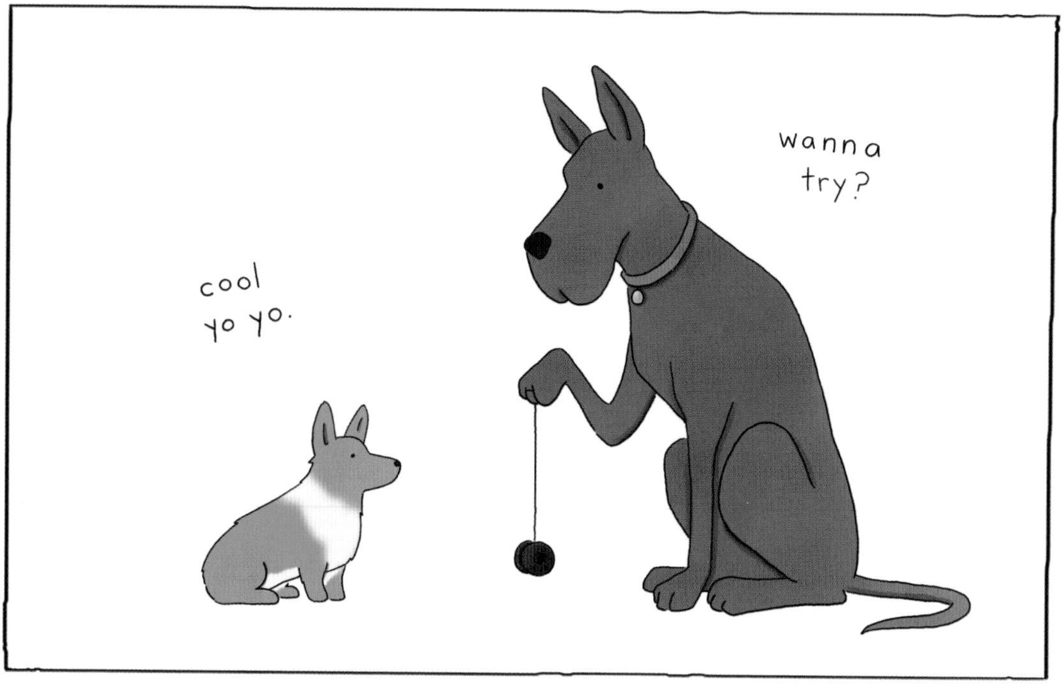
cool
yo yo.
wanna
try?

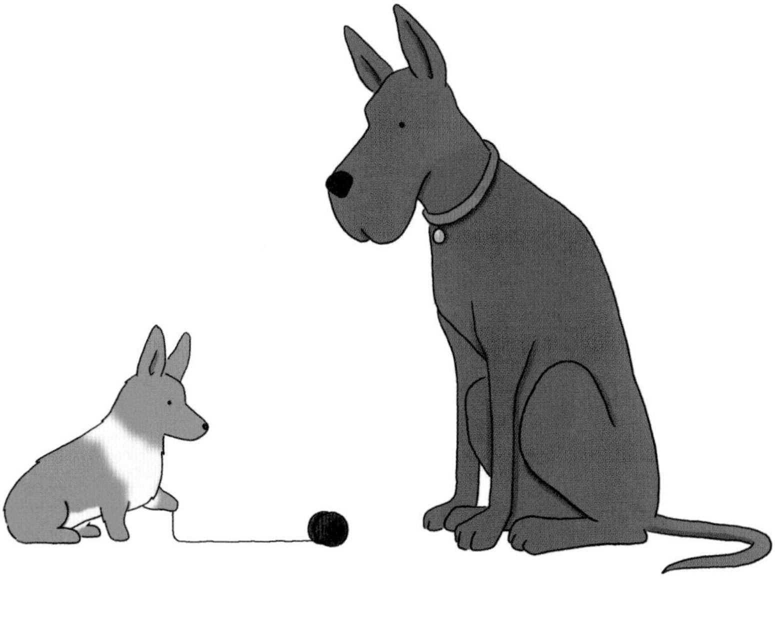

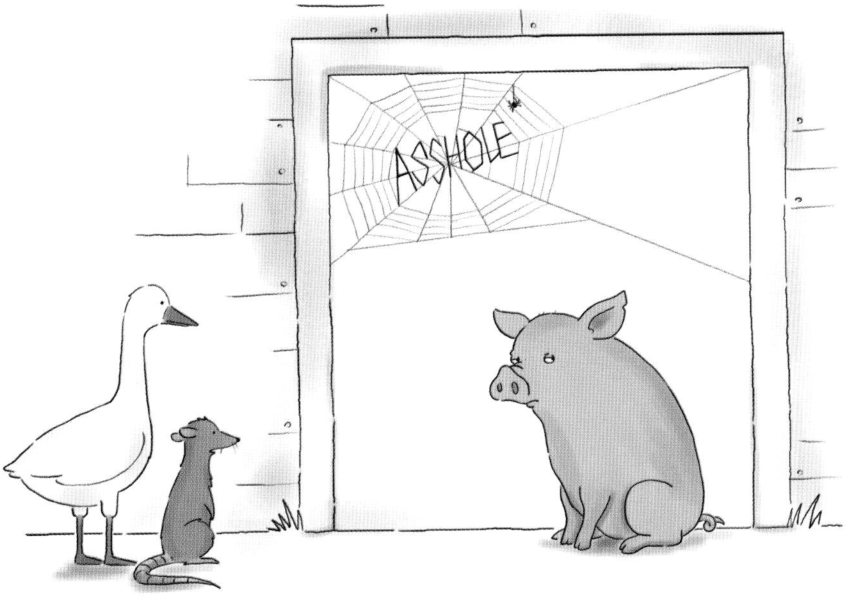
ASSHOLE

Looks like Charlotte and Wilbur are fighting again.

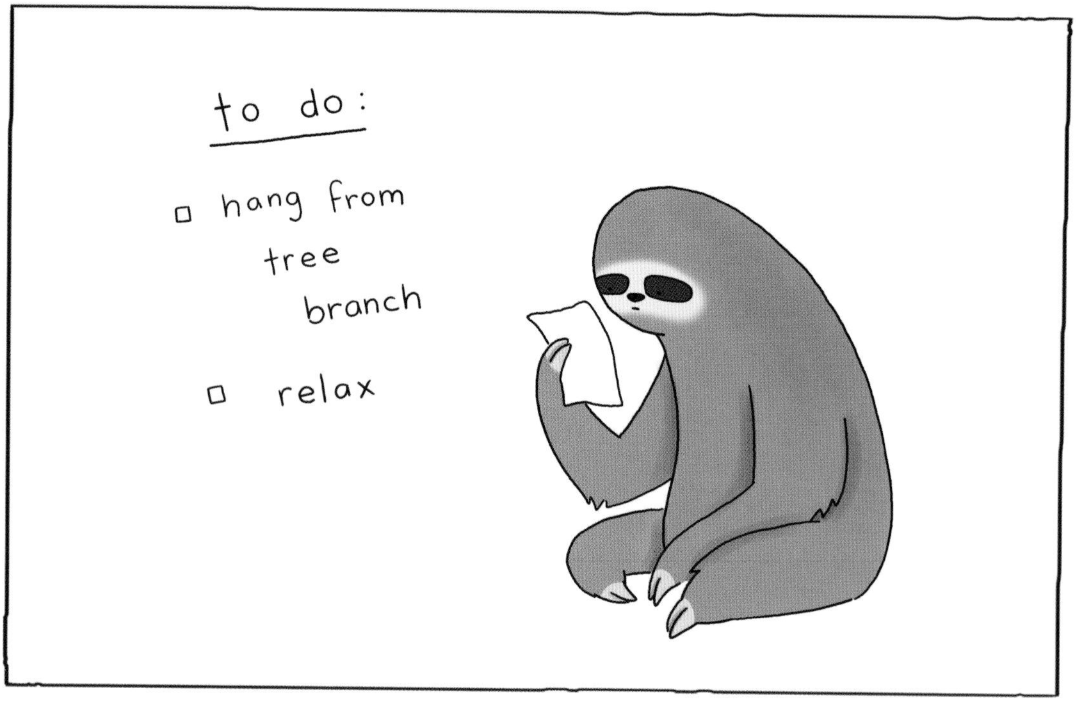
to do:
□ hang from
tree
branch
□ relax

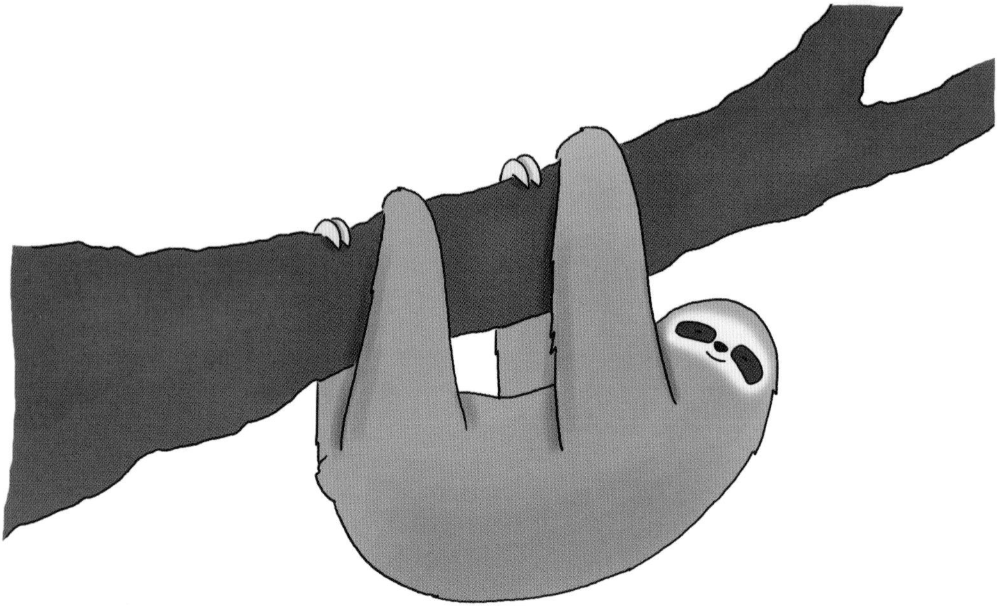

Acknowledgments

I would like to thank Kathleen Ortiz (agent extraordinaire), Joanna Volpe, Danielle Barthel, and everyone at New Leaf Literary for all of their hard work, inspiration, motivation, and encouragement. Bryan Konietzko for a foreword so lovely it made me cry into my breakfast (in front of a very confused waitress) the first time I read it. Jennifer Kasius and the entire team at Running Press, for all of their fantastic work on this book. Dana Kaye, my fabulous publicist. My web friends Christian Baker, Jeff Wysaski, and The Frogman, who have offered me much support via email, and were kind enough to reblog my comics and bring traffic to my site early on. Yannick Lejeune, John J. Boulet, and Arthur de Pins for their support all the way from France. Roxy Lange, who keeps my baby (and me) company while I draw. Anyone and everyone who follows my blog, especially those of you who have been there since day one. You guys are my favorite.

For my mom, who encouraged me to find humor and happiness in everything. My dad, who is the biggest fan of my comics and texts me every time I post a new one to tell me it's his new favorite. For my brother and sister, who are two of the best people ever. For my entire family for their unwavering love and support. For my wonderful friends, who I consider family. And for my husband Colin and our daughter Marlow, who fill my life with love and laughter.

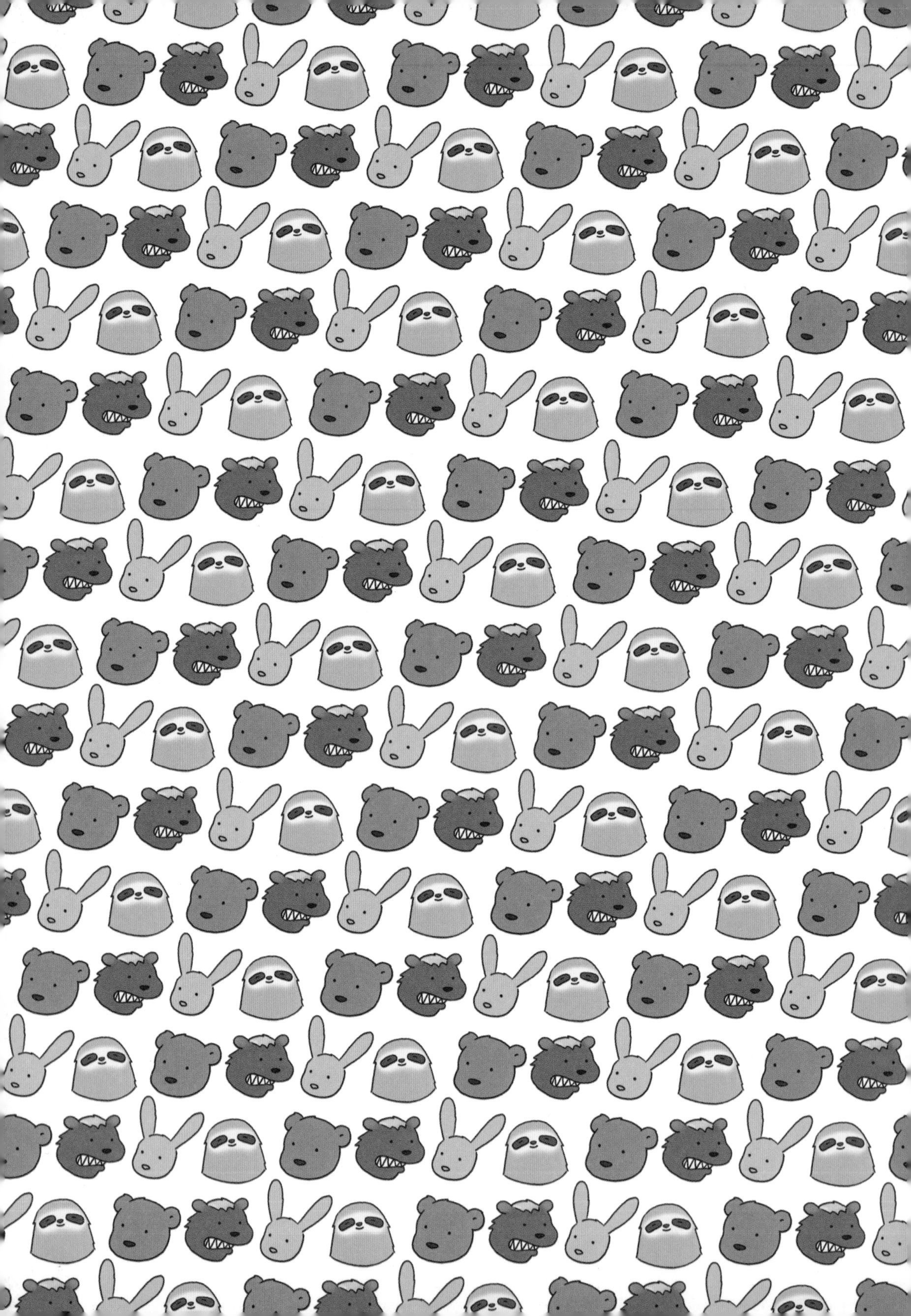